LOVE & ECONOMICS

LOVE & ECONOMICS

Why the Laissez-Faire Family Doesn't Work

JENNIFER ROBACK MORSE

SPENCE PUBLISHING COMPANY • DALLAS

2001

Published in the United States by
Spence Publishing Company
111 Cole Street
Dallas, Texas 75207

Library of Congress Cataloging-in-Publication Data

Morse, Jennifer Roback, 1953-
    Love & economics : why the laissez-faire family doesn't work / Jennifer Roback Morse.
        p. cm.
    Includes bibliographical references and index.
    ISBN 1-890626-29-5 (alk. paper)
    1. Family policy—United States.   2. Family—Economic aspects—United States.   3. Child rearing—United States—Philosophy.   4. United States—Economic policy.   5. United States—Social conditions.   I. Title: Love & economics.   II. Title.

HQ536.M574 2001
306.85—dc21   2001020103

Printed in the United States of America

All the members of human society stand in need of each other's assistance, and are likewise exposed to mutual injuries. Where the necessary assistance is reciprocally afforded from love, from gratitude, from friendship, and esteem, the society flourishes and is happy. . . . Society may subsist among different men, as among different merchants, from a sense of its utility, without any mutual love or affection; and though no man in it should owe any obligation, or be bound in gratitude to any other, it may still be upheld by a mercenary exchange of good offices according to an agreed valuation.

Society, however, cannot subsist among those who are at all times ready to hurt and injure one another. The moment that injury begins, the moment that mutual resentment and animosity take place, all the bands of it are broke assunder, and the different members of which it consisted are, as it were, dissipated and scattered abroad by the violence and opposition of their discordant affections.

Adam Smith, *Theory of Moral Sentiments*, II. ii.2-3.

Contents

Acknowledgments

I HAVE BEEN FORTUNATE to have the opportunity to present papers and lectures based on the ideas in this book. I benefitted from each and every one of the audience discussions generated by those lectures. I am grateful to the people who gave me these opportunities: P. J. Hill of Wheaton College, Gerry Gunderson of Trinity College, Fr. Michael Beers of Mount St. Mary's Seminary, Greg Gronbacher and Fr. Robert Sirico of the Acton Institute, Luis Ravina of the University of Navarre, Matthew Spalding of the Heritage Foundation, Mary Meade of the Brent Society, and Martha Dean of the Federalist Society. People who generously read and commented on the manuscript at various stages include Peg Brinig, Greg Gronbacher, Robert Nelson, Steve Rhoads, James V. Schall, SJ, Karl Zinsmeister, and the late Julian Simon.

First among my institutional debts is the Center for Study of Public Choice at George Mason University where I worked until 1996 and where the ideas of this book germinated. Among my students and colleagues there who contributed to this manuscript in various ways are David Levy, Roger Congleton, Mark Broski, OSB, and Tim Reichert. I must specifically express my gratitude to James Buchanan, founder of the Center, for creating an intellectual atmosphere supportive of unorthodox, cross-disciplinary research.

I must also thank the Hoover Institution for the Study of War, Revolution, and Peace for supporting me on terms that accommodate the growing needs of my family. John Raisian, the director of the Hoover Institution, in particular has been a most generous and understanding employer.

I gratefully acknowledge my debt to the Social Philosophy and Policy Center at Bowling Green State University, where I am a senior research scholar. The basic argument of this book appeared in a paper, "No Families, No Freedom: Human Flourishing in a Free Society," published in their journal, *Social Philosophy and Policy* (16:1, Winter 1999, 290-314). I am grateful for their permission to use this material in the present book.

My greatest single debt is to Ellen Frankel Paul, the deputy director of the Center. Of all the editors I have encountered in academic life, Ellen is simply the best at taking a stuffy piece of academese and turning it into something normal people would want to read. I can not easily express or repay my debt to Ellen.

Parts of this work appeared in "Truth and Freedom in Economic Science," in *Centesimus Annus: Assessment and Perspectives for the Future of Catholic Social Doctrine*," John-Peter A. Pham, ed., Archbishop François-Xavier Nguyen van Thuan, intro. (Libreria Editrice Vaticana, 1998), the proceedings of a conference sponsored by the Acton Institute for the Study of Religion and Liberty. I am grateful to the Acton Institute for permission to use this material. Likewise, parts of the book appeared in Spanish in "Religion y economia: la ciencia triste descubre el amor," (English title: "Religion and Economics: The Dismal Science Discovers Love") in *Economia y Religion*, Luis Ravina, ed. (Pamplona, España: Ediciones Univerisdad de Navarra, 2000). The argument about daycare appeared in abbreviated form in the May/June 1998 issue of *The American Enterprise*, the flagship magazine of the American Enterprise Institute, under the title

"Why the Market Can't Raise Our Children For Us." Some of the ideas in this book appeared in my column in *Forbes*. I am grateful to James Michaels and Betty Franklin of that magazine for their editorial instruction, and to my readers at *Forbes* for their instant feedback. The editors at the *National Catholic Register* came up with the title "The Mother of All Myths" for a column in which I made the argument presented in the chapter of the same title in this book.

Finally, I must acknowledge my debt to my family. It is customary for authors to express their gratitude for their family's forbearance during their long absences and general neglect during the writing of the book. I am unable to thank my family in this way. I made a conscious effort not to shoo them out of the way during the writing of this book. I did not want to convey to them that this particular project of mine was more important to me than my relationships with them and the performance of my duties to them. In fact, I take this opportunity to apologize to any of them who might have felt neglected by me due to my efforts on this work.

I most sincerely thank each and every one of them, husband, children, parents, siblings, and in-laws. They all contributed to lengthening the time of production of this book. But without each and every one of them, I would not have had anything nearly so interesting to say.

LOVE & ECONOMICS

The New "Problem That Has No Name"

WHEN BETTY FRIEDAN launched the modern feminist movement with *The Feminine Mystique*, she called the frustration of the middle-class housewife "the problem that has no name." Now we face a different and deeper problem that has no name. I call it the "laissez-faire family."

I have lived in a laissez-faire family, and I have learned from experience that it does not work. I was surprised to find that the laissez-faire family, in which each member pursues his own self-interest, does not make people very happy. A family held together by a series of contractual understandings, even the most reasonable and elaborate, turns out to be less stable than a family held together by that vague, much misunderstood, intangible quality called love.

When I first encountered the ideas of free market economics and libertarian political theory, I was captivated by their logic, consistency, and simplicity. But if I am completely honest with myself, I have to admit I was also enchanted by the application of those political and economic ideas to my personal life. I liked applying the Invisible Hand to my family life. I enjoyed believing that I could do anything I chose to do and still expect a reasonably good outcome, even if it was not "any part of my intention." I found the libertarian emphasis

3

on contracts as a tool for free and independent people particularly appealing. I had many difficult relatives. I found it convenient to ignore them on the pretense I had never voluntarily agreed to be in a relationship with them. I liked telling myself that it was my life and that no one could tell me what to do, not even my parents or others who loved me.

This book is not an attack on laissez-faire economics. Not only is the free market alive and well, it is the only game in town, in theory and in practice. I also do not attack libertarian political theory. When the topic is the proper relationship between the individual and the state, libertarianism is pretty much the right path. The question is whether these ideas apply as well to the conduct of our personal lives. I tried to argue by analogy from libertarian political and economic ideas to a full-fledged philosophy of life. This book is an extended reflection on why that analogy does not work.

This is not to say that there is no relationship at all between libertarianism and family life. I maintain that the freer we hope to be from artificial economic and political restraints, the more we need loving families. This need for stable, committed, loving families in turn places demands upon the behavior of individuals. But these demands cannot be enforced or even defined by the government in very much detail. The opposite of the laissez-faire family is not a government-run family.

The proper contrast to the self-centered approach to the family is the self-giving approach. Far from denigrating the individual, self-giving actually elevates the worth of each individual. Seeing oneself as a gift proves to be a greater act of self-valuing than seeing oneself as a set of desires in need of satisfaction or as a set of opinions in need of assertion.

~

THIS WORK had its beginnings in 1991 when my husband and I became the parents of two children. Our daughter was placed into our care at conception; our son, after two and half years of life in a Romanian orphanage. The developmental path of our daughter has been smooth, easy, exactly as the book said it would be. The developmental path of our son has been circuitous, painful, and slow, unlike anything we could have ever predicted. We had to provide explicit instructions for our son to learn tasks our daughter picked up effortlessly: making eye contact, making the most elementary sounds, playing peek-a-boo, noticing other people, even smiling. Our daughter easily takes pleasure in life; our son can barely relax, even when he is asleep.

Because of the radically different paths our children have taken, our family has had the opportunity to notice things we might otherwise have taken for granted. My understanding of the human person and society had been deeply influenced by free market economics and libertarian political theory, which have shaped my entire adult working life. As I came to realize how much I had overlooked, I concluded that my profession was overlooking much as well. I became motivated to think systematically about what I had seen and heard within my own nursery. Motherhood provoked me into writing this book.

The family performs a crucial and irreplaceable social function. Inside a family, helpless babies are transformed from self-centered bundles of impulses, desires, and emotions to fully socialized adults. The family teaches trust, cooperation, and self-restraint. The family is uniquely situated to teach these skills because people instill these qualities in their children as a side effect of loving them. Contracts and free political institutions, the foundations of a free society, require these attributes that only families can inculcate. Without loving families, no society can long govern itself.

Contracts are the tools used by free people to arrange their economic affairs for mutual advantage. But it is often not practicable to make provisions for every contingency that might arise during the life of the contract. Hence, people are vulnerable to opportunistic and predatory behavior from their contracting partners. When we have reason to be suspicious, we must make ever more detailed provisions for non-compliance and shirking. A person who fears that his contracting partner is about to renege must scramble to cut his losses. The potential gains from the contract can be substantially dissipated by this self-protective behavior.

Likewise, constitutionally limited popular government is the heart of a free political society. It is impracticable to make explicit constitutional provision for every contingency that might arise during the life of a republic. Citizens are vulnerable to constitutional interpretations that increase governmental power around the edges of explicit constitutional provision. The benefits of a government of constitutionally limited power can be greatly diminished if a significant set of the population tries, with the help of government, to "push the envelope" of what is constitutionally permissible.

A free society requires self-restraining, self-monitoring, self-governing adults. But we are not born as adults. Contrary to the romantic view, actual babies are not noble savages: they are just cute savages who have the potential to be civilized. They are totally self-centered, impulsive, and demanding. It is not a foregone conclusion that any particular child will be civilized.

There are many competing visions of what might be called a free society. At the libertarian end of the spectrum are advocates of a "night watchman state," a government that performs only the minimal functions of providing national defense, police protection, and a legal system to enforce contracts. A more conservative vision of a free society allows the government a greater role for inculcating and enforcing moral norms. A New Deal liberal vision of a free society includes the provision of a social safety net, financed through taxes, to provide economic security. The most expansive view of the government's role sees free political institutions allowing mass participation as the only defining characteristics of a free society. The government may do anything selected through democratic political institutions, no matter how intrusive.

The argument of this book applies to any of these visions of a free society, except possibly the last. Almost every society requires self-restraint on the part of the population. The freer the political and economic institutions of the society, the more necessary the skills of individual, personal self-governance. Conversely, without self-governing, self-restraining individuals, the scope of government will necessarily grow.

I make a libertarian argument for loving families precisely because libertarians take the most expansive view of personal liberty. If I can convince libertarians that their ideal political world makes demands upon individuals as parents and marriage partners, then perhaps others who are more willing to accept constraints upon their own behavior would be inclined to agree. In the first part of this book, I show that developing the basic attachments between parents and their children is a crucial social process for any society that hopes to remain free.

As we all know, maintaining a loving disposition towards all the members of our families can be one of life's most trying battles. Many families have members who are outcasts either by their own choice or by common agreement among the others. Most people have gone through crises with one or more family members, periods filled with so much tension that we wondered if we would be able to stand it. Most of us have had the experience of wanting to walk away from some of our family members. When we take the American individualist ethos to mean the right to do any non-aggressive act, we might easily conclude that dissolving our family ties is analogous to dissolving any other voluntary association.

But the family is not analogous to other forms of association. In the third part of this book, I show that there really is no substitute for the family in creating among children a disposition to cooperate.

The government certainly cannot replace the family in this all-important task. Some of the modern alternatives to the family are not adequate substitutes either: single and divorced parents have difficulty producing the qualities of cooperation and connectedness in their children. I do not say that it is impossible, just that the odds are against it. Likewise, children raised primarily by paid childcare providers often have social difficulties. The fact that all the adults voluntarily agree to a living arrangement or childcare plan does not guarantee that the needs of their children will be met.

The primary motivation for living up to the demands of love in the family must come from within the individuals. These are not demands that can be imposed by outsiders through threats or force. Certainly, the government cannot "make" people love each other; nor can it compel parents to perform the numerous tasks, in all their rich variety and subtlety, that responsible parenthood requires. If a libertarian minimal state requires loving families, then a libertarian social theory must inculcate an ethos of generosity and loyalty within the family.

This statement may cause consternation among the many Americans who have adopted a libertarian posture in their personal lives—and there are far more of these people than there are political libertarians. Many who consider themselves political liberals and even leftists have embraced a libertarian personal credo. This form of libertarianism means the right to do any peaceful, non-coercive act.

I can speak for myself when I say that libertarian political philosophy offered justification for behavior and attitudes I could not have justified any other way. I found it convenient to be able to say, "It is my life. I owe nothing to anyone." I found it comfortable to be able to say, "I am sovereign. I can do whatever I want." It was reassuring to believe that the great intellectual and moral tradition of Western liberty stands behind these statements.

But I was wrong when I said these things. As a matter of political philosophy, it may be perfectly valid to say, "I am not the property of the state. I owe nothing to the state," or "I owe much less to the state than it demands of me." It does not follow by analogy that, "I own myself. I owe nothing to anyone." The fourth part of this book explains some of what is wrong with these statements. I define love as willing the good of another person. The decision to love enriches and enlarges a person, even though there are many moments in the course of a loving relationship that require us to surrender our inclinations. I try to show that the decision to love is reasonable.

Having a sound working philosophy in the personal realm is just as important as having a sound political philosophy, for this is where people really live their lives. The real world is the world around the kitchen table, the world of the nursery, the world of the bedroom. (As an academic, I have always been sensitive about this question of the "real world" and where it might finally be located. I'm pretty sure it is at home.) Political ideas and institutions matter, it is true. But people live out their days wiping runny noses, visiting old people, practicing spelling lessons, packing lunches, and hearing about each other's days. This mundane world of ordinary chores, ordinary joys, ordinary problems, this is where any personal philosophy must bear fruit. It does not matter much if we have a perfectly consistent and elegant theory worked out on the chalkboard. If our domestic lives and our relationships are not satisfying, if our home life does not work, if our theories do not help us make sense of life's inevitable difficulties and disappointments, then our theories have failed us.

Part of developing a workable philosophy of life involves defining our idea of our own interests. Libertarians and their critics spend a lot of effort debating the concept of self-interest and its proper role in society. Much of that abstract discussion of political theory concerns "self-interest rightly understood," that is, how a reasonable person ought to understand his own self-interest. That discussion is motivated by the realization that some people cannot be safely turned loose to pursue their own self-interest. Members of street gangs, liars, and conmen cannot be trusted. Scholars who see the world through the lens of rational self-interest try to rescue their theory from the problem posed by these reprobates by arguing that antisocial behavior is not really in the interests of the people who engage in it.

My point is quite different. Self-interest, even rational self-interest, is not enough to provide the social glue for the good society. I want to show how a person develops a reasonable understanding of his own interest *and* a realistic understanding of his relationship to other members of the human race. After all, we are not born as fully rational adults, capable of grasping our true interests, able to make contracts and other agreements, able to defend our property rights and our other legitimate interests. We are born as helpless babies. The fact of infant helplessness is not peripheral; it is a central fact to any coherent social theory.

I shall not begin with an analysis of individuals in a state of nature. Political parables that begin in this way attempt to explain how a cooperative social order could come into being prior to the existence of government. State of nature theories explain how this primal social order might develop into a more complex system of social and political relationships. But all the individuals under discussion are fully grown and fully formed in their preferences, tastes, and beliefs. These individuals are prepared to make contracts with one another and to define and defend property rights.

But where did all of these fully formed, rational adults come from? Instead of beginning with a state of nature, let us begin where each of us begins life. Let us begin with the baby—helpless, needy, and immature.

Homo Economicus *and the Noble Savage*

Economic and political institutions can remain free only if they are largely self-regulating. Free societies need institutions that produce social order yet allow ordinary people to conduct their activities with minimal government interference.

The decentralized market economy is probably the most celebrated self-regulating social institution. Adam Smith's "invisible hand" insight shows that people pursuing their own self-interest can actually end up furthering the public interest through no intention of their own. Since Smith's time, free market economists have developed the Invisible Hand concept further through a construct called *homo economicus*, or economic man. Economic man is a rational person who calculates the costs and benefits of each potential action and chooses the action that brings him the most happiness.

But we are not born as rational, choosing agents, able to defend ourselves and our property, able to negotiate contracts and exchanges. We are born as dependent babies, utterly incapable of meeting our own needs—or even of knowing what our needs are. As infants, we do not know what is good or safe. We even resist sleep in spite of being so exhausted we cannot hold our heads up. We are completely dependent on others for our very survival.

In our experience as helpless infants, we learn some very important things: whether the world is a safe place that can be counted on to meet our needs; whether we in particular are worthy of living; and whether others can be trusted. We learn whether people respond to us favorably, and we learn ways to encourage them to do so.

Orphanage workers and developmental pediatricians have observed a "failure-to-thrive" syndrome in minimal care orphanages. Children who are deprived of human contact during infancy sometimes fail to gain weight and otherwise develop. All their bodily, material needs may be met. They are kept warm and dry; they are fed, perhaps by having a bottle propped into the crib; they contract no identifiable illnesses. Yet they fail to thrive.

Some scientists now believe that the presence of a nurturing figure stimulates the growth hormones.[1] Others believe that this psychosocial growth retardation is stress induced. In any case, observers report that orphanage children from former Soviet-bloc countries fall behind an average of one month of growth for every three or four months of orphanage life. Head circumference, which may signal brain development, is typically smaller for orphanage children.[2] Whatever the exact mechanism, failure-to-thrive children sometimes even die from lack of human contact.[3]

These children without families often have difficulty forming attachments to others. Even children who are later adopted by loving and competent families sometimes never fully attach to them or to anyone else. Experts believe that children who do not develop attachments in the first eighteen months of life will have grave difficulty in forming attachments later. If the parents of such children do not intervene by the time the child reaches twelve years of age, the prospects for successful future intervention are thought to be diminished to the point of hopelessness.[4]

The classic case of attachment disorder is a child who does not care what anyone thinks of him. The disapproval of others does not deter this child from bad behavior because no other person, even someone who loves him very much, matters to the child. He responds only to physical punishment and to the suspension of privileges. The child does whatever he thinks he can get away with, no matter the cost to others. He does not monitor his own behavior, so authority figures must constantly be wary of him and watch him. He lies if he thinks it is advantageous to lie. He steals if he can get away with it. He may go through the motions of offering affection, but people who live with him sense in him a kind of phoniness. He shows no regret at hurting another person, though he may offer perfunctory apologies.

As he grows into adolescence, he may become a sophisticated manipulator. Some authors refer to this kind of child as a "trust bandit" because he is superficially charming in his initial encounters with people and can deceive them for long enough to use them. In the meantime, his parents, and anyone else who has long-term dealings with him, grow increasingly frustrated, frightened, and angry over the child's dangerous behavior, which by this time may include violence, arson, and sexual acting out.[5] As the parents try to seek help for their child, they may find that he is able to "work the system." He can charm therapists, social workers, counselors, and later perhaps even judges and parole officers. This child is unwilling even to inconvenience himself for the sake of others.

Who is this child? Why, it is *homo economicus*—rational, calculating, economic man, the person who considers only his own good, who is willing to do anything he deems it in his interest to do, who cares for no one. All of his actions are governed by the self-interested calculation of costs and benefits. Punishments matter; loss of esteem does not. As for his promises, he behaves opportunistically on every possible occasion, breaking promises if he deems it in his interest to do so.

This is the child whom some social theorists might have imagined a "noble savage," untouched by corrupting adult influences. This is the child in the state of nature, who takes care of himself, who has no society around him, having survived a life that truly was "nasty, brutish, and short." But plainly this person is not fit for social life. Most people would call him a sociopath, and not dignify him with the label *homo economicus*. Certainly, this left-alone child bears no resemblance to anyone's notion of a "noble savage."

I did not describe *homo economicus* as an attachment-disordered child because I believe that any economist believes that this is how children are or ought to be treated. But the desperate condition of the abandoned child shows us that we have, all along, been counting on something to hold society together, something more than the mutual interests of autonomous individuals. We have taken that something else for granted, and hence, overlooked it, even though it has been under our noses all along. That missing element is none other than love.

Love Matters

At a conference for the adoptive parents of children who had spent substantial time in Eastern European orphanages, one mother remarked in the course of the discussion that her son "was fed like a hamster." The attendant at the orphanage had wired a baby bottle between the bars of the crib. The baby was able to eat whenever he wanted without anyone ever having to pick him up. The members of that particular audience knew exactly what she meant. Many of our children had been fed like hamsters, too.

All of us were dealing with the long term problems created for our children by having been treated like hamsters. They are shorter and smaller than average; they cannot control their bodies very well; they engage in repetitive, stereotypic behavior, like repeatedly throwing an object into the air or rocking, and even banging, their heads. They have severe delays in speech, language, and social skills; they have poor impulse control; they cannot draw inferences, especially in social situations; and, of course, they often have trouble attaching to other people. Even after the child has spent a long time with his new parents, he may still have these problems.[6]

If the human person really is nothing more than an animal, there ought to be no problem with feeding children like hamsters. But in fact such children have many problems. The issue is not simply poverty. Many normal children have been raised well by parents, or even in orphanages, with few resources. The problem is the idea of materialism, which holds that the person is nothing more than his body. Provide for the physical well-being of the person, and you have cared for the whole person. Provide enough material resources for society, and social problems are solved.

Materialism was a central part of the failed Marxist ideology and methodology. Economic science sometimes adopts its own form of materialism, at least as an explanatory strategy. Explain the material surroundings of a person or a society, and you can explain that person or that society. Control the physical circumstances surrounding the person, and you control the person. While materialism may be perfectly fine as a scientific methodology, it is implausible as a full-fledged philosophy of life.

Suppose materialism were literally and universally true. We might suppose that everything a mother does for her baby out of love could be imitated by a stranger using purely physical means. Rocking the baby stimulates the child's nervous system, helps with sensory integration, and prepares the child for the development of language. Perhaps all the benefits of rocking the baby could be duplicated by placing the child in an automatic rocking machine or swing. The presence of loving adults evidently stimulates the baby's growth hormones. Perhaps all the benefits of a loving family could be replicated by giving the child hormone injections. Breast feeding appears to help the child's visual acuity: the child is required to look up at his mother, from both directions (because she changes sides for feeding). Bottle fed babies are usually fed from one direction only. Perhaps this improvement in vision could be achieved by some artificial means: strap the bottle to the bars of the crib; place something in the vicinity of the bottle that might be as interesting to the baby as his mother's face; switch the position of the object from time to time so the baby had to look from both directions while feeding.

Materialism and Economics

We can apply one of great insights of the theory of free societies to the intricate set of interactions between parents and children. In the 1920s and 1930s, defenders of socialism used to argue that an economy could be centrally planned using scientific methods. They claimed that central planners could simulate the workings of the market economy by scientifically calculating the correct prices for goods and services. Setting the appropriate prices would lead people to have right incentives for production and consumption. This scientifically planned economy would be more efficient than the market economy, because all the duplication and waste of the competitive process would be sidestepped.[7]

Nobel Prize–winning economist Frederick Hayek argued that free economies would outperform centrally planned economies, pointing out that one of the major purposes of the market mechanism is to discover the proper prices. No group of people, no matter how intelligent, can discover the complete set of prices for every good and service, at every time, in an economy of any size or complexity. Much of the knowledge upon which the price system is based is tacit and implicit. People do things they do not fully understand, acting upon knowledge they truly possess but cannot fully express. Having knowledge of particular circumstances, places, and things, they incorporate what they know into their economic activity. But if a central planning commissar were to interview them about what they produce, how and why, they might very well omit crucial pieces of information.[8]

There is a strong analogy with the work of parenthood. Most parents cannot articulate the physiological and psychological significance of the activities they do with their children. Indeed, if you ask the mother of an infant what she did all day, she is unlikely to be able even to describe her activities except in the most general way. She might tell you how many times she changed his diaper, but she will probably forget to mention that she looked into the baby's eyes, wiggled his toes, and laughed while she imitated his baby babbling sounds. She might tell you she folded laundry and did dishes. But she probably will not remember that she rewarded every little noise her baby made, by smiling at the baby, or imitating the baby's sound, or having an imaginary conversation with him. Far more is going on between a normal mother and child than we would ever imagine in the absence of the horrendous counterexample provided by our little Eastern European orphans.

Hayek's last book was *The Fatal Conceit*, in which he criticized social planning of all kinds.[9] He argued that the attempt to control outcomes was based upon the "fatal conceit" that someone or some group of people could know enough to manipulate every detail of the social order. The authorities in the former Communist-bloc countries evidently thought they could raise children scientifically. This particular conceit of theirs was literally fatal to an unknown, but very large, number of children.

Tacit Knowledge

One consequence of viewing the parental role through the materialist lens is that we could convince ourselves that the parents' responsibility includes only the things currently known to affect the bodily well-being of children. But what parents do out of love for their children is much more extensive than this. Many of these acts of love, while observable in principle, are not really enumerable. Not even experienced parents or scientific observers can list all of them. People do what the child needs without necessarily having a complete understanding of what they are doing or why.

Reflecting on the neglected infant helps us appreciate the surprising importance of the simple activities parents do with their babies. Most parents rock their babies and look into their eyes without realizing that this activity wards off attachment disorder. Very few parents are conscious that they are stimulating their baby's vestibular and proprioceptive systems when they bounce the baby on their knees or lift him up overhead and wiggle him around. Most parents do not realize that they are teaching their child basic trust and reciprocity every time they play peek-a-boo. People have been playing patty-cake with babies for generations without realizing that this simple game stimulates the development of motor planning and coordination.

Many people have finally realized that Hayek was absolutely right about the importance of tacit knowledge to the smooth functioning of the economy. Yet the tacit knowledge required to raise children may be even more extensive and more important. Many parents today consider self-help books and parenting experts more authoritative than the experience of previous generations. While there is nothing wrong with scientific information about child development, it cannot fully substitute for the learning from experience and the passing on of experience that can only be done on a personal level.

A materialist might believe that we will one day know enough about the physiology of child development and behavior to understand how the ordinary activity of mothers and fathers affects the body chemistry of children. Once we understand that, a materialist might say, we will be able to provide substitutes for the ordinary activities of real parents, and we will have done all that is necessary.

But why should we believe that someday we will have this all figured out? We do not know, and in the nature of things cannot know for certain, what science will discover. Why should we assume that we will someday know enough to be able to provide material substitutes for every parental activity?

We have already discovered many surprising things about human development. It is just as reasonable to assume that the more we learn, the more we will realize just how important and irreplaceable parents really are. We may discover how to help children recover from one set of ill effects of absent parents, but we may very well discover yet another set of goods that parents had been providing all along through their ordinary and, dare we say it, natural activity. Therefore, in spite of all we learn about the links between parental care and the child's body, we ought not conceptualize the parent's role in quite this materialist way.

Love as Motivation

A materialist might respond that "love is not enough." Each of the deficiencies caused by lack of human contact can in fact be understood in a physical sense. We can detect the physiological pathways from the lack of human contact to the difficulties the child experiences. This demonstrates that the physical world is at the heart of everything. If we could control the physical environment, if we could provide enough corrective material contributions to the child's life, all the damage could be undone. The damage that cannot be undone is material as well. Kids who do not mature properly missed the window of opportunity for their neural pathways to develop. These children cannot be fully repaired. They will never fully catch up, no matter how much love their adoptive parents pour into them. This shows that materialism *is* true.

But it does not follow that since love is not enough in this extreme situation love is unimportant. We might state the proposition this

way: love may not be a sufficient condition for the proper development of the child, but love appears to be a necessary condition. More
than that, deprived children help us see that our common notion of
love is deficient. If we imagine love to be nothing more than sentiment, then the claim that love matters seems almost silly. But the
classic definition of love (which I will discuss in later) is "to will and
to do the good of another." This understanding of love has little to
do with feelings or emotion; rather, on this view, love is a decision
that provides the motivation for parents to continue to do what is
necessary for their child, even when they do not fully understand it,
even when they do not know what the final outcome will be.

Let me illustrate the principle of love as commitment with a very
different kind of example. My husband is an engineer—a prime can-
didate for a materialist. He also happens to be a sailboat aficionado.
If you ask him what keeps a wooden sailboat afloat, he will answer
without hesitation, "Love." He is obviously not making a statement
about physics but about human motivation. Wooden sailboats require
an enormous amount of maintenance. Without a person to pour
money, time, and attention into it, a wooden boat will sooner or later
sink into the harbor. And why would a person pour all of those resources into a wooden boat when he could have a fiberglass boat at a
fraction of the cost in time and trouble? He loves the boat.

When we understand love as commitment, we can see how love
is the necessary condition for the child to thrive. Far from being a
shallow sentiment that provides nothing but warm, fuzzy feelings, the
love of parents is the motive force that drives them to do what is truly
good for their child. Maybe a particular child needs hormone shots
or time in an automatic swing. A stranger in a white lab coat is unlikely to stumble over such a child and volunteer his scientific exper-
tise. It is the mother, with her irrational commitment to the child,
who will inform herself about her child's needs, march into the
doctor's office, and insist that her child receive these services.

Why Materialism Is Implausible

Materialism rests on analogies between ourselves and animals, but the analogies are never perfect. Animals respond instinctively. They flee from things that are dangerous to them: predators, competitors, and hazards. They are drawn toward things that are good for them: food, shelter, mating, and the care of young. Animals do not systematically behave in self-destructive ways. Natural selection has taken care of that problem for them by not favoring self-destructive behavior in the reproductive race.

But human beings can behave in self-destructive ways. We do not automatically do what is good for us or avoid things that are bad for us. The good for us is more than simple survival. We can live for a long time with no apparent dangers to our survival and still be miserable. The good for us is more than the absence of pain. We can sit in a room in perfect physical comfort with no intrusions, yet we can still become agitated. The good for us is more than reproductive success. The mere fact of seeing our genetic material survive into another generation is not enough to satisfy us. Which of us would go to his grave satisfied knowing he had sired a small army of evil children? Or unhappy children? Or children who hated him? Even if these children could successfully reproduce, no one would be happy with the outcome.

It is more reasonable to believe that the person is more than the sum of his body, especially because this view does not preclude assigning significance to the body. We can be fully appreciative of every discovery of science without taking the radical leap into materialism as a philosophy. To say that everything is controlled by the material and that we will one day understand exactly how is to take a giant and unnecessary leap of faith.

Materialism is fine as an explanatory strategy for scientific research, even for social science research. But this is quite a different proposition from the claim that materialism provides a complete account of human motivation or a full-fledged personal philosophy that helps make sense of human existence. One can make full use of every legitimate scientific discovery without adopting the materialist posture as the basis for one's personal life. At this level, we can say beyond any shadow of a doubt that materialism is implausible.

If we treat babies like hamsters, we do not end up with noble savages; we end up with a society full of *homines economici*. Understanding what the loving family does for babies and why it is important helps us grasp why the loving family is essential for any society freer than a police state.

PART I

BABIES AND TRUST

1

The Baby and Society

ONSIDER THE TINY INFANT, who enters the world attached to an umbilical cord. Only the most obtuse economist would claim that this small creature possesses the capacity for rational choice or deliberation; only the most doctrinaire contractarian would argue that this little newborn has property rights in any practical sense. The infant is helpless, needy, and immature. These traits have direct implications for communities that wish to survive for more than a generation.

Helplessness

The most obvious fact about the infant's condition is his helplessness. The newborn child is completely dependent upon others for the satisfaction of his most basic needs. The baby cannot have developed preferences, for he has had no experience of consuming anything. He cannot know what will please him, and even if he did know what would please him, he would have no capacity to bring it about.

Helplessness may be the only truly universal human experience, since no one can avoid passing through infancy. But the experience of helplessness is not unique to childhood. Adults are completely helpless in some situations and partially helpless in a great many more. We are powerless over most of our background: we must take as given the time, place, and culture into which we are born, as well as the characters and characteristics of our parents and other relatives.

We are just as helpless in the face of the biggest events of our lives: the time and manner of the arrival of children. We believe that contraceptives and modern reproductive technology give us control over these events. We even call it "reproductive freedom." But the fact is, as many women have discovered, this control is an illusion. We have only the power to say "no" to conception and birth; we do not have a positive power to make ourselves pregnant when and how we want to be.

When those children arrive, we do not have control over their characteristics. We have only limited control over their health and their abilities. We can with time and effort improve our children's abilities to do many different things, but we cannot make an opera singer out of a tone-deaf child or a basketball player out of a short kid. Nor will we ever be able to correct every medical condition. We might think that "someday" modern technology will make it possible to have complete control over the arrival of children: no more infertility, miscarriages, or stillbirths. Likewise, some futurists believe that we will one day control every aspect of our children's behavior indirectly through the choice of their genes.

However that may prove to be, no parent can seriously claim that he completely controls his children's behavior and decisions. It is easy to congratulate ourselves when our children please us or when they present no particular problems. When they are tiny and so appealing, we can convince ourselves that we created this little angel. We enjoy believing that we and we alone are entitled to full credit for all the good we see in our children. But if we are honest with ourselves, we know much of our children's goodness is simply a gift to us. When we are presented with difficulties in parenting, we are more ready to admit that we are not in full control of the situation. An economist might say that parents can control some of the "inputs," but they cannot control the final "output." As a mother, I can say for certain that anyone who enters into parenthood planning to control all the outcomes is in for a rude awakening.

Finally, we are helpless in the face of death—our own deaths and the deaths of others. Perhaps we hate this particular powerlessness more than any of the others, this powerlessness of old age and the inevitability of death. Some of us will live so long that we will have to surrender even the routine care of our body. The only way we can really take command of the situation is to take command of death itself. We can kill ourselves or another person, imagining that we are thereby empowering ourselves. But our power over death is, again, only a negative power. We cannot sustain life. We cannot cause ourselves to remain living, nor can we cause someone else to remain living. The only power we have is the power to kill.

In all of these situations, from birth to death, from cradle to grave, we resist the reality of our helplessness. The difficulty arises because we truly do have *some* power—as well as the responsibility to use it well—but our power is limited. We live between two solid walls of reality: our responsibility to act and the awareness that our power to act is limited. For some, the greater temptation is to sloth and abdication of responsibility. For others, pride is the greater temptation as they attempt to control situations that will not bend to their will.

Societies do much better if they face facts rather than ignore them. In particular, political philosophies and their accompanying social philosophies need to address the limits of human power. We are all completely incapacitated in infancy, and even adults at the height of their capacities are far from omnipotent. If philosophies and the societies built around them ignore either of these truths of human helplessness, negative consequences will follow.

Political philosophies that overemphasize the human power to control the world easily slide into utopianism. These philosophies stand behind elaborate social and political edifices designed to solve every problem and wipe away every tear, but like the Soviet Union and its satellites, these grand systems cannot survive a single century.

To its great credit, libertarian political philosophy has resisted the modern temptations of utopianism far more effectively than most of its competitors, for it fully recognizes the limitations on the human ability to change the world and the people in it. But libertarian political philosophy sometimes overlooks another facet of human helplessness: that people are completely incapacitated during infancy, and partially so in old age and illness. Libertarianism needs a social theory that looks more closely at the helpless people—children—who reappear in every generation.

This deficiency in libertarianism is dramatized in the characters created by Ayn Rand, one of the most radical and consistent individualists of the twentieth century. Her heroes have no childhoods. In *Atlas Shrugged*, Rand describes John Galt as being like Athena, springing from the head of Zeus, fully grown, armed and ready for battle. At very young ages Dagny Taggert and Francisco D'Anconia act more like adults than the adults around them. Howard Roark leaves home as a teenager in *The Fountainhead*.[1]

Critics of libertarians sometimes accuse us of advocating "atomistic individualism," meaning that libertarians believe that every person can and should operate as a completely self-contained individual. Often, these critics attack a position that no thoughtful libertarian actually holds. I think it is well to admit, however, that our inattention to family life and community responsibility have left libertarians open to the charge that we do not care very much about these matters. Amending libertarian political theory to take account of infant helplessness offers us one way to respond to the accusations that we are insufficiently sensitive to the social aspects of human life. By observing the infant, it is easy to see that atomistic individualism cannot be literally true. The human race could not survive beyond a single generation if every person truly acted as if he were unconnected to any other person.

Neediness

Helplessness is only part of the picture. The real problem with babies is that they are needy. They need food and clean diapers; they need shelter and protection; they need baths and clean clothes—and all these things on a daily basis.

If we consider only the physical needs of the child, we might be tempted to think that childcare could be mass produced. We might imagine that it is a menial work that any idiot could do. We could pretend that any caregiver is an adequate substitute for the child's mother and father. But children need more than easily predictable, readily observable, material things. They have intangible needs that are no less real. They need to be rocked and cradled; they need to be comforted; they need direction and guidance, correction and encouragement.

We are quickly disabused of this form of materialism by the slightest experience with actual babies.[2] We discover that each little person is born with a personality and temperament, with talents and dispositions, with needs and capacities. We find that the work of childrearing grows more, not less, demanding as children grow up. Delegating the care of children to strangers becomes more difficult the older the children are. When they are little, the instructions are simple and few because the child's needs are simple and few. As children grow older, it becomes more difficult to pass on to a caregiver the details of discipline, encouragement, and instruction. In this age of technological progress in almost every field, it is sobering to realize that the basic technology of raising children has not changed very much. All the reproductive technology, child psychology, medical knowledge, and educational research cannot take the place of loving adults. Children still need to be raised one at a time by people who love them.

Moreover, because our species has such a long period of immaturity and dependence, and because our dependence is so profound, taking care of babies is an extraordinarily time-consuming process. Therefore, someone must take care of whoever is taking care of the babies.

Some traditional, pre-modern societies, such as the Five Nations of the Iroquois, organized themselves in a matrilineal fashion. Women took care of their own children with the assistance of their mothers and brothers. Fathers played a relatively unimportant role, since the attachments between parents were relatively weak: blood relationships were more permanent than conjugal relationships. Hence, mothers took care of their babies and were in turn taken care of by their blood relatives.[3]

In many societies, the biological father takes care of the mother while she cares for their children. This seemingly natural arrangement can become complicated in societies that permit multiple marriages during the lifetime of the partners. The biological father's attention and resources become divided among the children of several wives, whether polygamy or serial marriage is permitted. In these situations, societies must develop additional constraints on the behavior of men to ensure that all children are at least minimally cared for. Such societies often end up with hierarchies among wives, with the man's "favorite" (or current) wife and her children receiving larger shares of the man's resources.[4]

The Christian solution to this problem was to insist upon the indissolubility of the marriage bond. Jewish law permitted divorce, but rabbis discouraged it in various ways. In this way, the Mosaic law foreshadowed the Christian prohibition of divorce. In Christian cultures, the responsibility for the care of children is assigned to the mother, and the care of the mother is assigned to the biological father. Because the marriage is permanent, the assignment of these roles is unique. Each child has exactly one mother and one father. Each father is committed to exactly one mother, and each mother is committed to exactly one father. Remarriage is permitted only after the death of one spouse, and the new spouse assumes the responsibilities of his or her predecessor.[5]

In many modern Western democracies, the responsibility for the care of the mother is concealed behind impersonal institutional arrangements. Sometimes, of course, the father takes care of the mother. But sometimes the mother is cared for by the state through systems such as welfare. In other cases, the mother earns a living and some third party, such as a day-care center or school, takes care of the children. Day-care workers take care of the babies, and the mother, in cooperation with her employer and through the magic of the modern economy, takes care of the day-care workers. There really are still three parties present, even in the case of a single mother who appears to be taking care both of the babies and of herself, completely unassisted. The third party for the single mother and her child is an institution that has no particular commitment or personal relationship to her.

Every society must face the twin facts of infant helplessness and infant neediness. We can state the proposition even more strongly: Society forms around the helpless baby. For every baby needs at least two persons to support him. This trinity of persons, however it is organized, is the foundation of the whole social order. This primal community forms naturally around an individual infant and his needs without any external encouragement. This community of the infant is as spontaneous as any social order could be. It ought to be an awe-inspiring sight for those who distrust organized government and centralized authority. The child appears in the first place because of the attraction between a man and a woman. That attraction arises naturally and spontaneously, requiring no direction from government or other persons. Everything about this little community emerges from the desires and needs of the people who compose it.

Libertarians like to call attention to the fact that not all order in society is created by centralized government and the institutions surrounding it. This insight certainly applies to the community around the infant. The fact that the family emerges independently of central authority does not necessarily mean that family life is chaotic, for it is an example of "spontaneous order," a naturally occurring social order that is the result of human action but not of human design. The concept of spontaneous order emerges as an element of social theory beginning with Adam Smith in the eighteenth century and continues with Frederick Hayek in the twentieth.[6] These thinkers focused on the economic marketplace as the paradigmatic self-regulating social institution, but the family is an even more fundamental example of an undirected social order that arises spontaneously from the needs and activities of its participants.

The family is and needs to be primarily a self-governing, self-regulating community. Under ordinary circumstances, families do not require extensive legal intervention or formal rule making. This community needs little more than a basic structure of formally recognized rules. Within these basic rules, individual family communities must govern themselves in all the myriad details of daily life. Intervention by the state into the ordinary lives of well-functioning families is ridiculous at best and grotesque at worst. All the same, these primal communities need rules of internal governance. Like the market and every other social institution, the family has a logic of its own. We will be happier if we respect that inner logic and recognize that we cannot make up the rules as we go along.

The Cycle of Trust

The combination of helplessness and neediness gives the child an instrumental need for other people. The child experiences his life in short bursts of neediness. He cries out for help. When help arrives, it actually produces two things for the child: satisfaction of the need and some capacity to trust other people.

We can think of this sequence of interactions as a cycle.[7] The process begins with contentment, progresses to the emergence of a need, then the cry for help, satisfaction of the need, and finally the return of contentment. Normal mothers and infants repeat this cycle many times in the course of each day. In the process, the baby becomes attached to his mother and comes to trust her.

The infant's dependence on adults is more profound than his need to resolve his discomfort, for only an adult can teach the child to trust. A child cannot become trusting all by himself, any more than he can hop out of the crib, open the refrigerator, and heat up a bottle of milk for himself. The baby cannot navigate through the cycle of trust without an adult partner. Some parents might think of their job as meeting the infant's needs at minimal cost to themselves, and they try to placate the infant in the most convenient way. These adults ignore the affect of their time upon the production of trust on the infant's part.

Parents might decide to spend a relatively small amount of time with their baby for several reasons. They may be unaware that they produce trust while satisfying their child's needs. Other parents may realize that their time affects their baby's capacity to trust, but the value of their time may be so high (that is, their wages may be so high) that they find it optimal to select a low level of time with the infant. This adult choses to spend relatively more money and less time on the care of the child. Finally, adults with few resources may be constrained by necessity to satisfy their child's needs at a very low level. The amount of time and market goods devoted to the infant may both be low. Perhaps the child is taken to a minimal-care daycare center or left at an orphanage. Or perhaps the child is left on the street to fend for himself as best he can. In all of these cases, the input of adult time is low, and so a low level of trust is produced.

If the child's needs are not satisfied, he does not develop any trust from particular episodes of neediness. But the unmet need creates something in the child that cannot be fully characterized as an absence. He is sitting there hungry or wet. He has a bloody nose or diarrhea. He keeps crying, his cries growing louder and more frantic. No one comes.

What goes through the child's vulnerable little mind during this episode? He may get angry or despair. The child who despairs may very well become the failure-to-thrive child who wastes away. The angry child perhaps has a better chance of survival. This angry child may very well become the attachment disordered child who allows no other person to truly matter. Many neglected children learn to stop crying for help. They have learned from experience that no one will show up. Crying is futile. They develop some other strategy for getting their needs met. But it is deeply pathological for an infant to be thrown back on his own resources.

When caring adults eventually appear in the child's life, they may misinterpret what they see. They may think, "What a good baby: he never cries." But there is something seriously wrong with a child who never cries. There are few sights more pathetic than an obviously needy child who does not cry—a child with a huge mess of diarrhea, a bloody nose, or a serious injury, just standing there, not crying or trying to comfort himself, resisting the assistance of others. In the normal cycle of trust, the child's neediness leads to the production of trust as a loving parent arrives with satisfaction and relief. But when the cycle of trust is broken, the unmet need produces a combination of rage and despair.

Immaturity

The human infant is helpless and needy. But perhaps even more important, the human infant is immature. The intangible aspects of growing up are more important and difficult than the simply physical aspects of maturing. After all, the body more or less matures automatically. When we tell someone to "grow up," we are not ordinarily shouting encouragement at his growth hormones. We are calling his attention to the fact that his actions need to change, and he is the one who needs to change them. We expect him to change his behavior, in part by changing the thoughts behind the behavior. We want toddlers to stop grabbing and pushing and crying. A child does not automatically share his toys or resolve his own disappointments: he has to be taught how to do these things, and this requires active instruction from adults.

As the child grows in physical strength and intellectual capacity, he needs to embrace even more complex behavior. We want him to moderate his own urges and desires. Crying out for food or feeding himself every time he feels a twinge of hunger is not appropriate. We want him to become capable of forming and maintaining more and more complex and demanding relationships. All of this requires guidance from adults, as well as real effort on the part of the child. This is the deeper part of growing up where parents and children are more likely to stumble. It is the mysterious part of parenting and the difficult part of growing up. We can perhaps get a deeper insight into this mystery by using an analogy from economics.

Economists claim that people respond to incentives in a systematic and predictable way: costs and benefits can be structured to influence a person's behavior. As parents, we rely on the truth of this observation all the time. We make some activities costly for our children, and we provide benefits to them for other activities. No one would deny that it is necessary to use costs and benefits, punishments and rewards, to shape our children's behavior.

We eventually find that these costs and benefits are not fully adequate to the task for two reasons. First, we cannot be present to monitor our children all the time and in every detail. This problem becomes more serious the more independent they become. It is not practical to rely exclusively on externally imposed sanctions. Even a full-time mother with only one child cannot monitor the child's every thought, word, and action.

Second, we cannot control completely what the child is willing to consider a cost or a benefit, except when he is very young and the set of sanctions very limited and obvious—and only then to a limited extent. But even a very little child may decide that watching mother get upset is fun or can take perverse pleasure in stirring up the whole household. The older a child grows, the greater the challenge involved in figuring out what will encourage good behavior and discourage bad behavior.

The two problems with costs and benefits are interrelated. Because it is impracticable to completely monitor the child's behavior, we teach the child to monitor himself. For the child to monitor himself, he must have some sense of what is valuable, what is right and wrong. The parents can and must teach this, but the child has the responsibility to incorporate the teaching into his own thinking and behavior. We cannot compel a child to internalize reasonable standards of conduct. Sooner or later, each new human being must choose whether to embrace such standards and make them his own. As one philosopher put it, we are all initially conscripts in the army of moral duty. But to be morally motivated, we have to volunteer.[8]

From the standpoint of the economist, we might say the following. We know that a person with a particular set of preferences will respond to costs and benefits in a predictable way. But we cannot predict what preferences a particular person will hold. No matter how many sanctions we impose and rewards we offer, we cannot completely change another person's preferences.

Economists say that the person's preferences determine how he will respond to a change in the costs of the activities that he engages in. A person responds to prices differently as an adult than he did as a child. The very things that a person considers as costs or benefits change with maturity. Parents hope to convey to their children which injuries matter and which should be ignored; which sets of rewards are worth pursuing and which are ultimately unsatisfying; which sets of peers should be emulated and which should be shunned. But the child must have some attachment to the parent for the parent to be a credible source of this kind of moral information. The child who has too many interruptions in the cycle of trust never learns to trust. Without that basic trust, adult authority figures must continue to use rewards and punishments, costs and benefits, as motivations for good behavior—or for even minimally acceptable behavior.

From Trust to Love

Every human being is born helpless, needy, and immature. Every episode of neediness has the potential to either produce or destroy trust. The adequacy of the parent's response to the need affects the child's trust in the parent: the child's hunger can be satisfied by being nursed at his mother's breast or by having a bottle propped into the crib. The parents create more trust on the child's part the more lovingly they meet his needs.

With reasonable and supportive parenting, the baby learns to trust that he will be taken care of. As the adult world responds to the child's needs, the child learns that it is safe and even beneficial to trust. Children of normal, loving parents learn that all their anxiety is not really necessary: Mom and Dad are going to show up and do what is needed. Children learn to relax into the care of adults who are in loving control of the situation. In the process, children come to know that there is more in life than the satisfaction of bodily appetites. They learn from experience that human contact and love are the great goods that ensure their continued existence. As a by-product of caring for their children's most basic bodily needs, parents call out their child's longing for human contact. The longing for human contact ultimately develops into a longing for the deeper attachment we ordinarily call love.

2

The Prisoners' Dilemma

THE INFANT'S LIFE IN THE FAMILY lays the foundation for larger social institutions based on trust. Most children learn as infants to trust their parents. Later, their parents entrust them to the care of teachers, scoutmasters, religious leaders, and babysitters. Children learn to trust other people and institutions in a moderate, mature way. Parents eventually allow children to walk by themselves in a crowd, go shopping, or travel to new places, with a reasonable confidence that the child will both survive and behave well.

The ability and willingness to trust is intrinsic to our human nature—and to our survival. Indeed, trust is as deep a part of our human condition as is the self-centered impulse that economists spend so much time talking about. The satisfaction of the infant's needs in a personal way leads to the development of trust and then to the capacity for reciprocity.

Even an infant can provide something of value and pleasure for the mother: the first smile. In this exchange of smiles for satisfactions, the child begins to learn the value of reciprocity, of give and take, in human relationships. The child's continued existence depends not only on the presence of adults but on their willingness to give to and provide for the child. In being cute, making people laugh, and en-

38

gaging others, the infant makes it easier for adults to provide help. An economist would say that adults find it less costly to give to a cute infant than to an obnoxious one.

The Prisoners' Dilemma gives us an appreciation of why the development of attachment and trust is so important. The Prisoners' Dilemma analyzes situations in which it is collectively beneficial for people to cooperate with each other, even though it is in their individual interests to be uncooperative. Social scientists use this scenario as a model for studying problematic cooperation.

The Prisoners' Dilemma takes its name from a hypothetical situation. Two people have jointly committed a crime and have both been arrested. The authorities do not have sufficient evidence to convict either prisoner. So they offer the following deal to each prisoner separately: If neither you nor your accomplice confesses, you will both go free, for we have insufficient evidence to convict you. If you confess, your accomplice will receive the full sentence, but we will give you a reduced sentence. If he confesses and you do not, you will receive the full sentence, while he gets the lighter sentence. If you both confess, you both get the full sentence allowed by law, for we will have enough evidence to convict you both.

Both prisoners will confess in this scenario as long as there is no possibility for communication between them. This is a dilemma for the prisoners because both would be better off if neither confessed. Since neither can be sure what the other will do, neither is willing to take the chance of being the only one to remain silent. Both prisoners confess and receive the heaviest sentence. The authorities deliberately place the prisoners in this dilemma to generate the best outcome for the whole society, namely to induce criminals to confess. The situation is a dilemma from the point of view of the little society consisting of the two prisoners. They would prefer that the authorities not offer them this tricky deal that results in both of them receiving the maximum sentence for their crimes.

There are many situations in which the entire society finds itself in a dilemma comparable to the dilemma of these two prisoners; many social interactions have a structure of rewards similar to that described in the Prisoners' Dilemma. I would be better off if no one littered in the park, but I cannot stop others from littering. Why pay the cost of cleaning up after myself if no one else has done so or is likely to do so? I would be better off if no one ever filed frivolous liability lawsuits. But since I am already bearing the social cost of many such frivolous lawsuits, why shouldn't I file a suit of my own if a plausible occasion presents itself? I am better off living in a world in which everyone keeps his promises and contracts than in a world without effective promise-keeping. But within the world of general promise-keeping, I am even better off by reneging on my own agreements when I can get away with it.

Theorists and experimentalists alike have shown that it is privately rational to play tit-for-tat in a prisoners' dilemma game, as long as the game has been started with a cooperative first move. In this context tit-for-tat means "I will cooperate with you, if you cooperate with me. If you defect from our (implicit or explicit) agreement, I will retaliate by refusing to cooperate with you in the next round of interactions."[1]

Think of the parent as the first mover in the child's life. The parent gives to the child in an unrequited way: the child's very existence is a gift. The child receives the gift of life as well as many other gifts from the parent. The child does not, and indeed cannot, reciprocate in kind. But the child does learn to participate in reciprocity. Sometime between the age of three and six months, the child learns the cognitively trivial, but socially complex, task of playing peekaboo— looking, with anticipation, for another person and delighting in the moment of eye contact. The only rewards for the game are laughter and looks. Ultimately, the child learns to take turns in a conversation. All these behaviors have elements of regard for others, of reciprocity, of mutual benefit and pleasure.

Some social scientists and economists have a tendency to use the contract as the model for every human relationship with reciprocity and to treat every interaction of mutual benefit as if it were an exchange. Yet it would be a mistake, a grave distortion of the situation, to describe the relationship of parent and child as a contract. Infants are far too primitive in their development to be offering consideration in exchange for promises, and the mutuality and reciprocity of their relationship with their parents is far deeper than contract, the trust far more profound than a contractual promise.

Trust and Trustworthiness

Besides the willingness to trust, the ability to be trustworthy also develops as the child matures. Restraining oneself is an integral part of being trustworthy. In fact, part of cooperating in the Prisoners' Dilemma is restraining oneself from taking advantage of opportunities for immediate gain. Both the willingness to trust and the ability to restrain oneself flow from the attachments of people to each other. The child learns to suppress some of his immediate desires for the sake of the comfort of others. He learns not to scream for what he wants. He learns to wait his turn and share his toys. These primitive forms of cooperative behavior require self-restraint.

Child development specialists have outlined the course of moral development in the following way: First, my parents will punish me if I do wrong. Next, my parents will not like it if I do wrong. Next, my parents might not find out, but if they did they would not like it. Next, I will not like it if I do wrong. Finally, I am not the kind of person who even thinks about doing wrong. External costs and benefits become less relevant with each step. The child moves from calculating the costs of disobeying, to calculating the probability of detection, to completely internalizing the prohibition. The child eventually incorporates the prohibition into his preferences and his view of himself. The costs and benefits become irrelevant for the child because he will not even begin to calculate whether it is cost effective to violate the rule.

For any of this progression of internalized prohibitions to take place, there must be a significant person in the child's life. This other person is significant precisely in the sense that the child cares what the person will think. This person's disapprobation alone becomes enough of a cost to deter bad behavior. The child's internal voice must say "We don't do that kind of thing" before the calculation ever gets started. That internal voice is the voice of the loving parent, the parent who proved himself trustworthy long before the child could even begin to demand reasons for anything.

Trustworthiness and the Time Horizon

Social theorists have shown that people are more likely to be cooperative the longer the time horizon of the relationship. In other words, people are more likely to take advantage of a stranger than a person they will have to deal with again later. Even if you feel nothing for the other person, the argument goes, but you know you will encounter him again in future interactions, you will be more likely to be cooperative and not press your full advantage. Even if you have no attachment to the other person, it will be in your rationally calculated self-interest not to exploit the other person if you know you will have to deal with him again. This argument is sometimes used to show how even people who have no attachments to each other could be induced to cooperate simply by following their rational self-interest. It is also used to justify "minimal morals": self-interest can be counted on to do the job that morals formerly had been asked to do.

But this argument assumes too much. It assumes that people have a time horizon long enough to take advantage of future potential gains. But it is not reasonable to assume that every person has an equal capacity for accurate calculation of future costs and benefits.

Nor can we safely assume that every person has an equal capacity for postponing benefits in the face of immediate costs. We know from casual and systematic observation that children have considerably shorter time horizons than do adults.[2] A great deal of moral training focuses upon teaching a child to accept delayed gratification. The length of a person's time horizon is not a given but is an important variable in determining the person's success in life.

With a bit of reflection, we can see that trust is a necessary element for teaching delayed gratification. Most people do not instinctively or automatically forgo future benefits when faced with immediate costs: they usually need to have their experience explained to them. Children need someone to tell them, for instance, that they have a stomach-ache because they ate too much candy, and they are more likely to accept that information and incorporate it into their thinking if they trust the person who tells them. Trust is the mechanism through which a person with normal attachments to others first learns to delay gratification and lengthen his time horizon.

Trusting other people is one thing that an unattached person truly cannot do. Unattached children have difficulty learning many ordinary things because they believe adults cannot be trusted. Imagine trying to teach a child how to ride a bicycle when the child secretly believes you want him to fall or playing catch with a child who flinches because he thinks you are trying to hit him in the head. Think of even something so mundane as washing the hair of a child who thinks you might drown him.

As adults, attachment disordered people have trouble participating in long-term interactions. The argument that repeated interactions in themselves induce cooperative behavior does not apply to them. Others are truly interchangeable for the attachment disordered person: he cares as much about a stranger as he does about his own mother. (Parents of attachment disordered children often report that they believe their child would willingly go home with a stranger.) He is willing to find new trading partners for every interaction.

But the attachment disordered person is extremely limited in the kinds of transactions he can carry out. He can only engage in activities that do not require a particular person to interact with him for long periods of time. Unless he can truly restrain himself in the short run, using his rational calculating faculty, he will not be able to do anything long term. One of the characteristics of these people as they age is that they continue to deceive people and find a steady supply of dupes.

The attachment disordered person is literally running the cost-benefit analysis on every opportunity for theft, lying, and cheating. Normal people do not even begin such calculations because they know if they do, they will find that some of the time crime will pay. In prisoner of war camps, some people confess, inform, or otherwise comply with the wishes of their captors. But not everybody does. Prisoners are offered various inducements, both negative and positive, for cooperation. People who manage such places have observed that once a person begins deliberating whether it is worth it to comply, their task is over. He will eventually comply; it is only a matter of finding the right combination of inducements. The person who never breaks is a person who never begins the calculation.

Trust and Economic Institutions

Trade in organized markets and exchange through informal barter are the most basic economic activities and are reciprocal behaviors. They require some willingness to trust and some capacity for trustworthy behavior.[3]

Experimental economists have observed that rats can be induced to do something akin to comparing costs and benefits. Rats will demand fewer food pellets when the cost of obtaining them is higher. In this very limited sense rats are rational economic actors.[4] But the experimentalists cannot induce the rats to trade. Rats will not exchange food or anything else with each other. Demand is the economic action of an individual in isolation; exchange is the economic interaction among individuals in a society. Rats can be trained to "buy" commodities from a food dispenser, but rats do not trade. They appear to be incapable of reciprocal behavior.[5]

We can compare a commonplace transaction in the grocery store to the rats buying from a food dispenser. A person observes the commodity offered for sale and the posted price and decides whether to buy it. If he decides to buy, he parts with the required amount of money. The store dispenses the commodity to him. The transaction is completed.

But many more complex transactions are not at all comparable to the rat tapping for food pellets. Some transactions take place over longer periods of time and require people to deliver goods and make payments at intervals. Other transactions are more complex because the commodities are more difficult to define precisely. Buyer and seller may have different conceptions of the good being traded.[6] In these types of transactions, a certain amount of trust is necessary for the transaction even to begin. If the parties are both trustworthy and willing to trust, the transaction can be completed at a far lower cost.

Imagine having a long-term contract, with thousands of dollars at stake over long periods of time, with someone who is calculating every short-term advantage. Contract law cannot be enough to protect people from "efficient" breaches of contract.[7] The world could not do the amount and kind of business it does if literally everybody acted opportunistically on every occasion.

The banking system provides a specific example of the economic significance of trust. The banking system is based on trust: trust that your money will be there when you go to withdraw it, trust that your loan will not be called in ahead of schedule. Without trust of this kind, the banking system would collapse, no matter how it was regulated and no matter how much deposit insurance was pumped into it. The banking system of Europe has its foundations in the activities of trading families and religious orders during the eleventh, twelfth, and thirteenth centuries.[8] One of the marvelous phenomena of economic development is the extension of those networks of trust, based on personal contact or highly developed reputations, into networks available even to strangers. Hayek described that system of trust among strangers as the "Great Society."

In the decade since the collapse of the Soviet Union, well-meaning Western economists have tried to graft a Western-style banking system onto that country. But the Russian people have been informing on one another, lying to the government, and generally doing what they could get away with for seventy years. Many of the economic and political leaders of Russia have had no scruples at all about lining their pockets with the money entrusted to them for the development of the country. No amount of formal regulation would be enough to overcome this fundamental lack of trustworthiness, especially in the short term.[9]

Trust and Political Institutions

As this example illustrates, trust and trustworthiness are important to politics as well as to economics. Public choice economists argue that public policy is made through a self-interested process.[10] Those who have the most at stake in the outcome of a regulatory decision, for example, have the greatest interest in getting themselves organized to influence the regulators. Typically, this means that producer organizations are favored over unorganized consumers. Well-defined, well-organized voting blocs tend to be favored over more ill-defined groups.

The modern democratic state offers many opportunities for the unscrupulous. The state is able to offer many favors in the form of tax breaks and changes in regulation. Because tens of millions of dollars can be transferred by the stroke of a regulator's pen, interested parties spend millions of dollars trying to influence the outcome.

Public choice economists refer to this phenomenon as "rent seeking."[11] There is a tremendous waste of resources in this process, as people spend valuable time either trying to live off the results of wealth transfer or trying to protect themselves from other predators. Most everyone realizes the destructiveness of this process: some people describe it as a "zero-sum game" or even as a "negative sum game." But once the process is in motion, no one can afford to step out of it. The temptation for this kind of antisocial behavior is too strong for most people to resist. An old-fashioned Catholic might say that the modern state is a massive occasion of sin.[12]

Americans have established many of our political institutions and instituted many of our public policies counting on the core of trust and trustworthiness that is created in individuals by their family life. Unfortunately, these public institutions contain so many temptations for antisocial behavior that the habits of trust have been eroded. People who continue to behave decently are exploited by the unprincipled. Much of the apparatus of the modern state was established in good faith by people who conscientiously believed that it would achieve its stated purposes. We overlooked the fact that we were creating temptations. We were counting on people to be public-spirited and to refrain from calculating the private benefits of taking full advantage of the system.

The state is parasitic on the core of trust created within the family. Perhaps the reason the state has not collapsed from the weight of its own corruption is that each generation continues to learn some of the core values of trust and trustworthiness upon which the continuation of mass political activity depends. The attachment between parents and children creates a capacity to form lasting attachments with other people. Other particular people become important enough to us that we are unwilling to take advantage of them, unwilling to sacrifice a long-term relationship with them for the sake of short-term advantage. Likewise, we exercise some forbearance in not attempting to harness the power of the state for our personal ends on any occasion that might present itself.

It is not good enough to say, as libertarians so often do, "We must make the state minimal. We must reduce and control the state so much that no one will be tempted to use it for his own benefit." The problem with this formulation is that it is unstable. A state with enough power to protect us from an enemy as powerful as the Soviet Union used to be is a state that can do what it likes with us. Even a minimal state has enough power to run a military establishment, legal system, and police force. This power can be harnessed by private interests if they are tenacious enough. Without an ethic of mutual forbearance among citizens, the minimal state is unlikely to remain minimal.

This is why a discussion of trust and reciprocity belongs in a discussion of libertarian political theory. Free market economics relies on the use of voluntary exchange and contracts. Libertarian political theory relies upon the use of political exchange relationships to a far greater extent than most other political theories do. We tend to describe these exchanges in rational, calculating terms.

But in the background of rationally calculating economic man, we economists and libertarians all along were assuming that the vast majority of the population comes to the economic and political realm with some very specific skills. The ability to trust and be trustworthy, the capacity for reciprocity and mutuality, these are "natural" in the sense that most everyone can develop them. But we do not come into the world with these traits: we have to acquire them. Under normal circumstances, children learn these skills so automatically, so effortlessly, so painlessly, that we scarcely notice the process at all. Trust and reciprocity are so much a part of the human condition that we take them for granted. We notice them only in their absence.

Economists, especially libertarian economists, have used individualism as a methodology for analysis and as an assumption about the human condition. Using the individual as the basic unit of analysis is valid, especially when the alternative is to use classes, nations, or races as the basic categories for social analysis. Beginning with the individual as the central focus, we can build up a larger theory of groups of individuals living and acting within a social context. But it does not follow that individualism is a valid assumption about the human condition.

Looking at helpless babies makes this point with special clarity. The individual baby cannot survive outside of a group of people who provide for his needs. Even within the context of methodological individualism, individualism is not an accurate assumption about the human condition or about human nature. The helpless infant becomes the focal point of a little community. While the adults are meeting the baby's immediate material needs, they are also building up the capacity for trust and reciprocity. The smooth functioning of the economic order and the self-governing political order depend on these qualities.

The economic order requires love. The love of the parents for the infant motivates them to give far more that they receive directly in return. The parents make the generous first move required to begin the process of mutual cooperation. Infants grow into children who are willing to give in return, to cooperate, to restrain themselves, to trust. Likewise, the political order requires love. Love among kin creates the capacity for forbearance. The stability of a modern democratic government depends directly upon an element of forbearance among citizens.

The political realm requires self-restraint, which is more likely to flow from affection than from calculation. Politics, which appears to be about power and force, actually depends upon loving families at least as much as upon patriotism or civic-mindedness. The economic realm, which appears to be comprised of impersonal exchanges of material objects among strangers, is based upon love.

PART II

The Contractual Mentality

∽ 3 ∾

Contracts in Libertarian Thought

T
HE INFANT NEEDS ADULTS in order to learn trust. Adults need
the infant to learn trust and be trustworthy, if they wish to
maintain anything like a free and open society. This places
obligations upon the adults. Adults cannot choose any way of life for
themselves and expect that the infant will grow up to become a self-
governing individual.

If I were writing this book during the Eisenhower administration,
I would not need to spell this out—I probably would not be writing
such a book at all. Adults at that time tacitly understood that the well-
being of children places constraints on adult behavior. They lived out
this understanding in their daily lives, in what they did and refrained
from doing, in what they celebrated and condemned.

It is probably fair to say, however, that few people in those earlier
generations could completely articulate what they were doing and
why. In fact, we can be sure that they could not because they were
powerless in the face of the cultural hurricane of the 1960s with its
revolution in sexual conduct, marriage, divorce, and childrearing.

It is beyond my scope to offer a complete explanation for how and
why so many cultural norms were uprooted within such a short period of time. But one part of the explanation surely is that the new

53

norms appealed to both ends of the political spectrum, albeit in slightly different ways. Without that broad appeal, it is doubtful that the revolution in family life could have swept through society so quickly and thoroughly.

The particular aspect of the new norms that appealed across the spectrum was the endorsement of behavior on the grounds of personal choice rather than the good of children. This appeal to personal choice in turn led to the language of contracts being used as part of the defense of the new norms. The language of contracts appealed to the political right: even people of conservative temperament endorsed social changes that amounted to revolutionary restructuring of family life. At the very least, if they did not endorse these changes, many on the right were unable to explain why they should not. It was the language of contracts, freedom, and personal choice that temporarily confused so many instinctive conservatives.

On the other side of the political spectrum, the application of the contractual mentality to the family is something of a puzzle. Left-wingers tend to endorse the idea that any sexual or family arrangement is fine as long as the partners agree to it. Yet it would be surprising to find these same people expressing that kind of tolerance toward other forms of voluntary agreement. People on the left are usually not persuaded by the claim that the employer and the employee voluntarily agree to a labor contract featuring low wages and long working hours. Most members of the lifestyle left would be revolted by the idea that country clubs should be entitled to exclude people from membership on the basis of race or religion, even though the club is a private organization and everyone in the club agrees to its terms. So the left's deference to personal choice and contracts in family life is somewhat anomalous. At least the libertarian position has the virtue of consistency. For libertarians, personal choice that does not harm anyone else ought not to be restricted—be it in employment contracts or marriage contracts.

Libertarians and economists place a high priority, for some very good reasons, on the use of contracts. When I say that the family is not a contract, I do not dismiss the contractual framework altogether. Rather, I reserve it for the contexts in which it most properly applies. At the same time, I am trying to enhance our understanding and appreciation of the family by analyzing the specific characteristics of the family in a more focused way. The next chapter shows why the language of contracts does not really apply to the family. The community around the infant cannot be held together exclusively by a contract. We distort our understanding of the family if we reduce family relationships to a contract.

Economists, especially libertarian economists, draw a sharp contrast between voluntary exchanges and transactions characterized by coercion. Market transactions and contractual exchanges are examples of voluntary exchanges. Each of the parties to a contract enters into the contract because he expects to be better off from the combination of what the contract requires him to do for the other person and what the contract requires the other person to do for him. Libertarians argue that these types of exchanges should be encouraged, or at the very least, not interfered with.

Libertarian and free market economists go on to observe that exchanges involving the government can seldom be characterized as completely voluntary. The government's powers of taxation and coercion stand behind its transactions: a parent dissatisfied with the government school system cannot excuse himself from paying property taxes; a taxpayer dissatisfied with the government's welfare system cannot withhold his donations from the tax collector.

Most libertarians argue even more strongly: in an "exchange" orchestrated by government, their presumption is that someone is being harmed or his interests compromised. Libertarians want to know, for instance, why a particular group requires the assistance of government to achieve its goals. In the absence of some compelling reason, libertarians presume that the group is using government to achieve their goals because they could not persuade people to go along with the transaction voluntarily.[1]

Contracts in Libertarian Political Thought

Most important political ideas are responses to earlier ideas that have played themselves out. Classical liberalism and libertarianism are no exceptions. Classical liberalism in its eighteenth- and nineteenth-century form was a response to absolutism. Absolutism is the political philosophy that claims the sovereign has absolute authority in the life of a country. In its early forms, the idea was sometimes expressed as the divine right of kings. God gave the monarch the absolute authority to do whatever he liked, and he was accountable to no power upon earth for the use of his authority.[2]

Twentieth-century collectivism is a variant of absolutism: these ideologies do not hold themselves accountable to anything outside of themselves. Collectivist ideologies such as fascism, socialism, or communism claim that the individual is subordinate to the state and its objectives. Collectivism holds that it is proper to subordinate the individual to the state because the state is in the service of some collective entity, the "nation" or "proletariat." The advocates of these ideas anthropomorphize collectivities, speaking about them as if they were persons, with goals, with needs, with desires. The individuals in these societies are swept into the service of the state.[3]

Classical liberalism and libertarianism are responses to absolutism and collectivism. Classical liberalism takes up the natural law tradition which argues that not every exercise of authority by the sovereign is legitimate. It is possible that even the monarch, the most powerful individual in a nation, could violate natural law, and this violation may absolve individual citizens from their obligations of obedience. Might does not make right; it just makes more might.[4]

In the classical liberal tradition, contracts play a key role. Contracts are one of the major ways in which people organize themselves to work together, either for their own private purposes or for public purposes. Behind this emphasis on contract is the insight that a contract is the tool used by free persons who are equals. No person is better than any other, so no one has a right to force a peaceful person to do something against his will. The belief that no peaceful person may be coerced is one of the key axioms upon which classical liberal reasoning rests.

Libertarianism, the twentieth-century variant of classical liberalism, has had more formidable opponents than its eighteenth-century predecessors, for the collectivist ideologies of our century have attempted to strip the person of his individuality altogether. Collectivism makes a comprehensive claim to the individual person, his property, his time, his loyalties, his efforts, his beliefs.[5]

The Nazis and the Soviets made demands for loyalty and obedience that no monarch ever could have contemplated or had the power to implement. No regulation of personal or economic life seemed too detailed or too intimate for the Soviets to attempt. And what can one say about the Chinese Communists who believe they have the right to do whatever is necessary to achieve their population control goals? Louis XIV of France declared "I am the law," but it is hard to imagine him considering requiring women to record the start of their menstrual periods in a public place. No king would have ever thought he was entitled to require doctors to murder an "illegal child" in the delivery room.

Libertarianism attempts to deal with the collectivist claim that the person is the property of the state to be disposed of as the state sees fit. The libertarian response is that the individual is the sovereign over his own life and property. The state, no matter how well-intentioned, may not strip people of their rights and their property. Individuals are prior to the state. This accounts for the sharp dichotomy between voluntary exchanges and government coercion in libertarian thought and for the high regard in which libertarians hold contracts. For many in the libertarian camp, an analogy between contracts and other transactions has become a "trumping" argument in a certain sense. If an interaction is like a contract, or can be described as a contract, that is a sufficient argument in favor of its legitimacy. If this is an exaggeration of the libertarian position, it is only a mild one. If this favoring of contracts is an overreaction on the part of libertarians, many would be inclined to say "So be it." Libertarians may, I think, be forgiven for overreacting. Something had to be said to counter the outrageous claims of collectivism. But classical liberalism paid little attention to familial relationships because these relationships were taken for granted, both by classical liberals and their opponents.

In fact, kinship bonds were so strong, and so taken for granted, that analogies with family relationships could be used as "trumping" arguments. If someone could plausibly argue that someone or something was "like a father," that would be a persuasive argument for obedience to the metaphorical father. Sir Robert Filmer wrote the famous work *Patriarchy* to argue for the divine right of kings.[6] His argument was that the king was like a father to his people. The people had an obligation of obedience to the king, just as children had an obligation of obedience to their father. When he made this argument in 1680, he evidently thought that a comparison between a father's authority and the monarch's authority would be persuasive to a great many of his readers.

When John Locke, one of the earliest classical liberals, responded to Filmer's argument, he spent a considerable part of his effort explaining why the analogy between a king and a father is not valid.[7] Filmer's argument would not have been plausible unless people lived in a social milieu that endorsed far more binding family ties than those to which our era is accustomed. Locke's famous rebuttal of Filmer would not have been necessary in a world of radically autonomous individuals completely severed from any family connections.

It is sometimes said that libertarians favor "atomistic individual-ism," as though each and every person could and should exist entirely independent of concern for others. I have already observed that this charge is usually an exaggeration. The grain of truth to that charge might be that libertarians have tended to neglect analyzing groups carefully. Many libertarians have become so apprehensive about claims of any kind of collective against the individual that we have neglected to elucidate responsibilities within family life.

But it would be unfair to place the entire blame for the extreme individualism of our time on the libertarian emphasis upon the in-dividual as a contracting agent or on economists who advocate the impersonal workings of the market. For there are a great many people, holding no identifiable political philosophy, who nonetheless embrace the view of the individual as sovereign, and for whom any voluntary choice is acceptable.

Collectivists themselves sought to weaken or break community and family ties. For a person with no family ties has no loyalties that might compete with loyalties to the state, the volk, the nation, or the proletariat. The Nazis made a point of closing down clubs of every kind. Hitler youth clubs replaced the German equivalent of Boy Scouts, church youth groups, and neighborhood groups. The Sovi-ets attempted to break down the family itself. They removed children from the home at earlier and earlier ages to be reared collectively in state-run crèches. They encouraged family members to spy on each other. The current Chinese policy of one child per family will have a very fragmenting affect on family life. For within a generation or so, people will have no relatives except parents and grandparents: no brothers and sisters, no aunts and uncles, no cousins. No family loy-alties will provide potential competitors to the loyalty people must feel for the state.

Every generation has a new set of problems with which to grapple. Our new problem is that the family bonds that earlier generations of political theorists could take for granted have become so weakened that the very fabric of social life is threatened. Men abandon their wives and children; women place even tiny babies into the care of strangers; husbands and wives do not really trust one another. So many adults have abandoned the responsibility for moral instruction of the young that we sometimes appear to be in danger of being over-run by a generation of illiterate barbarians. Even an infant in the womb is not safe from his own mother.

I think the generations of classical liberal thinkers who empha-sized the rights of the individual against the state may be forgiven for not predicting such a state of affairs. I would make an even stronger statement: even if this state of affairs were entirely attributable to the individualism in classical liberalism (which it is not), I can forgive them for not predicting it. At least classical liberalism saw the evils of absolutism for what they were.

Conclusion

This is how the libertarian dichotomy between voluntary, contractual relations and involuntary, coercive interactions arose. It was a re-sponse to the extreme absolutist claims that the individual is some-how the property of the state or the "child" of the state. Today's political libertarians who use this dichotomy between voluntary and involuntary relationships are trying to protect the individual from the monstrous demands made by the collectivists of our time. The di-chotomy is not, and was not intended to be, a completely exhaustive listing of types of relationships or interactions. The focus of the ear-lier discussion was on the relationship between persons and the state, between individuals and the collective. Nothing in the classical lib-eral concern about the tyranny of the state precludes a powerful lib-ertarian defense of the family.

With all of this in mind, let us turn to the business of breaking apart some of the old dichotomies: involuntary vs. voluntary; gov-ernment vs. individual; public vs. private; the market vs. the state;

coercion vs. contract. Breaking out of these categories will provide us some analytical room to talk in richer terms about the family. The family is the most basic category for analyzing social relationships—more basic even than contracts. The individual begins his life embedded within a family. The family precedes contracts as well as the state.

Kin relationships have elements of choice and elements that are not chosen. Blood relationships arise naturally, without any coercion from the state. Yet the institutions of the state may inhibit or support kinship. Without proper support from the state, or under active attacks from the state, even the most natural relationships among kin may not survive.

⋒ 4 ⋒

Why Marriage Is Not a Contract

T HE DICHOTOMY between a free society and an unfree one does
not rest exclusively on the distinction between what is voluntarily chosen and what is not. The more important distinction is between cooperative relationships and coercive ones, between
mutually beneficial relationships and exploitative relationships. Contracts are rightly revered by advocates of free societies because contracts are instruments of mutual benefit for people who want to
cooperate with each other. But contract is by no means the exclusive, or even the most important, method of cooperative behavior.
The contract is a very special form of cooperative relationship in part
because it is easily observed. We can see that the parties are cooperating because they have put their commitment to do so in writing.
Many other kinds of cooperation are loosely organized and only tacitly understood. They are no less important for having a less formal
character.

The community around the infant cannot be held together exclusively by a set of contracts. We distort our understanding of the family if we reduce family relationships to a set of contracts. My point
to my fellow economists is that this dichotomy between voluntary and
involuntary does not exhaust the possible types of interactions. Not

every relationship with mutuality can be characterized as chosen. Not every relationship with reciprocity can be characterized as an exchange. Familial relationships are not coercive in the usual sense, nor are they voluntary in the usual sense. This dichotomy, so familiar in libertarian and economic analysis, does not apply to the life of the family.

Marriage bears more resemblence to a contract than does any other family relationship. Marriage is embedded within contracts but operates quite differently from the typical contract and is better understood as a partnership than as a contract. Even the partnership analogy breaks down as we consider the aspects of marriage that connect the couple to their blood relationships. The family more broadly considered encompasses familial relationships that have no clear analogy with contracts or partnerships.

Marriage Is Not a Contract

Of all family relationships, that between a husband and wife bears the closest similarities to a contract. Unlike blood relationships, the conjugal relationship is chosen by the parties. A person chooses to marry another because he or she expects to be better off for doing so. Marriage vows are promises expressly and publicly exchanged, similar to the exchange of promises in a contract. Even in societies with arranged marriages, relatives of the couple do the arranging. No one outside the family attempts to coerce the family or the young people into a marriage.

At the most superficial level, a marriage is the sharing of a household by two adults and usually involves exclusive sexual rights. But at a deeper level marriage involves something much more. A successful marriage requires the complete gift of the self to the other person. It is not reasonable to give of the self at the same level unless there is a complete commitment. These are the key elements of marriage: commitment and self-giving to another person.

This explains some seemingly anomalous facts about modern marriage. For instance, it explains why people usually do not negotiate five-year renewable marriage contracts. On the face of it, we might have expected to observe this type of contract. After all, it corresponds to modern reality: we have observed just about every other form of negotiation over the traditional terms of marriage. Yet even people who know the probability of divorce know in their innermost being that a five-year renewable marriage is a contradiction in terms.

The centrality of commitment also explains a puzzling bit of social science data: people who cohabit before marriage are more likely to get divorced than people who do not cohabit.[1] Many researchers expected exactly the opposite result. They expected that living together would teach the couple about each other. They could learn whether they were right for each other. They could learn how to be married and thereby be better prepared for marriage. The theory behind this reasoning is that choosing a marriage partner is comparable to buying a car. Why not rent the car for a while before committing oneself to such a major purchase?

This reasoning might sound plausible for a glorified roommate relationship, but it neglects the importance of commitment. Living together without a commitment cannot in any way simulate living with a commitment. Each person can, in the back of his or her mind, imagine "If things don't work out, I can leave." This thought by itself can undermine the very skills necessary to keep a relationship functioning.[2] People end up calculating their advantage, much as the attachment disordered orphan is calculating what he can get away with. The partners become objects to each other, judged by whether they provide satisfaction. Moreover, the uncertainty of living with a sexual partner who might or might not be committed to you undermines the self-giving required at the heart of the committed marriage: we practice holding back on our partners; we practice calculating.[3]

If we were going to compare marriage with any commercial relationship, it would not be a contract. A better analogy would be a partnership.

Contracts and Partnerships

A business partnership has features in common with a contract, yet is more than a contractual relationship. A partnership is a voluntary exchange of sorts, since each member of the partnership contributes something to the joint venture and receives something for his efforts. A partnership has a contract as its foundation in that there is a set of legally enforceable promises establishing the relationship between the two parties. This basic contract establishes the relationship and brings it into being as a legal entity distinct from either of the two individual persons.[4]

The partnership differs from other contractual relationships in significant ways.[5] The contract between the partners does not govern every detail of the relationship's functioning. The partners do not attempt to specify every duty of each party during the course of their relationship: only the most basic duties are so specified. The contractual relationship between partners is not the end of the relationship nor the method for how the parties relate to one another. The parties expect to do a great many things of mutual benefit that cannot be included in the set of legally enforceable promises.

The partnership is more open-ended in duration, while a contract typically has a specified period during which transactions are to take place. In a partnership, the parties establish a relationship using a contract and then proceed with their business until further notice. The partnership contract establishes an ongoing framework within which business can be conducted.

Partnerships feature ongoing, joint decision making during the life of the relationship. In purely contractual relationships by contrast, the parties negotiate most, if not all, of the significant decisions prior to entering into the contract. In a partnership, the partners share responsibilities, decision-making, and risks. The partners make no attempt to specify all of the details of their relationship in advance. It might even be counterproductive for them to do so. The partnership allows two people to work together without fully specifying their responses to all possible contingencies.

Risk and responsibility do not, per se, favor a partnership over a contract. A contractual arrangement can allow for sharing of decisions, risks, and responsibilities. The primary difference between the partnership and the contract is that partners jointly cope with risk throughout their relationship. By contrast, a contract can be written that allows the parties to agree at the outset that the risks and responsibilities involved will be shared or allocated in some way.

For example, a sharecropping contract shares the risks associated with agriculture. In a typical contract, the tenant and the landlord evenly share the proceeds of the harvest. The risk of a low yield is shared to some extent by both parties. The party with the most (although limited) control over the yield is the tenant. The tenant not only supplies the labor but typically makes all the ordinary, day-to-day decisions about production. The landlord has the most knowledge about marketing the crop and finding the best price. The sharecropping contract thus divides responsibilities for decision-making and allocates the risk between the two parties.[6] The sharecropping arrangement is properly called a contract. Even though this arrangement might be renewed annually over the lifetime of both parties, no one would mistake it for a partnership.

Finally, partnerships are characterized by tacit, unstated knowledge, expectations, and responses. Each partner can count on the other to behave in certain ways because they know one another. They are not necessarily able to specify everything that each person will contribute to the enterprise. By contrast, explicit communication, rather than tacit communication, is one of the characteristic features of a contract.

Uncertainty and Uniqueness

A partnership is a reasonable response to two circumstances: the presence of radical uncertainty and the lack of a good substitute for the person with whom the partnership is being formed.

Economists sometimes make a distinction between risk and uncertainty.[7] The exact outcome is unknown in both risky and uncertain situations. But in a risky situation, reasonable probabilities of various outcomes are known in advance. Uncertainty refers to something quite different. In a situation of uncertainty, people cannot assign probabilities to outcomes. Sometimes, even which outcomes are possible cannot be accurately foreseen.

Insurance companies deal with risk in exactly the economist's sense. They have a reasonable estimate of the probability of a house burning down, or of a thirty-five-year-old woman surviving to age seventy. But they do not know which house will burn down or which women will survive. That the probabilities are known makes it possible for the insurance company to sell policies that are both helpful to the customer and profitable to the company. Hence, the relationship between the insurance company and customer is a contract and not a partnership: all the contingencies are well specified in advance, and the relationship is limited, both in duration and in scope.

But in a situation of true uncertainty, the sting of the unknown future cannot be alleviated through contract. For instance, a research and development project has an unknown probability of success. Even if a research team knows they will discover something, they cannot know, in the nature of things, exactly what it is that they will discover. No prudent insurance agent would offer an insurance contract that promises to pay a benefit to a researcher whose project fails. There is a "moral hazard" problem: the research team could pretend to discover nothing in order to collect the benefit. But more important, the insurance company could not assign a reasonable probability for the success of the project in the first place: the point of the research project itself is to discover something not presently known.

Because of this radical uncertainty, a research team might very well be better off organizing itself as a partnership. A full contract would require them to try to specify all contingencies and responses to them, but these are inherently unknown and unspecifiable. In a partnership, the partners can work more smoothly toward a response than if they had to renegotiate a contract each time an unforeseen event took place.

A sharecropping contract highlights this distinction between risk and uncertainty. The landlord and tenant negotiate over a set of readily foreseeable risks that occur with stable probabilities. They know the approximate probability of drought, excessive heat, and price fluctuations for the crop. The contract works reasonably well because the parties can specify the contingencies. The contract helps the parties plan for and respond to the risk of the situation. They do not face the same kind of radical uncertainty faced by the research and development team. The sharecropper and his landlord do not ordinarily face completely unforeseen events that could cause a purely contractual relationship to falter.

A second circumstance that favors a partnership is uniqueness. This is so obvious we might easily overlook it: people form a partnership because they want to work together. Each knows something about the other that makes that person seem to be the best person for the enterprise. This particular person is not interchangeable with any other person. Each partner believes that potential substitutes for the other partner are imperfect at best and at worst no substitute at all.

Perhaps each potential partner has specific knowledge or skill required for the success of the venture. By forming a partnership, both parties commit themselves to providing the partner with the full use of their own knowledge and skill. They need a pledge not to withhold what they know from the partner, but they cannot specify this promise in a legally enforceable way: a contract cannot say "I promise to tell my employer every brilliant idea that occurs to me." The partnership creates an incentive for each partner to willingly share ideas.

The uniqueness of the other person may precede the partnership and in fact be the motivation for entering into the partnership. The parties might expect each of them to become uniquely important to the enterprise as an outgrowth of the relationship. At the outset of a new business, there may be plenty of plausible candidates for the position of marketing manager. After a particular person has generated enthusiasm, good will, and a big mailing list, he may be substantially better than any new person that could be hired. It would not be surprising if the partners were to decide that including the marketing manager in the partnership would provide better incentives for energetic performance than a routine labor contract.[8]

Marriage is more like a partnership than a contract, for it is characterized by radical uncertainty in many dimensions. And of course, each member of the couple regards the other as unique.

The Uncertainties of Married Life

Since marriage is the complete giving and sharing of the self, there are uncertainties every step of the way. We are uncertain exactly who our partner may become and who we will become ourselves. Will we both remain healthy? Will we both continue to be employed at our current level of income and status? Will our needs change in ways we cannot fully predict?

As unanswerable as these questions are, these are actually the simpler ones because they focus on the two partners themselves. When we turn to questions that concern the relationship and its fruits, the outcomes become even more incalculable. Will the relationship be fruitful, morally and physicially? The relationship itself will change the people in it. The person who does the calculations at the beginning of the relationship is not exactly the same person who will be living within it twenty years later. Will the relationship help each of us to become better people? We cannot know how we will change and how our partners will change over the course of a lifetime.

The uncertainty inherent in living intimately with another person means that attempting to specify the expectations of performance would be impossible—and maybe even self-defeating. The contractual part of the marriage provides a basic framework within which the parties can work out their shared life. The spouses cannot attempt to specify in a contractual sense just what they expect of each other.

Sometimes couples try to formalize an agreement that will ward off a certain set of complaints. The agreement might be something like "The husband agrees to come home at 5:30 in the evening to be with the family." These kinds of agreements seldom work very well if taken by themselves. The problem is: be home with the family for what? Is the husband coming home to sit at the computer screen, or with the newspaper, or in front of the television? The couple can agree, in a quasi contractual way, that he should come home. But they cannot contractually demand that he be interested in other people, take part in family life, and be cheerful.

The problem is deeper than a scheduling issue and has to do with the attitude each member of the couple takes toward their shared time. This problem cannot be solved contractually. The solution has to come from a change in attitude, which by its nature cannot be brought about by a contract. A person's attitude can be observed, sometimes very accurately, but it is not the kind of thing about which a legally enforceable promise can be made.

As a matter of fact, the contractual approach can be positively harmful. The husband can say, "Well, you see, here I am home at 5:29. You have no cause for complaint"; the wife can respond, "You know very well that is not what I meant"; and so forth. Somebody has to give, generously, cheerfully, without worrying about receiving imme-diate and exact reciprocity. A person's needs can change from minute to minute. Surely no contract can do justice to this complex reality.

Sometimes people want to do nothing, but to do nothing together. The value of togetherness, apart from any other consideration, is one of the things that makes marriage, like all friendships, distinct from contracts. Couples do so many things for each other in a marriage. When just being there is enough, no one else except your partner can "be there" in quite the same way. The innumerable things that couples do for each other cannot be specified, enumerated, listed, or even understood. The attempt to specify by contract all the duties of a marriage partner would surely destroy the relationship. The most carefully drafted contract in the world can never be a substitute for a partnership.

The Uniqueness of the Partner

This observation leads us to the next circumstance that favors a part-nership rather than a contract: the uniqueness of the other person. Certainly in modern marriages, in which the partners select each other, they believe that the other person is the only person for them. Marriages end because "he was not the right person for me" after all. We have the idea that we could not be married to just anyone. Our betrothed truly is not interchangeable with anyone else.

Even in societies where marriages are arranged, the element of uniqueness can be important because only a portion of the unique-ness need be present at the beginning of the relationship. The unique-ness that develops during the life of the relationship can be just as important. It may be surprising, and perhaps a bit sobering, for us moderns to realize how often people in arranged marriages have lived together quite happily for a lifetime. One of the keys to their success must have been in honoring the fact that the partners become unique to each other. There might very well have been many other people who would have been just as suitable a marriage partner. But once the relationship was established with one person, that particular person became irreplaceable.

Part of the reason for this has to do with the sharing of experience. Long-married couples often develop a shorthand language. They can anticipate each other's reactions, thoughts, and ideas. Sometimes, even in their bickering, one can sense a kind of affection that could only be present after long and deep familiarity. And of course, a long-married couple shares memories upon memories upon memories.

For these reasons, it makes more sense to compare a marriage to a partnership than to a contract. Both in the business world and in married life, partnerships have contractual elements and may begin with a contract. In a partnership, both partners have enough at stake in the relationship that they have an incentive to do all the unstated but necessary things that can be known on the spot and in the moment. The contract is neither the end of the relationship nor the method for how the parties relate to one another.

There are some aspects to the partnership that are legally enforceable. If one of the partners has his hand in the cash drawer or is grossly negligent in performing his duties, the other may have legal recourse. Only the most obvious, readily measurable, readily observable infractions of the relationship can be the subject of litigation between partners. The parties must keep these most basic requirements of the contract for the partnership to be successful. While these are necessary conditions for a successful partnership, they are usually far from sufficient. There are a great many other things that the partners need to do, in good faith, that will never be legally enforceable.

Likewise, a marriage contract has certain basic provisions that can be (or used to be) legally enforceable. The marriage needs a basic level of fidelity and absence of violence between the partners. But simply satisfying these minimal requirements will never be enough to really make the marriage work. The husband and wife need to approach one another with generosity, with openness and a willingness to consider the other. These deeper requirements of the successful marriage cannot be litigated, contractually specified, or dispensed with. The marriage relationship presupposes compliance with contractual terms; the truly successful marriage goes beyond mere compliance into a generous sharing of the whole self.

More Than a Partnership

The marriage relationship is the one family relationship that most resembles a contract. The relationship between spouses is a chosen relationship, by parties of comparable status and capacity. In contrast, no blood relationship can be described as chosen by both parties. Nor can any blood relationship, with the possible exception of relationships between siblings or cousins, be described as a relationship between equals. The generations have a natural hierarchy associated with birth, maturity, and old age. Societies might vary in the relative status they assign to grandfathers, fathers, and sons, but every society takes some account of the natural differences in strength, capacity, and maturity between the members of different generations.

When we expand our vision to encompass blood relationships, the contract analogy for the family breaks down even more dramatically. To describe the relationship between parents and children as a contract, even an implicit contract, is to do violence to the reality of both childhood and parenthood; to describe the relationship between an adult child and an aging parent as a contract, or even a partnership, totally misses the point.

Considering these broader sets of family relationships reveals a deeper reason why even the conjugal relationship cannot be characterized as a contract or even as a partnership: marriages become embedded within blood relationships, almost in spite of themselves. The importance of blood relationships to the marriage appears even before any children arrive. We do not marry an individual person. We marry his whole family—and his family history. We choose our spouses, but we do not choose our in-laws. They come along with our spouse as part of a package deal.

I suppose no one would ever marry if he had to explicitly agree to each new relative one by one. Very few families could pass such a test. There are people in the family that we learn either to put up with or to avoid—and we can only avoid them part of the time. Sooner or later, somebody in the family will die or get married, and we will have to show up. All those in-laws will be there, and we just have to grit our teeth and go through with it.

This is one way that blood relationships fit neither the category of voluntary nor of involuntary. We enter into some of our relationships through choice, but by that choice we become connected to a whole set of other people, not exactly of our choosing but not exactly forced upon us either.

Choosing Parenthood Does Not Make It a Contract

The union between husband and wife typically produces offspring who has lives of their own. These new lives are bound to the couple by blood, not by choice, and certainly not by contract. Moreover, the couple have shifted from being in a chosen relationship to being in a blood relationship, at least indirectly, through their children. These children permanently alter the character of the relationship between their parents.

The members of the couple begin to relate to each other as parents. The relationship between them takes on a new importance as they realize that a helpless baby is counting on them not only to take care of him but to love each other. However much they might have cherished their independence, the arrival of a baby signals the start of a new era of interdependence in their lives. No matter how much they may have enjoyed their youth, no matter how old they might be when children finally arrive, the children let them know that now their own childhoods are definitely at an end.

The children extend the relationship of the couple beyond themselves. The chronological extension across time is probably the most obvious way in which the child extends the parent. But this is not the half of it. The responsibility for a helpless child pulls us out of our natural self-centeredness more thoroughly than almost any other situation.

To be sure, sexual attraction has the potential to help us moderate some of our self-centeredness, but that potential is not always fulfilled. Even interest in another person has a large component of self-centeredness, concern with our own pleasure and our own gratification. It is possible to have no more connectedness with a sexual partner than with a piece of comfortable furniture or a gourmet meal. We can focus on a sexual partner not as another person but as an object that gives us gratification.

The arrival of a new baby gives us, perhaps for the first time in our lives, the opportunity to find out just how much love we are capable of. We find out how patient we can be, how resourceful, how much sleep deprivation we can stand, how much pleasure we can take in the ordinary details of daily life. In this calling out of the parents from their natural self-centeredness, their real transformation begins in earnest.

The greatest distinction between the family and the contract occurs at exactly this juncture as well. Contracting partners carefully orchestrate their exchange before the transaction ever begins. The parties assure themselves and each other that no one is to be taken advantage of. Each party gives consideration. The parent-child relationship cannot possibly be carefully orchestrated. When a child is born, no one can possibly expect assurances of faithful performance of anything. Parents may not get a "good deal" from their child. In fact, in a certain sense, parents almost always give more than they receive from their children. I suppose no one would ever have children if they required advance assurance that they would receive a good deal. Perhaps that is why the modern birth rate has fallen below replacement. People enter into so many relationships with the idea that they are not to be taken advantage of that they expect similar assurances about childrearing. Once people begin calculating about their relationships, many conclude that the cost of children is too high for them to bear.

There will be many times over the course of their lifetime that parents will not want to carry out the duties of parenthood. It is straining the use of language to say that sleep-deprived parents voluntarily get up in the middle of the night to feed a howling newborn. Yet it is not accurate to say that the infant "forces" them to get up either. There are many stages of this most primal relationship to which the analogy to voluntary exchange fails to do justice.

It is not accurate to say that parents perform these duties out of contractual obligations to their children, or to society, or to anybody else. It is more accurate to say that they live out their commitment, even when it is uncomfortable or costly to do so. The faithful parent does not calculate at each minute, or even over the long term, whether caring for the children is cost effective, whether it is the best use of his time, whether he would be better off abandoning the children, or whether he would be better off living in a style that would be harmful to the children. To recalculate the basis of the commitment regularly would destroy the relationship.

Parent-child relationships also differ from contractual ones in their time horizon. The presumption of contract is that the parties are making an explicit exchange of promises for fairly well-defined objects or services and within a clearly delineated time frame. Lifelong contracts are unheard of in the common law. Lifelong labor contracts are expressly forbidden, suggesting as they do slavery or indentured servitude. Perpetual contracts are forbidden even in inheritance law. A corporation, which might appear to be a legal person with an infinite life, nevertheless cannot make a "lifetime" contract with an individual person. Nor can the corporation make a perpetual commitment to another corporation.

Yet the relationship between a parent and a child is in fact a life-long relationship, no matter what the legal institutions of our society might say. We do not cease to be our mother's child, no matter how old we are. Our mothers know this, even though we, as children, might resist knowing it. We might try to "divorce" our parents by never seeing them, by severing all contact with them. Sometimes people believe that leaving home is equivalent to being rid of their parents or that growing up requires them to discard their parents. But this is living a lie. They are our parents, no matter what we think of them, no matter how old we are. We carry their genes, their influence, their habits, their mannerisms, their language, their culture in our very bodies and deep in our minds. We deceive ourselves if we believe we can divorce ourselves from our parents entirely.

Beyond Contract to Cooperation

Contracts used in the wrong context and in the wrong spirit can actively inhibit a deeper and more genuine form of cooperation. Marriage is not the only relationship in which mere compliance with contractual terms is positively destructive. There are many situations in which it would be far more productive for people to be generous and contribute more to a common enterprise than they are specifically required to do.

For instance, the employer-employee relationship is more productive when people can move beyond a purely contractual arrangement. The combination of collective bargaining, large bureaucratic workplaces, and federal legislation has created the need for ever more detailed job descriptions. These detailed specifications of labor contracts in many cases disrupt the vitality of the workplace. "It is

not in my job description" is an excuse to do the minimum necessary. In this context, the attitude engendered by a contractual mentality is one of minimal compliance rather than maximal cooperation.
The attempt to specify every detail of a person's responsibilities destroys the spontaneity and the sense of partnership and teamwork.

It may be that in some work environments there was no sense of
partnership to begin with. That might be why the union could successfully organize in the workplace or why the workers acquiesced in
or even demanded federal legislation. But blaming the employer does
not change the basic problem. Regardless of whose fault it is that
there is no sense of teamwork, the fact remains that no contract can
take the place of a sense of partnership.

Even in the seemingly impersonal business world, an element of
teamwork and cooperation can contribute to the success of the business in a way that no mere contract could replicate. The attempt to
spell out every detail of each person's responsibility can convey the
message that his employer or partner does not trust him.[9] Partners
need generosity from each other. Employers and employees need
genuine cooperation from each other. Generosity can be in everyone's
interest.

The idea of being generous in the interest of some group has
gotten a bad reputation because collectivist governments have demanded many sacrifices of their citizens that really were not for
anybody's good. In spite of this, we observe that people really do
seem to have an impulse to cooperate with each other. People have a
desire to live together, to get along with each other, and, dare we say
it, to be generous with each other. We might even speculate that this
impulse to cooperate partially accounts for the success of the collectivist ideologies of our time. People like the idea of living in a big
cooperative society in which the group owns everything and everybody works together nicely for the benefit of all.

In fact, it is doubtful that the vast destructive systems of our century could have been sold to people by appealing to any motive other

than the wish for a world of magnanimity. Socialism and communism twisted those normal and noble motivations out of all recognition. These systems do not work because genuine cooperation cannot be extracted from people by force.

Begin with Generosity

The marriage relationship, then, is at the core of the family and the basis upon which the kinship network is built. Marriage is not a mere contract and is not held together by contract. Marriage is held together by love. Through the love between them, the married couple binds the other generations to themselves and to each other.

That is why this book about libertarian political theory and free market economics needs to talk about love. Some forms of cooperation are built upon a cautiously arranged exchange of promises made in advance of the exchange of any goods or services. But many other forms of cooperation are more spontaneous and less calculated.

Nothing in this analysis detracts from the basic libertarian understanding of contracts and their central role in regulating the interactions among free people. Libertarians advocate a world of minimal government. Our preferred substitutes for government are people working together through non-coercive institutions to bring about goods of common benefit. Contracts and the market are one example of such cooperation. But a civil society that would be a really good society requires many methods of cooperation. Generosity is required for almost all of them. Mere compliance, doing the minimum necessary to get by, will not be sufficient to create a society in which people enjoy living.

When we have a choice between a government solution to a problem or a contractual or market solution to a problem, by all means, choose the market. But if we have the choice between cooperation using a contract or cooperation that requires liberality beyond the reach of contractual obligation, by all means, reach beyond the contract. Not all situations allow a choice of methods. In some cases the circumstances dictate the form the cooperation must take. But where we have a choice, libertarians, of all people, must advocate the most generous form of cooperation that the situation can reasonably sustain.

American society has become encumbered by legalism. We have allowed the legal mechanism to take over every aspect of life. In the process, the legalistic mentality has squeezed out or corrupted institutions and relationships that ought to be dominated by teamwork and partnership. We can easily become obsessed with doing the minimum necessary to comply with the rules rather than cooperating in a spirit of magnanimity.

Yet I think there is some reason for optimism. For social institutions that have become encrusted with legalism have cleaned themselves out before. And they do this, not by making vast changes in institutional structure, not by purging all the wrong-headed people, but by a genuine moral renewal. These changes flow from the renewed commitment to live within the rules of the institution, with a spirit of generous abandon rather than with a grudging sense of obligation.

Generosity toward our spouses is an obvious place to start.

PART III

Why There Is No
Substitute for the Family

∽ 5 ∽

The Irreplaceable Family

THERE IS NO SUBSTITUTE FOR THE FAMILY in helping self-centered infants develop into cooperative adults. In the next few chapters, I consider and critique some plausible candidates for substitutes. Before doing so, I want to make clear exactly what I mean when I say there is no substitute for the family.

The statement that the family is irreplaceable can be interpreted in two ways. First, each child has two parents as a matter of biological fact. These two people play a unique role in the child's life, for better or for worse. No matter how poorly they behave toward the child or how irresponsible their decisions are, the child is indelibly marked by the two people who have given him life. The identity of one's parents is an irrevocable fact, a reality that everyone must face. From the child's point of view, his particular family is irreplaceable. Second, the family is irreplaceable as an institution. This is presumably the more controversial statement, since it appears to be flatly false. We can readily observe substitutes for the biological family. Step- and blended families, adoptive and foster families, and institutions such as day-care, schools, and orphanages are all in some ways substitutes for the biological family.

I am not concerned with every single activity of the family when

83

I ask whether there can be a substitute for it. The social institution known as the family can be considered an economic unit, a legal entity, a biological unit, or merely a group of individuals who relate to each other in a particular way. My concern is the family's role in creating attachment and teaching cooperation. I claim there are no suitable substitutes for the family in performing this task.

The primary job of parenthood is relational. Parents build relationships with their children and in doing so, teach their children how to build relationships with others. Families can create attachment and teach cooperation well or poorly. If we ask whether there is a close substitute for a particular family that is negligent and abusive, then of course the answer can sometimes be "yes." Usually, the best substitute even for that family is another, more healthy family. The question I am addressing is whether there is another institution that functions better than the family. The answer to this question is certainly "no."

The family is the child's first link to the rest of the human race. Parents spend a lot of time wiping noses and tying shoes, which might seem to be menial chores that any idiot could do. But as a by-product of fulfilling these mundane tasks, parents convey to the child that he matters to them, and he allows them to matter to him as well.

Grasping the crucial role the family plays in creating attachment and teaching cooperation shows us what to focus on when we must replace a non-functioning family. Even the most maligned of all institutional substitutes for the family, the orphanage, can produce tolerable results by keeping the needs of the child in focus. For instance, the economist Richard McKenzie recalls his experience growing up in an orphanage run by the Presbyterian Church. He encountered a teacher who both helped him believe he would amount to something and gave him an internal guide for his own conduct. Her opinion meant so much to him that for years afterwards "What would Mrs. Lester think?" was a question that guided his actions.[1] Likewise, Tom Monaghan, founder of Domino's Pizza, recalls his years in an orphanage run by an order of Catholic nuns. He remembers that the nuns gave him a sense of right and wrong. He describes one particular sister: "Sr. Barada, was my teacher for the first two years, as well as a virtual mother and father to me."[2] For all of the other problems they might have had, these particular orphanages gave the children in their care some crucial moral tools.

The example of the orphanage helps clarify another point about substitutes for the family. That those like Richard McKenzie and Tom Monaghan survived life in an orphanage does not make it an adequate replacement for the family. We would not take all kids from all parents and put them into orphanages just because these orphanages can do a tolerable job. The orphanage was a second-best solution, used because the best institution, the family, was not available.

Both McKenzie and Monaghan are deeply grateful to their orphanages. But presumably McKenzie would have preferred that his mother had not died and that his father had not been an alcoholic. Presumably Monaghan would have preferred that his father had not died and that his mother had been more willing and able to care for him. A tolerable substitute for a non-functioning or absent family does not constitute a full-scale replacement for the family as a social institution.

Two institutions might come to mind as possible substitutes for the family. From the left-wing statist corner, we might hear the claim that government programs could instill cooperation: we could inculcate this disposition in government schools and day-care centers. We could take children from their parents at ever earlier ages to assure that they are thoroughly trained and properly brought up for social life. From the right-wing careerist corner, we might hear the claim that the market could instill cooperation in children: We can hire someone to take care of our children who could for all practical purposes be parental substitutes. I shall devote a chapter to each of these two possible institutional replacements for the family.

The Family, Right or Wrong?

I have made a case that the family is an irreplaceable institution for the moral development and well-being of children. One might think, therefore, that I would favor policies that attempt to keep or return a child to his biological parents under any circumstances.

Each and every family ought to strive for family unity and preservation. But I do not say that the state should pursue a policy of attempting to preserve each and every biological family. To say that the family is a unique and irreplaceable institution is not to say the family, right or wrong, must be preserved.

Some current child welfare policies and family law trends strongly favor keeping the child in the custody of blood relatives. Child protective service workers have a policy of family reunification whenever possible.[3] There are also a small but significant number of cases in which biological parents have demanded the return of a child they had relinquished for adoption, sometimes after a considerable time. The child welfare policies that seem to require that the biological family must be preserved at all costs reduce the family to mere biology. Believing that the family is the best and most natural teacher of cooperation and attachment does not entail the belief that each and every family does this without effort. Giving birth to a child is not a guarantee that a mother will bond with her child. Providing a sperm is no guarantee that a father will help to shape his child's moral environment. People have to make decisions to do these things.

A public policy that places too great a weight upon reuniting children with their biological parents supports the family only in the most superficial sense. If the claims of biology trump other considerations of the welfare of the child, the implication is that physical proximity to the biological parents is the child's primary need. But the child needs appropriate care, not abuse. The child needs stability, not continual reshuffling. The child needs moral guidance from people who are themselves capable of exercising self-restraint.

The family reunification policy is backed up by temporary foster care while the biological parents attempt to pull themselves together. The idea is that placing children with families is better for them than keeping them in institutions: a foster family appears to be more like a real family. I know from personal observation that many foster families are made up of wonderful, generous, loving people who do a great deal of good for the children in their care.

But there is one crucial aspect of attachment that the foster family cannot provide: stability. The foster family cannot credibly say, "You are our child and no one will ever take you away. We will never get rid of you." The very premise of foster care is that it is temporary. The foster care system cannot replicate the crucial aspect of permanence of family life for the child.

The current policy of pulling the children in and out of the custody of their biological parents is supposed to give the parents an incentive to shape up, so they can have the child back. This is using the child as bait rather than addressing the child's needs. Parents suspected of being unfit lose custody temporarily. Child welfare agencies give the parents counseling, job training, and other services in the hope of being able to return the child.[4] The assumption behind the current policy is, "If only we can pump in enough services so that the child can be returned to his mother, everything will be fine. The child needs to be with his mother, as long as she isn't too abusive. Everything the child needs will flow to him automatically from being in the physical presence of his mother." I doubt that any defender of the foster care system would say exactly these words. But that is the message the policy conveys.

Richard McKenzie, in his memoir of growing up in an orphanage, offers his own testimony that he certainly preferred the orphanage in which he grew up to the available alternatives: an alcoholic father or indifferent aunts, none of whom could do anything about his out-of-control behavior. The orphanage was also preferable to being in the foster care system, in which he might have returned to those relatives at any time. In the process of writing his memoir, McKenzie contacted many of his orphanage "classmates" or "siblings." More than one of them said, in effect, "I am grateful I was not in foster care."[5]

Preserving the Family

Nevertheless, the fact that some families fail should not lead us to conclude that the family as an institution is dispensable. The failures of some parents should not become an excuse for public distrust of all parents. Rather than jumping to the conclusion that no parents should be trusted or presuming that children are better off in daycare, we should see how the actual characteristics of well-functioning families can be supported or replicated in families that are not doing their job well. Strengthening the family to make it easier for it to do its legitimate and necessary jobs should be the first object of social attention. The family as an institution is far too important for us to throw up our hands when signs of strain appear.

Finally, it should be said that even when families fail, we should acknowledge that it is just that: a failure. We should not avert our eyes from the destruction that is caused by adult negligence. We should not excuse negligence by describing it as an alternative lifestyle that we have no right to judge. We certainly do have the right and the responsibility to make judgments about appropriate behavior. The resilience of children does not excuse negligence by adults.

Let my voice be counted among those who encourage families to do all they can to keep themselves together and loving each other. Inculcating an ethic of fidelity is one of our most pressing national social priorities. If we can hold the family together at the individual and personal level, we would have less need for grand schemes to replace the family at a societal level.

∞ 6 ∞

The Mother of All Myths

THAT LARGE NUMBERS OF CHILDREN live without fathers has become an accepted fact of American family life, even though these children and their mothers face numerous hardships. Many people from across the political spectrum insist that helping single mothers should be a high priority of public policy. Those who resist this suggestion are dismissed as mean-spirited or as wanting to turn back the clock to the dreaded fifties.

I offer a different argument: There is literally no such thing as a "single parent." Some third party is always in the background, helping the mother who is unconnected to the father of her child. The third party may be her biological family, but more often the third party is an impersonal institution. The person who appears to be raising a child all by herself has substituted for the other parent some combination of market-provided child care, employment income, and government assistance.

Although some women become single mothers because of the death of their husbands, by far the largest percentage of fatherless children become so from decisions made by one or both parents. Some children have divorced parents, while others live with never-married mothers.[1] I propose that we see these decisions for what they

are: decisions to substitute impersonal institutions for human relationships. The issue is whether any institution, no matter how well
funded, can be a genuine substitute for the other parent, particularly
in helping the child build attachments.

Social scientists have accumulated an impressive body of evidence
showing the difficulties that children in single-parent families and
stepfamilies face. The child who does not live with both parents has
lost something of value.[2] Children from mother-only families obtain
fewer years of education and are more likely to drop out of high
school; they have lower earnings in young adulthood and are more
likely to be poor; they are more likely to marry early and have children early, both in and out of wedlock; they are more likely to divorce;
and they are more likely to commit delinquent acts and to engage in
drug and alcohol use than children from two-parent families.[3]

Children of single parents are more likely to have academic problems.[4] In one study, children from disrupted marriages were over 70
percent more likely than those living with both biological parents to
have been expelled or suspended; those living with never-married
mothers were more than twice as likely to have had this experience.
Children with both biological parents were less likely to have repeated
a grade of school.[5] Children in single-parent families have lower math
scores. In one study, students who attended schools with a high concentration of students from single-parent households also had math
and reading achievement scores that were 11 percent and 10 percent,
respectively, lower than students who attended schools with a higher
concentration of two-parent households. This suggests that the presence of children from mother-only families adversely affects other
children in the school.[6]

Children living in single-parent households are also more likely
to have emotional and behavioral problems. The children outside of
two-parent families had between 50 and 80 percent higher scores for
indicators of antisocial behavior, peer conflict, social withdrawal, and
age-inappropriate dependency. Such children also had between 25

and 50 percent higher scores for indicators of anxiety, depression, headstrong behavior, and hyperactivity.[7] Children of divorce are statistically more likely to be depressed than children in two-parent families. The impact of divorce on girls' depression seems to be an indirect effect, generated by poor parenting and increased parental conflict. For boys, on the other hand, nothing seems to compensate for the sense of sadness that boys experience at the loss of their fathers.[8]

One might think that the income differences between single-parent and two-parent households might account for some of these differences between the children of the two types of households. But income differences account for only a portion of the differences. The relatively large number of non-whites among single-parent households does not account for the whole constellation of problems. The effects of single motherhood are consistent across a large number of racial and ethnic groups.[9]

All the reasons that single-parent households have difficulties arise from one basic fact: The job of child rearing is too big for an individual person to do. No social arrangement can alter the basic fact of the dependence of mothers on some source of assistance in providing for their children. The modern arrangements that claim to liberate women from dependency actually mask their dependency by transferring it from the father of the child to some other person or institution. There is a tragic irony in this, for the father is more likely to have an interest in and commitment to the mother and her child than any other person or institution.

Granted, in comparison with married mothers, the single mother is more independent of her child's father. But she is more dependent on the good graces of her employer, the competence of her childcare provider, and the energy of her blood relatives. Mothers of the baby boomers and earlier generations were not as dependent upon people outside their own home. Yet mothers in the 1950s typically had a far more secure commitment from their husbands than do today's women. Even today, with the instability of marriage in general, most husbands are more committed to their wives than are the other people upon whom unmarried women necessarily depend.

The dependency of motherhood is by no means a parasitic dependence. The mother is producing something of value to herself, the child's father, and the wider society. She is producing (if I may be pardoned for using a rather cold-blooded expression) a civilized adult. It would be more accurate to say that the mother and her assistants (whomever they may be) are engaged in a team production process. Her dependence is more accurately described as an interdependence. There is nothing undignified or inappropriate about this interdependence, but the alternative to depending on the father is not complete independence.

Substitutes for the Father

If fathers are thought to be inherently unreliable or dangerous it seems unreasonable to assume that some other person is more reliable or less dangerous. There is no particular reason to expect a man who is not the child's father to be more committed to and loving toward the mother and child. In fact, there are good reasons to expect him not to be.

Sociobiologists argue that the biological father has a selfish interest in protecting and preserving his own child and its mother.[10] Whether sociobiologists are correct in assigning the full weight of this paternal bond to genetics, there is little doubt that biological fathers contribute more to the care of children than do stepfathers or others with no genetic relationship. According to a British study of child abuse, a cohabiting boyfriend is thirty-three times more likely to abuse a child than a married father who lives with the mother.[11] The cohabiting but not married father has the same genetic interest in the child as does the married biological father. But these fathers are twenty times more likely to abuse their own children than fathers who are married to the mother of the child.[12] This suggests that a commitment between the parents contributes to the child's safety independent of biology. Moreover, marriage is safer for women than cohabitation, whether or not children are present. Though some theorists and feminists argue that women are in danger from any man at all, the empirical evidence does not bear this claim out.[13] Cohabiting women are more likely to suffer severe violence from their partners than are married women.[14]

But the mother needs the father of her child to be committed to her for reasons that go beyond the basic safety issue. Commitment between the parents contributes to the child's ability to attach to people. Cohabitation is not good enough, suggesting as it does a temporary or conditional relationship. There will be many moments in the life of a mother where a conditional commitment is not enough: the moment when the washing machine leaks all over the floor, or after she has put in a load full of diarrhea-soaked bedding soiled by a sick child during a night that was sleepless for mother and child. The short-term calculus of an uncommitted partner would surely be: "There has to be a better (more attractive, smarter, more pleasing) woman for me than this exhausted wreck." No mother can feel secure if she has continually to wonder whether her partner still calculates that she is good enough for him.

What difference does this make to the child? A helpless baby, overcome by his own neediness, needs to relax in the care of adults who are in loving control of the situation. He needs to trust his mother; his mother needs to be able to trust her partner to take care of her so that she can relax in her role in the child's life. Her effectiveness as a mother is diminished if she has to worry whether her boyfriend will come home, or whether the child support payment is really in the mail, or whether the babysitter will really show up on time for her to go to work, or whether her employer will fire her if she does not. The baby needs the mother to provide stability for him; the mother needs the father to provide stability for her.

Perhaps the most unsettling aspect of cohabitation is the resistance of the couple to commitment. In some cases, the couple celebrates their independence from each other. Some cohabiting couples have the attitude that they do not need anyone—including the person who is acting as their child's other parent. Unfortunately, this is the fantasy of an attachment disordered child. However appealing this posture may be for an adult, it is pathological for a child. Any couple with this attitude, married or not, is at a disadvantage in facilitating attachment in a child, for they convey an implicit message through their relationship: "I stand aloof from you; I do not entrust myself to you." Building attachment with a child requires the child to entrust himself to his parents. If the parents are unwilling to entrust themselves to each other, it seems unreasonable to think that they can credibly convey to the child that he should entrust himself to them.

One might think that replacing an absent father would alleviate some of the children's difficulties. A stepfather does typically bring additional income to the household, and children are safer with a stepfather than they are with biological but unmarried parents. Commitment trumps genetics as an inhibitor of violence.[15]

Nevertheless, consistent with the hypothesis that relationships are more important than increased resources, introducing a "new father" into the picture does not necessarily solve the child's problems and may add some new ones. Children in stepfamilies show more developmental difficulties than those in intact nuclear families. The adjustment of children in stepfamilies is similar to that of children in one-parent families.[16] For instance, children with stepfathers have approximately the same high risk of repeating a year of school as do the children of never-married mothers, around 75 percent.[17] When a stepfather enters the home, children exhibit more behavior problems compared with their peers who live with both biological parents.[18]

More parental involvement in children's lives reduces problems at home and in the school, but the presence of a stepfather is a double disadvantage to children in this regard. Stepfathers spend less time with children than do biological fathers, and the presence of a step-father reduces the time mothers spend with their children. This may be why the children of stepfathers have more behavior problems than children who live with two biological parents.[19] The emotional issues in stepfamilies can translate into lowered academic achievement. One study specifically examined the relationship of family structure, time spent with children, and academic achievement.[20] Children in two-parent families received the highest grades of any family structure. In all cases, the time fathers spent with children had a positive impact on their grades, but the effect was not significant enough to mediate the impact of family structure on grades.

One explanation frequently offered for the relatively poor performance of stepfamilies is that the introduction of a new parent disrupts established loyalties and creates conflicted loyalties.[21] The mother may be unwilling to allow the stepfather to share the parental authority that is part and parcel of creating attachment. It is all too easy for her to say, "These are my kids, not your kids. You don't really understand them. You are being too hard on them." A stepfather would have to be very self-confident to persist in trying to establish his moral authority in the face of his wife's opposition.

The various institutions that attempt to provide substitutes for the father's economic support are not good enough either. No employer can be committed to a mother and her child the way the father could and should be. Likewise, no government program can be sufficiently committed to them. Neither an employer nor the government has any particular reason to be reliable. The woman's ability to rely on her employer for economic support depends not on her needs and the needs of her child but on her usefulness to the employer. The public assistance check might arrive with regularity, but support from the state depends on the vagaries of politics, not on the needs of the mother and child. Moreover, the relationship between the woman and these institutions is just that: institutional. There is nothing personal about the interaction between the employer or public welfare officer and the mother. Not only do they not care about her very much, they might not even know who she is or who her child is.

These arrangements replace the father with a check, but a mother needs much more than money. She needs moral support as well as financial support; she needs someone to lend a helping hand; she needs encouragement, to be told she is doing a good job. If she is getting nowhere in her approach to a particular problem, she needs someone with whom to talk it over. When she looks bedraggled and harried because she has given the last ounce of her energy to her child, she needs to be told that she is beautiful. No employer or social worker is going to do all that for her.

The Irreplaceable Contribution of Fathers

The father's contribution to his child's well-being is irreplaceable. Fathers who are present in the home contribute far more material resources to the welfare of their children than noncustodial fathers do. Indeed, it would be almost impossible for noncustodial fathers to contribute as much. When a father inside a family buys a house or a car or plans a vacation, he is making these purchases and plans for his whole family. In this way, the bulk of his earning power is devoted to the welfare of his family. The average married father annually contributes about thirty thousand dollars to the welfare of his children in this way.[22]

The noncustodial father, by contrast, sends a check. His financial contributions, on average, amount to about three thousand dollars per year. When he buys a house or car, it is primarily for his own use, not for the use of his children. And his purchases for himself compete with money or gifts for his children. But the father's financial contributions to the material welfare of his children are a relatively minor matter. When we begin to look at the more subtle problems, problems of poor behavior or distressed feelings, we begin to see why there is no close substitute for a father.

The father's unique contribution to the moral development of children is something to which we are almost blind at this moment in our history. We scoff at the idea of gender-specific roles for parents. Yet as feminists never tire of telling us, the father is the most physically powerful figure in the family. It would be surprising if this obvious physical difference between parents played no part in creating distinct strengths and weaknesses in the separate parental roles. The real question is not whether men and women are different but how the difference allows each to contribute something unique to the moral development of children.

Inside a functioning family, the father's power is harnessed for the good of his children. His strength allows him to enforce a given set of rules. Children need limits on their behavior, even though they resist limits. Appropriate and reasonable limits allow a child to feel safe. It is not that mothers cannot set limits, but the presence of the father, even in the background, gives those limits greater authority.

A misbehaving child needs to be corrected, and this is often unpleasant for both child and adult. A chastised child also needs to be brought back into the warmth of the family, to know he is still part of the family. Sometimes, but not always, being comfortable makes it easier for a child to behave well. On the other hand, sometimes being a bit intimidated or in awe makes it easier for a child to behave well. It is a rare parent of either gender who can switch back and forth between these two modes effortlessly at all times. In general, mothers want their children to be happy, fathers want their children to behave well. Children need both to be happy and to behave well.

Sociologist James Coleman has observed that sometimes teachers and students conspire to do as little work as possible.[23] It is easier for the teacher to let children do what they want and for the children to harass the teacher into letting them do nothing. However, Coleman noted, if there is an independent testing authority, the teacher can direct the students' opprobrium to that authority. The teacher can teach to the external standard without seeming to be the "bad guy" who spoils the students' fun. With this division of labor, the teacher is not forced to bear all the responsibility for setting standards and evaluating performance. He is more free to instruct when someone else has set the standard and enforces it. Indeed, it is impossible for a single teacher to adhere to rigorous standards in an environment without any external standards. The pressures, both inside and outside the classroom, to conform to a lower standard are simply too great to resist.

Something comparable takes place inside the home. The parent who spends the most time with the children is in continual danger of being worn down by their testing of limits. While children are still developing an internal sense of right and wrong and their capacity for self-control, they have a tendency to press against limits set by the family rules and to test the willingness of authority figures to enforce the rules. The presence of a father is of immeasurable value to the mother in her efforts to set and enforce limits in the home.

It is not that I advocate mothers saying "wait until your father gets home" as a disciplinary strategy. The fact that the father will eventually come home adds to the authority of the mother, whether she specifically invokes it or not: the child knows perfectly well that his father is coming home. The child needs to learn that he ought not to do everything that he can do. Who better to demonstrate to the child the importance of self-restraint than his father, the most powerful person in his little world? The father can convey the message at lower cost and with greater credibility than anyone else can.

There is a social counterpart to this division of labor inside the family. In many neighborhoods, women set the standards for the behavior of children, and men enforce these standards. The men do not need to use their muscle or push people around. The mere presence of a male authority figure is often enough to deter misbehavior. According to James Q. Wilson, "neighborhoods without fathers are neighborhoods without men able and willing to confront errant youth, chase threatening gangs, and reproach delinquent fathers. The absence of fathers deprives the community of those little platoons that informally but effectively control the boys on the street."[24] Empirical research bears out Wilson's observation: the presence of single-parent households in a neighborhood is more closely connected to increased crime than the presence of non-white or low-income families.[25]

This brings up the second irreplaceable contribution of the father: protection. I suppose many people would sneer at the thought of a man's protection being relevant, much less irreplaceable. But modern technology has not brought with it an automatic moral advance for every member of society. Each person needs to receive moral guidance, no matter how much wealth or sophistication his parents may possess. And as we know, there are plenty of people who are not instilling the most basic moral principles in their children.

Statistics show that young girls in fatherless families are at greater risk for abuse by men outside the circle of their families and their mothers' friends. Children without resident fathers are more vulnerable to predatory behavior, both sexual and physical, by people outside the family. It is as if predators sense the defenselessness of a fatherless girl.[26]

But this is only the most obvious of the ways in which fathers protect their families. They can and ought to offer moral protection as well. The father has a special duty to prevent morally offensive material from entering the home, whether it is in the form of violent television programming, rock music with sexually explicit lyrics, or objectionable friends.

The media usually portray men as the perpetrators of physical violence or sexual aggression. The father who remains silent in the face of such portrayals can appear to condone them. The father must establish and maintain the distance between himself, as the most powerful figure in the family, and the abuses of power so often presented either in the media or by experience. Precisely because the father is physically powerful, he is the one who must protect the family morally as well as physically. Although a good father must distance himself from the abuse of raw physical power, the proposals for androgynous parenting are too extreme.[27] The father needs to harness his power for the good of his family. It is not in the interests of the family for him to renounce the use of power altogether. Nor is it in the interest of the family for him to refrain from making moral judgments about acceptable behavior, both inside and outside the family.

Why is it particularly the father's responsibility to offer moral clarity and guidance, including negative consequences? Because it is too hard for mothers to do. Many mothers have known full well that their son or daughter had embarked upon a disastrous course of action. The most common reaction, by far, of mothers is to weep, beg, and plead.[28] By contrast, fathers are more likely than mothers to threaten additional negative consequences, including his own wrath. Fathers will throw a wayward son or daughter out of the house, sometimes for his or her own good. It is, for some reason, easier for fathers to give what is sometimes called "tough love." It is the fashion in popular psychology to insist that children are entitled to unconditional love at all times. But there are times and contexts in which love itself requires that a parent make significant demands on a child. This produces a kind of love that is not entirely unconditional, a love that insists on good behavior.

I know from experience that my own instinct is to protect my children from feeling bad. There are times that my husband makes demands of them, demands that make me as uncomfortable as they make my children. It took me a long time to see that his perspective is frequently far more realistic than mine. His insistence on higher standards of behavior has been appropriate. Even when I know he is right, I often cannot bring myself to make those same demands myself. Sometimes, the best I can do is to suppress my urge to protect my children from discomfort and let my husband do and say what needs to be done and said.

Where the father's role is not sufficiently appreciated, a tragic situation can develop. A child embarks on a course of action that will lead to trouble. His mother pleads and begs for him to behave. His father threatens serious consequences: loss of car privileges, strict supervision, or, at the extreme, eviction from the home. His mother then pleads with his father for leniency, and his father's authority and insistence on good behavior is undermined. The child gets away with bad behavior, gets worse, and the cycle repeats. The family collapses from the child's bad behavior and the mother's undermining of the father's authority.

The Parental Model of Teamwork

Ideally, the parents' relationship should demonstrate cooperation. A woman raising a child alone cannot model cooperative behavior all by herself. The single mother can perhaps teach cooperation through instruction or by example with people other than the child's father. But married couples have a built-in advantage in giving an example of cooperation.

The most important relationship by far for the child to observe is the relationship between his mother and his father. If they get along reasonably well most of the time, he learns that this is possible, as well as learning something about how it is done. If there is no father in his home, he will not see the same level of intensity and duration in a relationship as he would with an intact married couple for parents. Whatever else the child might see about his mother's relationships with other adults, he will see that his father is for some reason not present.

Cooperation between the parents can be very helpful in teaching reciprocity, especially in the area of disciplining and correcting children. Most children would naturally and happily ignore that their behavior sometimes causes problems for others. Children need to know that their behavior affects others. Some children need help just to notice other people: they resist even the slightest interruption of their little plans. When an adult confronts a child with unpleasant information, or with a necessary interruption of the child's agenda, it is often not an enjoyable experience for either the adult or the child. Yet the very process of compelling them to notice others helps children to learn reciprocity. This kind of correction and instruction leads the child out of his natural self-centeredness. Parents who can "double-team" a tough child have a tremendous advantage. They can back each other up when the inevitable wailing and screaming begins, or they can take turns dealing with a difficult child. But to do any of this the parents need to be a team.

Changing the Debate

The correlation of child well-being and living with both biological parents is present in the raw data of most studies. The debate among scholars centers on the extent to which this can be accounted for by differences in resources typically found in single-parent households. The debate then turns to ways in which society can offer additional resources to support the children of single mothers. But most studies show that children of single parents still do worse even after accounting for differences in economic status. This suggests that the children are harmed from the loss of the relationship itself, not simply the loss of resources.

It is almost as if policy makers and academics wish they could find any way possible to help children short of stating the obvious fact that they would be better off if their parents were married. The goal seems to be to find the minimal set of human relationships that a child can have and still turn out tolerably well or to find the least adults must do for their children. This minimalist posture is not confined to academic advocates and people who themselves are divorced. People from across the political spectrum seem to be saying "What do I have to do in order to maintain my position that divorce or single parenthood is not harmful to children. How much money does society have to spend to make up for the loss of the relationship, so that I will not have to give up my belief that parents are entitled to any lifestyle choices they want?"

One of the unspoken premises behind this minimalist position is that it is unreasonable to expect or even encourage people to get married and stay married. But asking stepfathers or cohabiting boyfriends to behave like biological fathers is every bit as unreasonable. It is unrealistic to expect men to work as hard on a relationship with another man's child as he would with his own child. Likewise, proposals to "crack down on deadbeat dads" are red herrings. It is unreasonable to expect that a father who has been expelled from his home in a nasty divorce will contribute the same amount of money that he would if he were part of a functioning family. It is more straightforward and more sensible to expect men and women to work together to maintain their marriages in the first place.

I propose that we shift the terms of the debate. Fiscal conservatives, including libertarians, are often accused of minimalism regarding money. Their demands for financial accountability are frequently countered with the accusation that they want to spend the least money necessary to achieve tolerable results. But the stinginess that is so repugnant when applied to money is even more repugnant when applied to relationships. Surely we cannot bring ourselves to believe that children have no need for stable, committed human relationships, as if children were potted plants that need a bit of physical care but can otherwise be left on the shelf. Once we realize that children thrive when they live with both parents who are married to each other, we need to have a serious reason for withholding that arrangement from them. We expect taxpayers to make some financial sacrifices for the sake of needy children, and we criticize as hard-hearted those who resist those sacrifices. It is every bit as reasonable to expect parents to make sacrifices for their own children, including the sacrifices necessary to maintain a relationship with the child's other parent.

I propose that we confront these relationship issues with more generosity toward children rather than with stinginess. Instead of asking how little do we have to do, the questions instead should be "What do children need from their parents in order to thrive? How can we adults support each other in maintaining our marriages?"

Some defenders of the current regime of easy divorce argue that divorce is better for everyone concerned than the continuation of a bad marriage. No one wants to see women and children remain in the home of an abusive husband and father, but we ought not to exaggerate the number or intensity of bad marriages. Research shows that some children do benefit when their parents divorce: children whose parents were in a "high-conflict" marriage. But, children whose parents had a "low-conflict" marriage were worse off if their parents ended the marriage: "Children who live in homes in which parents seldom fight, but then divorce, show relatively high levels of psychological distress and unhappiness. . . . the dissolution of a home that they thought was stable is an unwelcome and disturbing event."[29]

How many divorces really represent the dissolution of high-conflict marriages? Spouse abuse is not a factor in the vast majority of divorces.[30] The vast majority of married women never experience physical abuse. Unmarried, cohabiting women are more likely to be abused by their boyfriends than wives are by their husbands.[31]

Spouse abuse is a red herring. The question is whether ordinary women married to ordinary men should make the effort to sustain their marriages. Any one of us can unilaterally create a high-conflict marriage by starting quarrels or overreacting to perceived slights. We can easily deceive ourselves that we are entitled to a divorce because of the very conflict that we created ourselves. With an insignificant number of exceptions, both parties contribute to the quality of the marriage. The good news is that with an insignificant number of exceptions, any one of us can unilaterally contribute something positive to the quality of our marriages, by the quarrels we do not start, by the "slights" we overlook, and by the benefit of the doubt we give our partners.

Private Interests and Public Interests

An unmarried parent is at an inherent disadvantage in trying to teach a child how to cooperate in an adult relationship. It is not that it cannot be done, but the job is more difficult and the odds are against its success. Common sense and statistical evidence concur on this point. Yet it is often difficult to persuade people that they ought to sacrifice their own interests for the sake of another person's, even if the other person is their own child. I suppose very few people defend single motherhood as a positive good for children. More commonly, the defense is on behalf of the mother: single motherhood is superior to the alternatives and is not too harmful to the child. A small cottage industry has developed among social scientists who defend the proposition that single motherhood is just an alternative lifestyle choice. Single motherhood can be made to work for the child as well as the mother if only the public sector will commit enough resources and if only public opinion would become more supportive.

But the losses to both mother and child are deeper than these arguments suggest, too deep to be fully repaired by money from strangers or platitudes from acquaintances. The loss to the child is the loss of the opportunity to be in a day-to-day relationship with both of his parents. The loss to the parents is the loss of the opportunity to experience the life-transforming power of being in a loving relationship with another adult.

Many women believe this is no longer possible and have come to this conclusion for a variety of reasons. This one has been abandoned by her husband or lover: she is a single mother by necessity. That one wanted more than her husband was seemingly able to give her, and so she left him: her actions have made either her or her husband a single parent. This one watched the continual bickering between her own parents and concluded that marriage was a bad risk: she decides to become a single mother to avoid the trouble of having to deal with a husband. That one believed that giving herself to her career would make her happy and so postponed marriage for so long that she cannot find a partner: she decides to have a child on her own rather than remain childless. Each woman has her unique story. It would seem to be impossible to say something to and about each one of them. Yet the one thing that unites these single parents is that they are unable or unwilling to sustain a relationship with an adult.

The most militant of single mothers take pride in their independence from men in general and their child's father in particular. It is quite true that men can be difficult, even impossible at times. Yet we women are no picnic ourselves. We humans, men and women alike, are all imperfect, sometimes difficult or even impossible for other people to deal with. It is the easiest thing in the world for us to focus upon the flaws of others, but it is a mistake to separate ourselves from the rest of the human race by asserting that the other person's faults are too grievous for us to live with, as though ours were insignificant in comparison. It is certainly a mistake for us women to declare ourselves automatically superior to all those with xy chromosomes.

I suspect that relatively few women are single mothers out of a principled commitment to some kind of feminist separatism. Probably the vast majority of single mothers, and single fathers for that matter, would be willing to be in long-term relationships, but they cannot see how. Perhaps some people construct an entire theory of the inherent unreliability of the opposite sex based upon their own particular disappointments. Probably most do not even generalize as far as this but come to a more modest conclusion. They conclude that it is not possible for them to sustain a marriage for a lifetime, and remain agnostic on the question of whether it is theoretically possible for someone else to do so. Most would prefer to be in life-long relationships, if they could see how.

So this question of whether lifelong love is possible takes on some urgency, not only for children but for adults. It is not necessary to pit children's need for stability against the interests of parents in long-term happiness. Parents would like to have a lifelong, loving relation-ship that is satisfying to them: very few get divorced for sport. If people could see how to keep their marriages alive, most would gladly do so.

We might go so far as to say that even women who are single mothers by choice would have been better off if they had known how to sustain a relationship with a man. The plan to become a single mother is a plan to separate oneself into compartments: in one com-partment is my sexual activity; in another is my desire to have a child and my love for that child; in yet another is my relationship with the father of my child. Perhaps that last compartment is completely empty. Perhaps the woman has made a conscious decision to get herself pregnant through a casual encounter with a man she has no intention of being intimately involved with. In this case, she essen-tially uses the man and her own sexual attractiveness as instruments to achieve her private goal of having a baby all to herself. Or per-haps she has herself impregnated through an anonymous sperm do-nor, creating a radically fatherless child.

In any event, the woman's sexuality becomes fundamentally di-vorced from its two organic purposes: personal intimacy between two adults and the bringing forth of a new person. Sexual activity be-comes reduced to a recreational, or a purely instrumental, activity. A baby can be produced without an intimate relationship with a man or even without a direct encounter with a man. Sexuality has no necessary connection with being intimate with another person. This deconstruction of the self into separate compartments creates losses for anyone who does it, whether they realize it or not.

The members of a married couple need not compartmentalize these parts of the self. These three aspects of one's self are intimately and inexorably intertwined in marriage. My love for my spouse directs my sexuality exclusively toward him. Our love for each other produces a child whom we both love. Each of these aspects of the self reinforces and nourishes the others.

It is easy to see how a woman in today's world could conclude that sexuality, intimacy, and childbearing could be and perhaps should be placed into distinct cubbyholes of one's life. We all receive plenty of cultural messages telling us that sexual activity has no necessary connection with either procreation or deep personal intimacy. The organic connection that naturally exists between sex, procreation, and intimacy is almost hidden from public view and excluded from discourse. When people are able to discover that the intertwining of these three deepens and enriches every aspect of their lives, it is as though they have stumbled onto a great secret unknown to any other member of the human race. It is time for married people to come out of the closet.

The Analogy with the Market

The apparent dilemma between the interests of the child and the interests of the parents resembles the apparent dilemma between the public interest and the private interest in the economic marketplace. Libertarians and free market economists are fond of pointing out the convergence between public and private interests in the economic sphere. This convergence is not immediately evident to the untutored eye. It might appear that the interests of the producer and the consumer are in conflict. But upon closer examination we see that the producer's interest in earning a living induces him to provide something of value to the consumer at a price the consumer is willing to pay. As Adam Smith taught us so long ago, it is not from the public interest that the butcher and the baker provide us with our daily sustenance. They do it out of their own interest in earning a living.

But not just any definition of "interest" will generate this convergence. Consumers who think they are entitled to something for nothing will not be satisfied with the producers' insistence on being paid. Businesses that demand a monopoly in trading or production will not find it in their interest to provide consumers with the best quality product at the lowest possible price. For this happy coincidence of interests to occur, both consumers and producers need to be reasonable. For the public interest and private interests to converge, both consumers and the producers need to play by appropriate rules that apply to everyone. Such rules allow people to do well by doing good. Private interests in earning a living and in purchasing commodities at modest cost overlap enough that people are not trapped between their needs and their morals.

We can say something similar about the interests of individuals within the family. Children have an interest in the stability of their parents' marriage. Parents do as well. But not just any definition of the parental interests will generate this happy coincidence of interests. As Adam Smith would have been the first to point out, businessmen do not automatically define their own interests in such a way as to coincide with the public interest. They need to be tutored to do so. Similarly, people entering into married life need to channel their understanding of their own interests in such a way as to minimize social disruption, as well as to increase their own happiness.

This is not as impossible or oppressive a task as might be imagined. A series of uncommitted sexual liaisons may sound appealing to teenagers, but reality seldom lives up to these heady abstractions of personal fulfillment through unconstrained sexuality.[32] Nor does anyone really become happier from a series of attempted marriages, all of which end in disruption. People who initiate a divorce probably do so because they expect they will be happier. Yet the fact that second marriages have a greater rate of failure than first marriages suggests that many of these people are disappointed a second time.[33]

Adam Smith also would have been the first to observe that businessmen need an appropriate framework of laws to constrain and channel their interests into socially productive paths. Smith knew that businessmen would gladly cheat the public if they thought they could get away with it. This is one reason why Smith and generations of his followers have insisted upon rules that reduce the incentives for businessmen to conspire against the public and upon a system of open competition in which no business is granted special trade privileges by government. The economy in Smith's time (as in our own) was riddled with grants of monopoly, exclusive trading licenses, and the like.

We now have ample evidence that men and women alike are fully capable of playing each other for dupes in the courtship and marriage market if left completely unconstrained by law and social custom. No-fault divorce sometimes leads high-income men to dump faithful wives in favor of new, younger, "trophy wives."[34] Skewed judicial interpretations of custody rules can lead women to banish their husbands from the family while demanding a lifetime of child support.[35]

We who came of age during the sexual revolution perhaps underestimated the load that the informally enforced social norms of sexual conduct really carried. Those norms have been criticized as an oppressive double standards. Perhaps in some ways they were.

But who could have imagined the extent and depth of the changes in acceptable behavior over the course of such a short time? Men now assume that they are entitled to sex after just a few dates. On college campuses "hooking up" has taken the place of dating, going steady, or courtship.[36] "Responsible sex" used to mean being prepared to get married and raise a child. Now it just means using a condom. A gentleman used to marry a woman he impregnated. Now a woman is lucky if the guy offers to pay for an abortion. Some women who want a child have a casual liaison with a man and never tell him that they have become pregnant. It is not that these things never happened before, but when people did such things, they could expect to be criticized and possibly ostracized. The loosening of all these constraints on sexual conduct has lead to a weakening of the marital bond, as well as to an increase in sexual activity outside of marriage. Weakening the marital bond has led to an increased number of children with divorced parents.

One might have thought that the increased availability of contraception would have offset the effects of increased sexual activity outside of marriage. But more children are born outside of marriage today than ever before. We certainly cannot count on wider availability of contraception to stem the tide of illegitimate births. The contraceptive mentality might even be part of the problem. Contraception separates sexuality from commitment to another person and to the children that might result from the relationship. The compartmentalization of the person is part and parcel of the problem of single motherhood.

The combination of changing legal rules about divorce and social norms of sexual behavior has induced people to change their view of what is in their interest not only at the moment a marriage ends but throughout their lives. People who enter into a marriage they suspect will be impermanent will make different plans than people who expect their marriage to be lifelong. Women might very reasonably assume that the risk of being left on their own with small children to support is sufficiently high that they must work to protect their income stream and job security. These women might maintain their careers even when they might otherwise have preferred to be home with their children. That decision in turn, may have repercussions in every aspect of the marriage. Ultimately, the ease or difficulty of divorce will influence the care with which people choose their marriage partners in the first place.

Whatever else we might say about the pre-Sexual Revolution combination of social norms and legal rules, we can at least say this much:

the current set of constraints on men and women alike are not strong enough to help them keep the commitments of permanence and stability that would be beneficial to their children. The current situation creates perverse incentives, that is, incentives to do things that are not really in one's long-term interest or in the interest of others.

It was all very exciting in the 1960s and 1970s to look forward to a lifetime of freedom from commitments and entanglements. With the benefit of hindsight and experience, we can see that the ability to sustain those commitments is a great gift that produces deep happiness and satisfaction. We have forgotten much of what we once knew as a society about sustaining lifetime commitments. A great many adults are now ready to relearn whatever they can about lifelong marriage, for their own benefit as well as for the benefit of their children.

The child needs help learning to develop attachments to other people and to cooperate with other people. The married couple has an inherent advantage over a single person in teaching children how to be in relationships. The increased number of children being raised by single parents is cause for concern in that these children have a distinctive pattern of intellectual, social, and emotional difficulties. There is now an overwhelming amount of evidence that children need two parents in a stable marriage.

Although it might seem that the child's interest in stability conflicts with the parents' interest in happiness, there is a deeper sense in which their interests converge. We can improve our own situation by redefining what is in our interests. This is the area in which we actually have the most power. We do not have to wait for vast changes in public policy or big shifts in public opinion. Of all the things we might do to effect social change, changing our attitudes is one of the things we can do for ourselves.

Big Brother and Big Daddy

R EADERS OF PUBLIC POLICY BOOKS are wont to ask "What are
the policy implications?", meaning "What should the government do or not do?" I have deliberately postponed discussion of government policy because libertarianism holds that society
exists prior to government. Governmental policy need not determine
the ultimate outcome of a social problem. I prefer to focus first and
foremost on the choices we make as individuals. Nevertheless, government can dissipate the moral energies and basic goodness of
people in society by making appropriate individual behavior more
costly and difficult than it otherwise might be. The maxim "First, do
no harm" applies to governmental actions that affect the family.

The government is not likely to be successful at replacing the family. I focus on three particular characteristics of the modern state and
relate them to three broad areas of policy making relevant to family
life. The modern state's policies are financed by taxes, selected by
majority rule, and administered by bureaucracies. The state may attempt to supplant the economic function of the family through its
taxing power. The state may attempt to replace the family as the primary provider of moral education for the young by selecting a moral
curriculum through some kind of democratic process. Finally, the

state has a necessary role in protecting children from abusive parents. The state's methods will almost certainly involve the use of the blunt tools of bureaucracy, and this in turn will be less effective than more personal instruments.

The Trouble with Other People's Money

Two kinds of consequences flow from government attempts to replace the economic function of the family. First, the recipients of the economic support have less need for support from their family. Those who receive money from outside the family tend to remove themselves from the daily life of the family. Second, an infusion of cash into a family can undermine the ability of the parents to place sanctions on inappropriate behavior by the young. This can be disastrous when the young people still need assistance in growing to maturity.

Social Security, the granddaddy of all social assistance programs, collectivized the care of the elderly.[1] Working people pay a payroll tax earmarked for the payment of retirement benefits to the currently old. Old people receive retirement benefits from the general fund of these taxes, regardless of the contributions of their own children. Young people do not have to care directly for their own parents and old people do not have to rely directly upon their own savings or their own children for care and financial assistance. Socializing the care of the elderly has had two kinds of consequences.

First, public payments for the care of the elderly have contributed to making the family less necessary as a source of support. A higher level of pensions provided by government is correlated with lower birthrates. People who do not rely on their own children for support in their old age need not take into account the impact of their childbearing decisions. Social Security will be there, even for people who never had any productive children themselves. People who might otherwise have planned to have several children can instead rely on the collective support of other people's children.[2]

People who must rely on their children in their old age have a focused incentive to assure that those children become and stay productively employed. Under a social insurance regime like Social Security, a couple can plan their retirement whether or not their own children are productive. How many parents would stand for their adult children avoiding work or responsibility if those parents knew they would have to rely on those same lazy children for support in their old age? How many parents would allow their children to squander family resources in an effort to "find themselves" if the parents themselves might be economically destitute when the adult child remains permanently lost? Parents have far greater incentives to monitor and sanction the behavior of wayward adult children when their own old age support is at stake.

Second, the combination of economic support from a government source rather than a family source plus the natural desire for privacy has led many elderly people to live independently of their children, lured out of the family by this combination of incentives. It strains the imagination to think that so many elderly people would be living so far from their children in huge sunbelt retirement communities if individual retired people had to rely directly on their children for support. As a result, the accumulated wisdom of the elderly has been pulled away from the younger members of the family. Older people are less available to provide advice for young mothers and care for grandchildren. New mothers must rely on child-rearing manuals and day-care centers. Older couples are less available to provide their adult children with a longer-range perspective on making marriage work. Retired workers are less available to offer counsel about work and finances.

Providing income from a public source means that people are less dependent upon their family members, which in turn means reducing the connections among family members. We are less apt to be compelled by financial necessity into relatedness with family members. We are only connected to each other if we want to be, and to the extent that we want to be. We are sometimes inclined to retreat into our little households of a few carefully chosen people, so that we do not have to deal with family relationships very deeply. We withdraw into our jobs, so that we can avoid the intense relationships of home and relate to non-relatives in a more remote fashion than is required of us in the family. We create an artificial sense of independence. We can indulge our desire to be alone, less accountable for our actions.

We might think this is a good thing. People should be in relationships because they want to be, not from financial necessity. But we need not draw such a sharp dichotomy between emotional affection and financial necessity. Why not be connected in both ways? Maybe the generations would learn to accommodate each other if we were compelled by financial necessity to remain in close relationship. Perhaps we would learn to do things we know are good but that we are not necessarily inclined to do. Surely not every old person is a meddlesome, cranky old fool. Surely not every young person is a self-centered, immature boor. It is certain that we would all be very different kinds of people if the young had direct responsibility for the elderly, as well as the opportunity to interact with them.

It is convenient for us who are young to forget about old people if their financial needs are taken care of. We are tempted to think we do not need to do very much for them. But elderly people want and need attention from their children and grandchildren. The money from the government does not take the place of such attentiveness: a check does nothing for loneliness. We tend to forget that not so very long ago families maintained a continuous responsibility for each other from birth through old age. Old people used to live with their families rather than alone or in segregated institutions. Our current living arrangements of two generations at most in a household are an aberration in the history of the human race.

This, then, is the ultimate trouble with the government spending other people's money for the support of one part of the family. Other people's money relieves us from some of the personal responsibility for the other members of our family. Parents are less accountable for instilling good work habits, encouraging work effort, and creating an environment in which young people can prosper financially. Young people are less accountable for the care of particular old people, since they are forcibly taxed to support old people in general. All the members of the family are less accountable to each other for the impact of their everyday behavior on each other.

Removing the Moral Heart of the Family

If removing the old people from the family has lessened the mutual influence and support between adult family members of different generations, the policy of making welfare payments to young unmarried mothers has undermined the teaching authority of the family. Although recent welfare reforms have alleviated this problem, we may be dealing with its accumulated impact on family relationships for a considerable time.

Imagine a young woman who is part of a family in which early marriage is common. Perhaps she is a member of an ethnic group such as African Americans, Italians, Native Americans, or Hispanics. In an environment undistorted by welfare, this young woman might marry in her teens or early twenties. She and her husband would not be completely independent of the community. Her parents and her in-laws would support the young couple as they continued to grow into their new responsibilities as parents and spouses. They might receive advice, financial support, and a place in an already established social network. They might be allowed to share housing with their parents, uncles and aunts, or siblings, for a few years until they are better established. Now some of the help they would receive would probably not be too comfortable for them. They might sometimes be told that they are not doing things correctly or that they need to shape up. Disapproval of bad behavior offers a certain amount of corrective information to an immature couple. They need that input, precisely because they are young. But young people do not always enjoy it.

The introduction of welfare benefits changes the calculations all the way around. The young woman can have a baby, perhaps earlier than she otherwise might have, but not outrageously so. She can have enough money to get her own apartment. She can be out from under the watchful eye of the adults of her family and of the family of the man who, under other circumstances, might have become her husband. She no longer needs that uncomfortable help from adults that she might have otherwise received. She gets to be "independent" of her family. She appears to be more grown up because she lives on her own. But she is less accountable to the older members of her family. She has less opportunity to learn what she needs to learn from them. She may have to make many painful mistakes that she could have avoided had she remained connected to her family.

From the adults' point of view, the young woman's independent source of income removes one of the major tools they had for enforcing reasonable standards of conduct. They can no longer credibly say that they will not support the daughter unless she behaves. They do not need to say it: both the adult and the daughter realize that she does not need them under the system of state support. She can do what she wants without negative consequences at a much earlier age.

Some downplay the problems of teenage pregnancy by observing that there have always been teenage mothers. In former times, women got married and pregnant at earlier ages. Teenage sexual activity and teenage pregnancy, the argument continues, have always been with us.

The worry is that today's teenage mothers are less inclined to get married and stay married. Most young wives from previous generations remained married for a lifetime. Their children did not display the kind of pathologies that the children of today's unmarried teenage mothers do. Marriage had a maturing effect on women and their husbands. Single motherhood supported by welfare payments does not have the same effect. Nor does the experience of absentee teenage fatherhood generate anything like the same maturation that a young married man would have as he supported his wife and baby with the guidance and support of older people in the family.

Many of today's teenage mothers are not supported by husbands, parents, and in-laws. They are supported by the state, which cannot offer moral instruction, marriage counseling, and child-rearing advice.[3] We would almost certainly not allow the state to do the kind of intensive monitoring necessary to assist teenage mothers in maturing. But even if we did permit it, we would almost certainly be unable to accomplish it as effectively as could the family that immediately surrounded the young woman and her husband.

This is the problem with other people's money. The state can support members of families by transferring income to them. But in doing so the state pulls the props from under the structure of the family. The family members who receive the money directly from the state have less incentive to be accountable to the other members of the family upon whom they might have had to rely, and the members of the family who do not actually receive the money look on helplessly.

The programs of the state are sometimes appealing because they claim to take account of each and every person. Virtually every person over a certain age is eligible for Social Security; anyone with low income can qualify for means-tested programs. These programs give the appearance of being all-encompassing. Private programs, by contrast, might overlook someone. Not everyone will save for their own retirement; not everyone will take care of their own children.

But this appearance is deceptive. Everyone is covered or included, in principle, but people do fall between the cracks of the state-run programs. We should consider that the real goal of these programs is, or ought to be, much more than passing out money to people. The goal, especially in programs that involve children, ought to be to help them become responsible adults. This requires more than money. The more expansive the state's objectives become, the more likely it is that people will not have their genuine needs met. It is no overwhelming objection to private efforts that they are not all-encompassing: neither are the state's efforts. The state simply has greater pretensions.

The Trouble with Voting

Some might argue that the state itself should try to instill behavioral norms in children. We need not forcibly take children from their parents: just provide a combination of taxes and subsidies that will induce mothers to conclude that paid employment for themselves and day-care for their children makes the most financial sense. Then people would leave their children at state-run day-care centers, staffed by state employees trained to teach cooperation, and to enhance attachment. This scenario might have some appeal if we assume that our particular brand of state-provided day-care would actually be provided. But if we make the more realistic assumption that details of the day-care would be worked out by some political process of voting, or political give-and-take, the appeal quickly fades. Set aside the knowledge problem I alluded to earlier. Overlook the difficulties inherent in trying to create a system that would actually accommodate the needs of each and every child. Just focus on the fact that a government-run program for creating attachment and teaching appropriate cooperative behavior must make political decisions about how to accomplish these objectives.

For instance, teaching cooperation might mean eliminating all competitive aspects of the children's interactions. Or teaching cooperation could just as easily include a substantial component of aggressive team sports in which winning requires teamwork. Families routinely makes these judgements for each of their children. It is not uncommon for a family to decide that one child would be devastated by contact sports and should go out for the swim team, while another needs football with a former drill sergeant for a coach. This individual adaptation is less likely to take place if the a society tries to determine moral and developmental curriculum through voting.

Let us rule out a couple of relatively unlikely cases. We can safely rule out the case in which everyone in America shares the same views about children's behavior, relationships between children and parents, and the appropriate way to teach cooperation. That kind of consensus is not likely to emerge any time soon. We can also rule out, at least for the sake of argument, the case in which one group successfully and completely dominates the policy making process. We each have our own private nightmare: maybe your worst fear is that the Christian Coalition would select the moral curriculum; maybe you wake up with cold chills from a dream that Hillary Clinton and the Children's Defense Fund have taken over public schools, after-school programs, and preschool day-care centers. Let us instead offer the democratic process the most favorable set of assumptions and examine a situation with genuine voting among groups of people with different views. Suppose a political entity assigns itself the primary responsibility for inculcating appropriate social behavior and attitudes in young people. What is the likely outcome?

Political scientists and economists have studied majority rule voting rather thoroughly and have learned that decisions made by majority rule often have the undesirable properties of instability and arbitrariness. These properties can arise if no one policy can beat every other policy in pair-wise majority rule voting.

For instance, policy A might beat policy B, while policy B might beat policy C. But instead of A beating policy C, as one might expect, policy C can actually beat policy A. When this happens, the results of the election will be arbitrary, because the outcome will depend on procedural rules rather than on the preferences of the people. The results can be incoherent because mutually contradictory policies can emerge from a logroll ("I'll vote for your program if you'll vote for mine"). And the policy outcomes can be unstable as the voters rotate through the set of possible majority coalitions.[4] Each vote is a fair majority rule vote. But the outcome of the series of elections does not represent anything like "the will of the people" since there was no unified will of the people available to be expressed in these preferences.

When, during the 1950s, political scientists and economists began discussing the problem of voting inconsistencies, they were unsure about how important they were as a practical matter. After all, voters do not appear to cycle endlessly through a set of proposals. Democratic assemblies do ultimately make decisions that have some stability. Are voting inconsistencies merely a chalkboard trick? The apparent deadlock can often be broken by the use of procedural rules. For instance, many democratic bodies have a rule against reintroducing a defeated motion. This rule breaks the endless cycle of alternatives, but it makes the outcome depend entirely upon the order in which the proposals are considered.

When the procedural rules are the decisive factor, the person who controls the agenda and the order of consideration can determine the outcome. In theory, the agenda setter always wins. In practice, he does not. Nevertheless, he has a substantial enough advantage that political parties expend enormous energy attempting to capture positions, such as committee chairmanships and the speakership of the House, that control the legislative agenda.

An election can reveal a consensus if one exists, but an election cannot create a consensus. In fact, the electoral process will only highlight the divisions among the groups. Elections can exacerbate existing differences because people will not sit by idly while their deepest beliefs and strongest preferences are trampled upon by the majority. Instead, defeated voters will find some way to attach themselves to a different coalition that will give them a better result. The trouble with majority rule is not that it oppresses minorities. The deep problem is that there is always a dissatisfied *majority* that can form around a new, if slightly different proposal. The losers look around for a part of the winning coalition that they can siphon off to form a new majority for a slightly different proposal. Perhaps the new proposal incorporates features of the winning proposal (which is now the status quo) with some other feature that makes it less objectionable to those who were first defeated.

The only constant feature of an issue like this is change. The legislators will be unable to leave the system alone. One dissatisfied group after another will put together a slightly different coalition to promote a new wrinkle in the law. Every year will see a new reform or improvement or at least amendment. Considering how often we have seen "education reforms" or "tax reforms," this kind of realigning of coalitions probably takes place more readily than we might think from simply looking broadly at the party platforms or ideological orientations of legislators.

Instability is costly and inefficient in tax law. But tax accountants and tax lawyers are grown-up people who plan for a certain amount of uncertainty and change. Young people, however, have a need for some stability in the moral messages they receive, in the programs they participate in, and in the rules they are expected to obey. The instability itself can seriously undermine the government's efforts to inculcate ethics in the young. This is especially pernicious if the message we are trying to convey to the young is that certain standards of behavior are universal and timeless. In short, an electoral process cannot produce moral consensus if one does not already exist. The cultural and educational processes that might make such a consensus possible must take place prior to the actual election.

Limiting the Scope of the State

In spite of this inherent instability, we can make some predictions about the general direction of the voting process. Suppose we began from a position in which the vast majority of people agreed to a substantive moral code. It would not be too far-fetched, for instance, to assert that most people in America in 1787 agreed to the moral code embodied in the Ten Commandments. If we allowed people to vote on a moral code, the competitive process would begin to unravel the sanctions surrounding violations of the moral law.

For even people who know right from wrong sometimes do wrong. And when they do, most people find it easier to be absolved at minimal cost than to admit that they were wrong. Even people who believe an act is wrong will have a tendency to vote for the politicians who give them minimal penalties. Sooner or later, some politician will seize upon arguments that claim the act was not really wrong in the first place. People with a bad conscience find it convenient to agree.[5] The competitive process will have a tendency to drive the moral code toward the most minimal standard. This is one of the processes driving the phenomenon Daniel Patrick Moynihan has described as "defining deviancy down."

Therefore, the moral and ethical system underlying the polity must be secured outside the political process itself. It is also important to limit the scope of the state so that fewer occasions present themselves for the systematic watering down of moral standards. If we have to vote whether to lower a certain moral standard, the matter is probably already decided. The most secure moral standards are those that are taken for granted, that form the background for people's thinking.

Perhaps some will respond that the government once actively supported the Judeo-Christian moral code. The public schools actively taught and promoted that ethic for many generations. So what is meant by the claim that the government cannot promote a specific and substantive moral code through its schools? Granted, the American public school system once inculcated the civic religion of republicanism against a backdrop of Protestantism. Despite differences in emphasis among political parties, responsible political leaders were completely at ease advocating patriotism and devotion to America's founding principles. The country was overwhelmingly Protestant, both in confession and in culture.

The major exceptions were Catholic and Jewish immigrants, at whom the educational system was substantially directed. These groups established their own religious schools that taught respect for the American civil system while preserving their own religious traditions. Catholics established an extensive system of parochial schools, while Jews established Hebrew schools at least for weekend religious instruction and sometimes for a complete alternative to public school education. In neither case did they attempt to force the public school system to respond to their religious views. This was an entirely practical position to take in an era of low taxes, cheap land, and minimal government regulation. It was far simpler to establish private schools than to try to lobby for change.

But in the 1960s, the consensus about both the civic religion and the Protestant religion changed. The combination of the Vietnam War, the Civil Rights movement, and the Sexual Revolution dissolved whatever consensus might have existed about the meaning of the American experiment. The Protestant religious majority lost its consensus during the same period. These religious groups, who in earlier days had been mainstays in the support of the civic religion, fragmented over the very same political questions that shook the body politic. The religious groups had the added difficulty of trying to strike a balance between their roles as activists for social change and their more traditional roles as preachers of the Gospel and the Ten Commandments. The basis for the consensus within the public school system was destroyed.

At roughly the same time, the government began to undertake far greater social responsibilities than it had ever attempted to do. This changed the emphasis for many religious and civic groups from across the ideological and theological spectrum. Lobbying the government to control the outcome of one grand national decision became the focal point of social activism for groups that formerly might have sponsored their own orphanages, hospitals, and educational and poor relief efforts. These distinct groups previously had gone about their business with relatively little concern about the specific details of the efforts of other groups.

The result of the national government taking over so many of these functions of religious and private associations was to politicize the society to an ever greater extent. Given this trend of increasing politicization and polarization of the society, it is not surprising that people came to look upon the schools as the breeding grounds for the next generation of voters and political activists. The schools became ever more politicized and hence polarized.

It is not clear to me whether we can ever again have a society that enjoys the kind of approximate consensus about moral education that America once enjoyed. There was an era in which Protestants went to the public schools and read from the King James Bible; Catholics went to parochial schools, read from the Vulgate, and learned Latin; and Jewish children went to Hebrew school (at least on Saturday), read the Torah, and learned Hebrew. Yet they all learned to use English as a common language and to revere roughly the same things about the American experiment in self-government. All things considered, that society was less politicized and less polarized than ours is today. That society enjoyed more consensus about the proper standards of behavior that should be inculcated in young people than we do today. And it is without doubt that the America prior to the Vietnam War did a better job of educating the young, both academically and morally, than does America today.

Limiting the scope of governmental activity provides the best hope of achieving both reasonable moral standards and anything like consensus. A limited government broadens the sphere in which the distinctive religious and ethnic subcultures can create their own institutions. Limited government also reduces the number of occasions that demand consensus about things people are unlikely to agree upon.

The Trouble with Bureaucracy

In addition to the problems associated with voting, state programs are also typically administered by bureaucracies. This is a particular problem for government programs that relate to children and their welfare. I will focus on the problem of detecting and correcting child abuse, and area in which the state must surely play an important role. But a comparable analysis could be made for any bureaucratically administered programs, whether for education, medical care, or mental health.

I suppose most people understand the word "bureaucracy" to be something of a smear word. Probably the tamest image of the bureaucratic experience would be a day at the Department of Motor Vehicles. It is downhill from there to an audit by the IRS. What exactly is the problem with bureaucracy that the very word evokes images of standing in long lines, confronting uncivil civil servants, and generally feeling frustrated?*

The purpose of a government bureaucracy is to administer a program or law enacted by a legislature. The workers within a bureaucracy are either civil service employees or appointed by the executive branch. These workers are agents of the governor or president who appointed them or of the legislature that finances their activities. Formally, the bureaucracy is accountable to the institution that created it and the executives that appoint its members. But the average civil servant seldom lays eyes on these people. The legislature requires the bureaucracy to follow specified procedures ensuring that its mission is carried out. The primary accountability of the bureaucracy is to these procedures. Workers in the bureaucracy are held accountable to a set of procedures, forms, and guidelines.[6]

The administrators of the program must be limited in the amount

---

* I confine my discussion to government bureaucracies, even though some private sector bureaucracies have many of the same characteristics.

of discretion that they can use. In fact, the whole point of a civil service bureaucracy is to limit the amount of discretion that government employees have. This limit serves two purposes. It protects the employees from political pressure that they would have to endure if they possessed significant discretion. It also protects the public from abuse by either unscrupulous or politicized bureaucrats.[7] This lack of discretion might be acceptable if the institution were doing something as simple as passing out money.[8] Bureaucracy as a tool to provide child protective services is even more problematic.

The legislature and bureaucracy must define child abuse in such a way that it can be easily distinguished from activity that is not abusive. We cannot define it in a way that requires the social or child protective workers to use much discretion or judgment. We define it to include the easily measured, easily observed. A bruise counts; emotional scars do not. Neglect does not count, unless it is gross neglect of the most basic needs for physical care. Parental drug or alcohol addiction might count as abuse from which children could legitimately be rescued. Parents' sitting constantly in front of the television in an electronically induced stupor probably does not count as abuse.

There are two types of mistakes that child protective service workers could make. True child abuse could go undetected or unsanctioned or non-abusive parents could be wrongly accused of child abuse. The cost of the first type of mistake is that children remain with abusive parents, continue to be abused, and do not have the opportunity to be adopted by better parents. The cost of the second kind of mistake is that a good enough family is disrupted, children are placed in foster care or shelters that might well be worse than their original family, and the authority of competent parents is unnecessarily undermined.

The costs of wrongly accusing an innocent family are most likely to appear at the stage of initial entry into the child protective system. In most jurisdictions, the child protective service workers are required to respond to all accusations. They are not usually allowed to make a judgment that the allegation is frivolous in itself. They usually have a very limited scope for discretion that would permit them to say, for example, that the person making the anonymous phone call is drunk, or incompetent, or a vindictive estranged spouse, or a spiteful neighbor. The child protective service worker might have a very strong intuition that a particular allegation is unfounded. But she cannot prove it until she investigates, and the investigation process itself may be devastating to the family. The social worker is more likely to be in trouble if a child is harmed than if an innocent family is inconvenienced. So she is likely to go forward with an investigation of a complaint she feels sure is groundless, both because the law requires her to do so and because her incentives to minimize aggravation to herself encourage her to do so.

The potential for insufficiently protecting a child is more important once a child is in the child protective system after a genuine instance of abuse. A case worker might know perfectly well that a family has minimal prospects of ever shaping up enough to provide an adequate home in which the children can attach to the parents and learn reasonable social skills. But she has to prove it. All too often the social worker cannot prove her case in a court of law, which requires more than intuition, gut feeling, and tacit knowledge. She must be able to articulate her reasons for believing that parental rights should be terminated or that parental visits should be denied.

This cuts to the heart of why relying on government as the primary provider of child protective services is inherently problematic. The information required to make a proper judgment about which children should be returned to or removed from their parents is often too subtle to be fully articulated and explained in courts. Child protective workers must justify their decisions with reasons they can articulate, backed up with evidence they can demonstrate. But often the decisions involved in parenting cannot be fully articulated. Not every justifiable action can be fully explained or accounted for.

Understanding the context of a given family's decision necessarily requires some judgment. We do not want social workers to make life and death decisions for families using nothing more than gut feelings. We want them to be able to prove their case in court, precisely because so much is at stake in the outcome of the court's decision. There may be plenty of clues that signal to the social worker what the outcome ought to be. We all often form our impressions based on body language, noise levels, sights, and smells. These things cannot be completely and accurately conveyed to the court.

We would not want courts to make decisions based on this kind of shooting from the hip. Yet this is often the information that tells the story most completely and truly. Sometimes, close relatives and neighbors know exactly what is going on and have a perfectly sound judgment about the situation. These people are often not very articulate to begin with, and the information upon which they base their judgments would be difficult for anyone to articulate. It is not the kind of information that can be or ought to be used in a legal proceeding.

There will always be situations in which the family has collapsed so dramatically that the children are entitled to another, better family. And in those cases, the state will play a necessary role in verifying the collapse and recognizing the new family as the legitimate family. But if the state-run child protective service bureaucracy is almost sure to be wrong or inadequate in all but the most extreme cases, what can be done to protect children? Is there some decentralized system that can help protect children from abusive parents or, better yet, prevent parents from becoming abusive in the first place?

The Decentralized Approach: Mediating Institutions

The best way to deal with child abuse, obviously, is prevention. The statistics cited in an earlier chapter point to one very basic preventive tool: marriage. Married parents are far less likely to abuse children than unmarried cohabiting parents. Single parents are more likely to abuse children than married parents. If the child lives in a two-parent household in which one parent is not his biological parent, the evidence suggests that the child is much safer with married stepparents than with a cohabiting couple.

This is the ultimate decentralized solution to child abuse and neglect. Assign the responsibility for care of the child to the people who have the greatest interest in him: his biological parents. Keep these biological parents committed to each other for the maximum benefit to the child. Teamwork between them can help prevent burn-out: commitment to each other multiplies their commitment to the child and his well-being. Nothing the government can do to help the victims of child abuse is likely to have nearly the impact on the well-being of children than parents' staying married to each other.

The rate of child abuse among married parents is lower than among other types of parents, but still not zero. What decentralized non-governmental strategies can either reduce the incidence of child abuse or offset its worst effects when it does occur? The family's chief strength is also its weakness: the family is small. Two parents can know and respond to the needs of their own children. But small size becomes a weakness for the family if one of its adult members becomes incapacitated, or disappears, or is irresponsible. In these cases, the families need other people around them to help. Who is available other than the state and its agents?

There are numerous social institutions, sometimes called mediating institutions, that operate in the social space between the family and the state. These mediating institutions might include churches, neighborhoods, schools, Scout troops, parent cooperative sports leagues, and the like. These social institutions other than the state that support the family do much more than the state can do, or ought to attempt to do. The mediating institutions are closer to the family and have a better chance of knowing what is actually going on. They can support the family more effectively because they are more personal institutions than the state. Most of the time, what the family needs is personal help, not bureaucratic help. Even when the family needs moral guidance or instruction, the state is about the least effective instrument for that task.

Isolation is the enemy of good parenting.[9] People who live in social isolation need not be accountable to anyone for their actions. Regular, meaningful contact with people outside the family places a restraint on how abusive the parents can be. People will notice if the children are hurt or timid. People will notice if the children do not appear at regular intervals. Another family member or neighbor might restrain a distraught parent who could get out of control, if left on his own.

But this is a small part of how being embedded in a network of social relationships protects children from abuse. Families that participate in a variety of networks are less likely to be abusive in the first place. Sometimes, seeing another person do the things we are inclined to do can exert a moderating influence of its own. We can get a clearer idea of the impact our behavior has on others by observing another person do what we do. We might think, "I don't want to be like that. I need to cut that out." In this way, simply being around other parents can operate as an important moderating force on parents who might have a bad temper or who might have developed bad habits. The embarrassment of doing something in public, perhaps to someone other than one's own child, can help a person see that he might have gone over the line at home on some occasions. All of these actions and reactions help keep a parent from abusing the power that is inherent in the parent-child relationship.

Extended families, aunts and uncles and grandparents who live close enough together, can provide support as well as accountability to a couple with children. The members of extended families have an interest in keeping the family functioning as a unit rather than displacing the parents as the primary caretakers. If they live close by, they can have the knowledge necessary to understand the context of difficult or troubled relationships. If all else fails, members of the extended family can take over some or all of the responsibility for caring for the children if the parents are unable to do so appropriately.

Neighborhoods seem to be almost a thing of the past. Yet there are still some places in which children all walk together to the neighborhood school and play together after school. These relationships can develop among the children because the parents in such neighborhoods are all looking out for each other's children. Children can go from house to house comfortably. In such a neighborhood, an abused child stands out quickly. Parents have quite a few safety valves in such a free-ranging neighborhood. No one mother has the full responsibility for entertaining her children at all times, because at any given time her kids will be at someone else's house. On other days, she might have half the neighborhood at her house. Unlike a paid day-care provider, each mother has some scope for saying, "not today, I'm too tired or busy. See if you can all play at Bobby's or Janice's house." Children whose parents are bad tempered end up spending most of their time at other houses in the neighborhood. Everybody figures out quickly which houses no one wants to go to and why. Children whose parents have the time and patience for enjoyable activities end up with quite a few other kids visiting. Even bad-tempered parents start to figure out that some kinds of things are enjoyable and beneficial for children. More children go outdoors; fewer stay inside watching television or playing video games. These kinds of social networks are not organized or planned. Things do not always run smoothly; sometimes things fall between the cracks. But on average, the mothers and fathers in child-rich neighborhoods work together pretty well.

Attached to these neighborhoods sometimes are neighborhood schools, a public school, a neighborhood parochial school, or a local church cooperative preschool. A group of people can develop a sense of community much more quickly if all their children walk together to the local school than if everybody is driving in different directions to private schools outside the neighborhood. Mothers who bring their small children to school every day come to know one another. When those same mothers also see each other at the same grocery store or the same park or local library, they are more likely to become closer to one another. The teachers and principal can contribute much more if they are part of the neighborhood community. They can work with the parents rather than suspecting them or undermining them.

James Coleman's concept of "social capital"[10] concerns the family's web of social networks and relationships.[11] Coleman argues that a school that is embedded within a rich network of social relationships will do a better job educating the children. A study tested Coleman's thesis by using information about individual students and their families, as well as information about the school.[12] This study reported that more parental interaction with other parents increases the average math and reading scores of the school. These effects persist even after controlling for the average socioeconomic status of the families attending the school. In other words, the benefits from creating rich social networks among parents can accrue to schools in poor neighborhoods, as well as in more affluent ones. This study and Coleman's general approach is consistent with the idea that rich social networks are beneficial for children.

When I was a little girl, about half of the fifty kids on our block went to the local public school, and the other half went to St. Michael's, the parish school. At the Catholic school, the school lunch program was partially staffed by mothers who volunteered. All the moms on our block made a point of working at the cafeteria on the same day. Some of the teachers at St. Michael's were members of my mother's bridge club. Every two months, the club would meet at our house. We children (who were supposed to be in bed) would sit at the top of the stairs and listen to our teachers talk about the goings-on at school. It would have been hard to keep many secrets in that school and neighborhood. A case of serious child abuse would have certainly stood out.[13]

It goes without saying that churches play a role in protecting children. Churches at their best are integral parts of the community. Churches instruct parents about their responsibilities, offer places for families to come together for a variety of reasons, and to some extent monitor the behavior of their members.

The institutions closest to the individual family are in the best position to help. Equally important, these mediating institutions are in a better position to help people help themselves. An individual or family can be a more effective participant in a neighborhood association or a cooperative basketball league than they can in the government, even in the local government and certainly in the federal government. The participation of the individual and the family teaches them how to solve their own problems by giving them experience in coming together with other families to solve a problem of mutual concern. This kind of activity strengthens the community, as well as strengthening the individuals. Mediating institutions that are local and limited can strengthen the community precisely through the process of strengthening and empowering the individuals. State organized and orchestrated activity does not have this property.

Little by little, all this community activity that both supports and monitors the family has been replaced or shoved aside. The state has taken over greater authority for teaching and monitoring. Neighborhoods have become empty as women have become convinced that paid employment is the only worthy activity of dignified adults.[14]

Neighborhood schools were assaulted by busing. Children, white and black, were bused so far from their homes that they could not participate in after-school activities. The children they went to school with were not the children they played with at home. And anyway, there was little time left over for play after the long bus ride. Neighborhood schools have taken another great blow by the general poor quality of public education that has driven parents to private schools.

These are the very parents who, in earlier generations, might have been at the core of the community around the school.

These mediating social institutions support the family. They do not replace the family even when they operate at their best. These institutions play an essential role in the protection of children from parents who abuse their parental power. These institutions can both detect and deter child abuse.

The state, even in its most necessary and legitimate role, does not replace the family as an institution. The state's unique role is to provide a legal framework within which the other, less encompassing institutions of society can do their work. When all else fails, the state may have to take steps to protect children. But we ought to view the state as a last resort rather than delude ourselves that it has the ability to do very much more. The personal, local institutions that surround the family in its immediate environment have the greatest capacity and must bear the greatest responsibility for encouraging competent parenting.

My suggestions for protecting children without the help of the state require decent behavior from ordinary human beings. At the same time, government programs also require decent behavior from the ordinary people who work within them. Every aspect of the decentralized approach requires people who are able to look at another person as an individual endowed with dignity and rights. Every one of these mediating institutions, however imperfect, however limited, moves us one step away from the depersonalized apparatus of the state and toward a more personal and humane society.

I now turn from the government to an institution dear to the heart of libertarians: the market.

❦ 8 ❧

Institutionalizing Childhood[1]

PARENTS USE MANY SERVICES AND COMMODITIES that they purchase on the market. Are these services purchased on the market substitutes for the family itself? Few people would offer an affirmative answer to the question posed in this way. But the question can be phrased in a more controversial way: Is paid child care a substitute for parental care? Many people are deeply committed to giving an affirmative answer to that question.

The family's job is to build relationships. Parents must build bonds with their children and teach them cooperation and reciprocity. We cannot pay someone to do our relationship work for us. Excessive or inappropriate use of market services can interfere with this irreplaceable work of the family.

Advocates of the free market have a particular responsibility to address this question, for we are sometimes drawn into the periphery of debates around it. Some advocates of the market take delight in pointing out the responsiveness of the decentralized market to women's demands for paid child care. This argument is frequently made in debates about whether and how much the government ought to subsidize child care. The market will give people what they want, it is claimed, at lower cost and with greater sensitivity to more subtle aspects of their true needs than will any governmentally provided service. Therefore, let the market provide child care and keep the government out of it.[2]

But this is not necessarily the end of the argument. For there are premises embedded within the argument that free market advocates ought not to concede so readily. For example, the argument assumes that the work of parents, and particularly mothers, is not especially important. Therefore, providing a low-cost substitute for mothers' time in the home presents no particular problem. Another more insidious form of this premise is the idea that the work women do in the market is more socially valuable than the work they do in the home, at least for high-wage women. In other words, some women are too important to take care of their own children.

To argue that women want day care and that therefore the market will provide it is to assume that women's desires are completely given. This is not entirely true. Many women, of various beliefs and of all income levels, have been seduced by a peculiarly American ideological mix of left-wing self-esteem feminism and right-wing income-maximizing capitalism.

A woman under the influence of this ideological cocktail might believe that she must prove herself independent of and equal to men. Her self-esteem depends upon the status and income of her job. The worst stereotype of capitalism is that the value of a person is reduced to his value in the market. It is ironic that the American feminists have done so much to indoctrinate women into this distorted view of themselves.

Some professional women think it an admission of weakness or defeat to acknowledge that they enjoy taking care of children. We are supposed to believe that child-care is mind-numbing, spirit-killing drudgery, and only work outside the home is fulfilling. These are not reasons for labor force participation that women would come up with spontaneously in the absence of any feminist tutoring. For many feminists, the overwhelming argument in favor of women working is that women with paychecks are more powerful than women without any income of their own. Those of us who admire the free market as a social mechanism agree that dollar power is real power. Each individual with a dollar is just as powerful as any other individual with a dollar. We sometimes tend to agree with feminists that working outside the home empowers women.

We should not concede this premise too readily. We forget that dollar power is not the only kind of power. Losing control over what happens to one's children is, for many women, a devastating loss of power. Surrendering day-to-day contact with one's children, giving up the ability to influence their development and surely count as losses of power from the viewpoint of most parents, fathers and mothers alike. The power of an independent income is important for a person who plans to be financially independent but not nearly so important for a person in an ongoing relationship.

Finally, we know that the principle that the market will provide does not mean that every family can hire Mary Poppins to provide full-time care. Childcare can only be a rational choice if the cost is lower is than the woman's own wages. For women of moderate income, the only way this can be accomplished is through economies of scale in childcare. Group care will necessarily be the market-provided solution for the vast majority of women of modest means.

Commitment and Attentiveness

I noted in an earlier chapter that the institutional substitutes for the father's paycheck do not meet the needs of the mother and her child, especially their relationship needs. Neither an employer nor a government agency have reason to be committed to the mother and child. The same can be said of a paid childcare provider.

The baby needs the paid mother substitute to be present and attentive to his needs. The adult must come when the child cries. The adult must make a good effort to figure out what the crying signifies.

This can be an impossible task because sometimes babies cry for no apparent reason at all. The adult might try everything he can think of to console the child: offer food, change diapers, or rock the baby. When the crying finally stops, the adult might still be mystified as to what it was all about. In these situations perhaps more than any other, it is important that the adult be present. The caregiver cannot simply throw up his or her hands and say "I'm leaving. This is too hard." We sometimes observe the very sad state of affairs in which the childcare provider *is* more committed and more attentive to the child's well-being than the parents are. If she is, this is most likely because the parental commitment level is so low.[3] The nanny or babysitter does not particularly have reason to be more committed.

But even the best of babysitters quits, changes jobs, or moves on. No mother can count on a paid childcare provider's being committed to her for the duration of her child's early years. It might happen, but there is absolutely no reason to count on it. The childcare provider might do a perfectly fine job with the child, but what mother really wants her child to attach to the babysitter instead of herself? I have known women who quit their jobs when their children started calling the nanny "mommy."

I am aware, of course, that many people defend infant day-care as beneficial to children. But social science research disputes the claim that group care meets the social needs of infants.[4] The need for contact with children the same age does not really emerge until the toddler years. Newborns do not need to interact with each other. Other infants are competitors for adult attentiveness. If infants need any contact with other children at all, most probably they need the doting attention of older siblings. Infants also "take in" quite a bit of information by watching the activity around them. Older brothers and sisters provide role models for talking, crawling up the stairs, walking, and eating with a spoon, among other activities. An infant in a day-care center is unlikely to receive the kind of rich and varied attentiveness that is possible inside a family.

There is an irony to the following pair of facts. Modern families evidently have a preference for small families. One of the arguments against large families is that children in small families can receive more attention from their parents. On the other hand, modern families seem to have a preference for leaving their children in group care, sometimes at very early ages.

Very high quality day-care centers proudly announce that their child to adult ratio is four to one for children under two years old, ten to one for preschoolers, twenty to one for school-age children—and they accept infants as young as six weeks old. I have many friends who home school their children. Some of these families have as many as ten children. I cannot think of a single such family that has four children under the age of two, or ten preschool children, or twenty second graders. Yet professional families with one or two children routinely leave them in group care facilities in which such child-adult ratios are common. Children of large families at least have each other. Does anybody really think that children are better off with no siblings and no time in the home? We baby-boomer mothers and modern career women seem to be rather schizophrenic about this matter.

The Knowledge Problem

There are inherent limits to how much responsibility and authority parents can delegate to the people they hire. These limitations are another example of Hayek's idea of tacit knowledge. To illustrate, let me summarize my activity as a stay-at-home mom on any given day. How are the basic jobs of instruction, direction, and guidance to be done with any particular child? One of my children has such a tender conscience that she bursts into tears at the realization of having done something wrong. The other requires a small two-by-four to even get the message that he has done wrong and needs to apologize. One child plays every minor injury for maximum drama. The other child is so impervious to pain, and so resistant to accepting help, that if you hear a whimper out of him, you should call for an ambulance. And the subtleties of settling quarrels! Who really started the fight? It looks for all the world as if big brother pushed and shoved, but little sister can be an irresistible provocateur.

Then there is the job of providing encouragement, skating that fine line between managing the child's frustration by not asking too much too soon and making legitimate and necessary demands for improvement and advancement. I know these children are fully capable of persuading a stranger that they cannot do very much. On the other hand, there is no point in asking them to do something that is so far beyond their capacity that I might as well be asking them to solve a differential equation.

They need help in their social interactions with each other and the other children in the neighborhood. They need more than a generalized instruction to share and be pleasant. Sometimes they honestly do not understand how to do what they are supposed to do. They would like to persuade another child to play with them (on their own terms, of course), but they have no idea what to offer them or how to speak to them. Sometimes, they are sorely tempted to do or say something they know they are not supposed to do, but they cannot quite see how to stop themselves or how to manage the frustration inherent in controlling their impulses. The gap between what they want to do and what they are supposed to do is too broad for them to jump. They need some coaching not only for their actions but for their words and even their thoughts.

As the child gets a little older, helping him learn to manage his frustration is a more important objective than helping him find strategies to get his own way. "That toy belongs to him. He doesn't have to let you play with it." "You wouldn't like it if he took your toys." "Don't you have enough toys? You need to be satisfied with what you have." Knowing when a particular child is ready for a new level of self-restraint, knowing what level of abstraction he can grasp, knowing how much frustration he can tolerate and helping him move to a new level, all of these are part of the daily work of motherhood.

Now I ask: Who am I going to pay to do all this? How am I going to give instructions of sufficient detail to a babysitter? The "market" cannot handle this problem completely. Of course, there is nothing wrong with hiring some help. But it is not possible to completely delegate the innumerable tasks that go into raising any particular child.

As a matter of fact, when people are particularly pleased with a nanny or babysitter, they often express this fact by saying, "she is just like one of the family." This statement means that this person has slid into the routine of the family and has grasped its unstated rules, norms, and expectations. I have never heard someone praise a childcare worker by saying "He is an employee" or "She works for her paycheck." Parents say this kind of thing when they are at the end of their rope with someone who cannot draw any inferences or take any initiative.

The Analogy with Central Planning

There is an analogy between the use of information in the care of children and the use of information in an economic system. Economists have pointed out a contrast between centrally planned economies and decentralized, market-based economies. One of the key differences between the two basic types of economic systems arises from the ways they use information.

Hayek's fundamental critique of centrally planned economies was that such a system squanders a vast amount of implicit, personal, local information about scarcity, production, and preferences.[5] Hayek pointed out that all the work of a massive team of technocrats in Moscow could never take the place of the information that all the individuals in the production process routinely acquire and use in the ordinary course of business in a decentralized market economy. People cannot always articulate everything they know. They use information without being fully aware that they are using it. They see a high price for something and automatically switch to a different lower-priced substitute. Some small problem emerges, and people routinely solve it without realizing that they have simply taken it in stride. The use and generation of this information are inherently difficult to report to the central planners.

Raising children collectively is comparable to centrally planning an economy. Each child is unique, and each family is unique. No child can be raised "by the book," despite what some child-development experts might lead us to believe. The amount of variation among children in personality, strengths, weaknesses and developmental paths means that each and every child has to be raised individually and personally. Child rearing is not something that can be done in a systematic, check list kind of way. Parents always have to "wing it." Sometimes parents do something that seemed to work, but they cannot entirely explain what they did or why it worked.

Despite what we might think from the tremendous physical demands of caring for infants, leaving children with paid help actually becomes more difficult and complicated the older they become. This is because an infant's needs, while seemingly endless, are simple and few: change the diapers; give the bottle; rock; put to bed; bathe once in a while. It is conceivable that all these needs could be written down, checklist style.

As a child matures, his needs become more complicated. Attentiveness to the growing child's needs comes to mean more than their immediate satisfaction. The child really needs to learn to take care of himself. He needs to learn to feed himself, dress himself, and take responsibility for his own toileting. The child who remains dependent on adults for these tasks is attached to them in a certain perverse way. But socially constructive attachment is not just a skin graft between the adult and the child but rather the ability to participate in reciprocal interactions with other people. Demanding that adults immediately satisfy his needs is most emphatically not reciprocal behavior. A five-year-old who refuses to feed himself can hardly be called cooperative. The adult who is still dressing a ten-year-old is not teaching that child anything about reciprocity or cooperation. The child needs to learn how to give and to do some things for himself.

Much of this knowledge about the child's needs is tacit, difficult to articulate and specify. When is this particular child ready to learn this particular skill? How much frustration can this child tolerate in attempting to learn something new? This tacit knowledge sets a limit on how much care of their children parents can reasonably delegate to others. It is possible that one trusted babysitter or relative could have sufficient intuitive feel for the child's needs and personality. But often it is much easier for the adult to just do what the child wants rather than to take the time to teach a new skill. It takes very dedicated paid help to put up with the costs of time and frustration involved in teaching such skills.

Advocates of socialism once imagined that an ambitious system of scientific management would allow them to organize the entire economy more efficiently than the decentralized market mechanism. Central planning would avoid all the wasteful duplication of effort that uncoordinated competition requires. It would end destructive competition for scarce resources by allocating scarce resources scientifically. Everyone would be wealthier because so many resources would be freed up for productive use rather than being squandered in a wasteful duplication of effort inherent in the competitive process. Central planning would usher in a new millennium of prosperity and abundance.

These advocates did not realize that they could not artificially replicate the market with an army of technocratic experts and a scientific plan. They did not realize that the market process itself generates the information they would need to use in order to make an efficient allocation of resources. Without the workings of the market, the central planners had to make up information as they went along. Inevitably, they overlooked crucial information that ordinary participants in a decentralized market economy would have routinely used.

Advocates of paid childcare have made similar audacious claims. Paid child care would relieve intelligent women from the drudgery of meeting the endless demands of small children. Paid childcare would release a tremendous amount of productive energy into the economy as these intelligent women enter the labor force.[6] Children would learn to become independent of their mothers earlier rather than being smothered by overprotective, underemployed, frustrated mothers. Children would become better socialized by being among their peers at earlier ages. Paid childcare is not only an adequate substitute for parental care, it is actually superior to a mother's care.

Tacit knowledge comes into play in a particularly poignant way in the rearing of children. Hayek argued that the central planners, in the nature of things, could not know everything that ordinary players in the economic arena knew and used. The cost of trying to centralize an economy was that all that information was squandered. The economy became stagnant and less efficient as a result.

The cost of losing localized, individual knowledge possessed and used by the ordinary inarticulate parent is far more profound than simply an economy going bust. Paid childcare providers do not have the same interest in the child as the parents nor the same incentives to invest in learning about the child. The people who have the incentive and the interests, namely the parents, cannot invest the same amount of time in learning all the detailed particular things about the individual child if they are spending the majority of their waking hours away from the child. The child grows up unknown. The child's visible material needs may be met, but his deeper intangible needs may not be.

Those of us who accepted the arguments in favor of paid child care did not realize how much knowledge our mothers really needed as they raised us. We did not realize how much individualized attentiveness we actually had received and how difficult it would be to pay someone to give our children what we received. Our mothers discovered what we needed in the process of being in a relationship with us. They could not easily convey to strangers everything they knew, and everything they routinely, if inarticulately, used. We did not realize that our mother's help with homework blunted the impact of being in educational institutions not necessarily geared to our individual needs. We did not realize how much our parents and older siblings helped us work out difficulties in our relationships with school friends and neighborhood children. Those talks around the kitchen table, or in the car, or before bedtime gave us more than we realized, guidance that cannot easily be replaced by a nanny or a day-care worker. We did not realize how much we received from long-term relationships with our siblings, relationships that cannot be replicated by classmates in a school or day-care center.

As for the claims that freeing women from the drudgery of child care frees them to do productive and satisfying work, these claims are packed with hidden assumptions. Not all work in the market is really so glamorous and fulfilling. Instead of an intelligent and educated woman staying home to enrich a few members of the next generation, she is stuck in a law office doing house closings and title searches. Instead of introducing her own children to great literature and world history, she is stuck in a university office, grading a pile of illegible midterms written by other people's children. The work of providing direction and guidance to young people requires knowledge and intelligence far more subtle than a great many jobs in the paid labor force.

Women are only now coming to realize what many men have known all along: working is not always fun. Most of the jobs that most men do in the paid labor force contain large elements of drudgery. The generations of men who have gotten up in the morning, day after long day, to go to work have not done it because the job is intrinsically fulfilling. Most of them, much of the time, did their jobs out of love of their families. Love of their wives and children keeps men going to their jobs as truck mechanics and cab drivers. It is often a sense of duty that keeps men standing on the subway platforms waiting for a crowded train to take them to their offices day after day. The drudgery of caring for small children is nothing compared to the drudgery of factory work. For many men, the tedium of their ordinary jobs is relieved by their coming home to a loving, if noisy, household.[7] Many a man has been humanized by his wife and children.

Hayek attacked central planning as an alternative to decentralized market organization of economic activity. Central planning replaced a personalized and localized institution with an impersonal and bureaucratic one. In a similar way, paid childcare replaces individual, personalized child rearing with more institutional, impersonal arrangements.

The Quality of Non-Parental Care

Day-care enthusiasts hope that paid caregivers can substitute for the work parents do with infants and preschoolers. Some studies show that some children, usually girls, benefit from the preschool experience. These studies track one or two measurable indicators such as language development and cognitive skills.[8]

But when other researchers attempt to study more subtle things like children's behavior or the quality of the attachment between children and their parents, the case for day-care is not nearly so favorable.[9] One study showed that children who have spent extensive time in day-care at early ages tend to be more aggressive than children raised at home. "More aggressive" means being "more likely to hit, kick or push; bully or threaten, swear and argue; not use strategies like discussion or walking away to deal with difficulties, and to be rated by teachers as having aggressiveness as a serious deficit of social behavior."[10] Another study showed children whose mothers were employed for over thirty hours per week during the child's first two years were less cooperative.[11]

Studies tracking children as they mature through the preschool years suggest that day-care children become more aggressive. Children in non-maternal care during their first year of life do not necessarily behave differently during that year. But the children cared for outside the home in their first year are more likely to be aggressive during the second and possibly later years as well.[12] Researchers do not have a complete explanation for what they have observed. But this illustrates how complex the developmental process really is and cautions us about visionary schemes for completely replacing maternal care.

Most alarming of all has been the finding that day-care children have weaker or insecure attachments to their parents than children reared at home.[13] Poor attachment does not necessarily lead to the kind of psychopathic behavior of the neglected orphan. But some of the symptoms of attachment difficulties reported among day-care children are less extreme versions of the problems exhibited by the profoundly neglected child. One of the clinical definitions of attachment is proximity-seeking in times of stress. One test used to identify attachment difficulties is the "strange situation" or the "stressful situation." The observer constructs an unusual or stressful situation for the child. The child's mother or other parental figure will be available to the child. The key question is: will the child turn to his mother for comfort during this time of stress? If he does, he is said to be attached. He is classified as having insecure attachment if he does not turn to her spontaneously or if he actively resists her attempts to offer help and comfort. Children with modest attachment difficulties turn to their mothers if the situation is stressful enough. Severely disturbed children may be so poorly attached that the greater the stress to which they are subjected, the less likely they are to turn to their mothers. The severely attachment-disordered child turns in on himself, neither seeking comfort nor accepting comfort if it is offered. In this way, the attachment issues lie along a continuum, with the kind of attachment difficulties experienced by orphanage children being an extreme version of those experienced by children in extensive and early day care. Modestly insecure attachments, while not leading to the extreme psychopathic behavior reported for severely neglected children, nonetheless are correlated with a whole series of very real difficulties. Oppositional behavior, such as having temper tantrums or being unwilling to comply with adult instructions, is symptomatic of insecure attachment. Securely attached infants are better able to tolerate brief separations by eighteen months.

Children with secure attachment histories are more socially competent with peers, tend to be less socially withdrawn and hesitant, and more self-confident and tolerant of frustration. In contrast, when the mother-child bond is insecure or ambivalent, the child is less willing to explore the environment, more inclined to be fearful, and more likely to withdraw from social activity. As being cared for oneself increases the possibility of expressing concern for other people, secure children are more sympathetic to the distress of others. They are less likely to be judged by anyone in their early school years to have serious behavioral problems, while being less emotionally dependent on teachers. However, they are also better at getting help and capitalizing on adult assistance or using attention and direction in ways that promote further intellectual and social development.[14] In all these ways, secure attachments are correlated with positive outcomes for the child. If non-parental care weakens the attachment between parents and children, we have reason to be concerned even if the children do not develop a full-fledged attachment disorder.

One study of attachment among 149 healthy first born infants, administered the Strange Situation Test for parents of one-year-old children. For the mother-child reunion, children in full-time child care (more than thirty-five hours a week) were more likely to be insecurely attached than children in other types of care.[15] For father-child reunion, fully half the boys whose mothers worked full-time were insecurely attached. The study also examined dual security: is a child attached to one or both of his parents, or neither? For boys whose mothers work full-time, 29 percent were securely attached to both parents, 36 percent were securely attached to *neither* parent. For all other boys, 59 percent were attached securely to both parents, while only 8 percent were unattached to either parent.[16]

These kinds of results are not confined to one or two studies. Several different researchers have performed "meta-analyses" that combine the results of several studies done by different research teams. In one such analysis, calculations based on five separate studies of children from working-class to middle-class married couple families showed that infants in non-maternal care for more than twenty hours a week are 1.6 times more likely than their counterparts with less non-maternal care, to be insecurely attached to their mothers.[17] In another meta-analysis of studies worldwide, the researchers estimated that regular non-parental care increased the risk of children developing insecure bonds by 66 percent. These authors noted that if this increase were related to disease due to environmental factors, it would be considered extremely serious and would lead to public health initiatives to combat it.[18]

More recent studies show complex interactions between the quality of care and the sensitivity of the mother to her child. Children of less sensitive or less responsive mothers are at higher risk for being insecurely attached to their mothers. This risk is greater if these children are in low quality day-care. That is, high quality care out of the home seems to mitigate some of the effects of maternal insensitivity. But, perhaps surprisingly, these same children are more likely to be insecurely attached the more hours they spend in day-care. Researchers hypothesize that these children need more time with their mothers "to develop the internalized sense that their mothers are responsive and available to them." [19]

Researchers who are skeptical about the link between day-care and attachment difficulties take comfort from the fact that attachment difficulties do not appear in every study.[20] Nevertheless, parents trying to make an informed decision are entitled to know something about the circumstances under which these difficulties do appear. Attachment difficulties appear to be more consistently reported for boys than for girls. Different kinds of behavior problems emerge for children who are shy than for those who are not. The prevalence of negative effects of child care vary with the number of hours the child is cared for away from home.[21]

Some arguments in favor of day-care imply that parents are in general incompetent and that children are better off with professional care than with amateur parental care. But even the most obtuse of parents can figure out whether his child is a boy or whether his child is under three. Even couples who are deeply committed to professional work can make marginal adjustments in their hours at work if they know that something substantial might be at stake. In other words, parents can readily evaluate some of the known risk factors by themselves.

I am aware that each and every point mentioned in this section has its detractors. The child development experts and psychologists argue heatedly among themselves about the effects of non-parental care on children. Some of the arguments are far from being the disinterested, detached debates that the public might expect of scientific discourse.[22] The average parent probably has no idea that such a debate is even raging. We have all been repeatedly reassured by numerous experts that day-care is good for children, or at least not too harmful. We see it on television, in books, and in magazines. Our pediatricians tell us not to worry about day-care. Parents are not well-served by overgeneralized headlines that reassure us—"Better Behavior in Day Care, Federal Study Finds," "Mother-Child Bond Not Hurt By Day-care."[23] Parents need the more nuanced information that sound studies provide.

The Hazards of Institutions

Comforting headlines that conceal subtle problems do not simply appear out of nowhere. There is a small but influential group of people in our society who want a more expansive role for the government in family life. Institutional childcare forms a central part of their vision.

The publicity surrounding a recent federally funded study provides a case in point. The headline from the *New York Times* read: "Superior day care linked to higher adult achievement." At a news conference at the Department of Education, one of the researchers said "The so-called efficacy question, whether you can affect development in the preschool years, is resoundingly in the affirmative. It has become crystal clear that if you wait until age three or four, you are going to be dealing with a series of delays and deficits that will put you in remedial programs."

But this high-profile report obscures the fact that the study itself has almost nothing to do with any day-care decision the average *New York Times* reader is ever likely to face. The reader does not learn until the fourth paragraph that the 111 children in the study were chosen because they were poor and at high risk for educational failure. We can see how unrepresentative this group of children is by one of the outcomes billed as a sign of success: of the children who received the intensive day care, 35 percent had attended some college by age twenty-one, while only 14 percent of the control group had attended college.

Only as the story continues do we discover the likely motive for overstating the results. "A group of experts (is) scheduled to meet in Washington next week to applaud France's universal preschool program." The purpose of the headline was to muster support for universal, taxpayer-supported day-care from infancy. Universal care means care for rich kids and poor kids, wanted kids and neglected kids. The most charitable interpretation we can put on this episode is that somebody's enthusiasm for his preferred public policy ran away with him. The worst we could say is that someone is deliberately spreading misinformation trying to generate support for a far more extensive intervention than the findings of this study warrant.[24]

As the reporting on this particular study suggests, advocates of paid parental substitutes sometimes try to convince us that institutional care of children is superior to home care. At least, high quality child care workers probably give care superior to that given by parents or relatives. Our kids are actually better off without us. They are better off in the care of specialists who know more about child development than the average mother. This mistrust of the parents of preschoolers is similar to the mistrust some professional educators display toward the parents of school-age children. Parents do not know enough to educate their children. Turn the children over to the school. Let the experts handle the situation.

Institutionalizing childcare is a policy that tends to centralize and homogenize society. An activity that could be done in individual, private homes is farmed out to the commercial sector. Although private sector childcare is undoubtedly superior to child care controlled and provided by government, home care is undoubtedly better still. We should not let the care of our children slip out of our hands too lightly. It is too easily an entry point for governmental and political controls that very few sensible people would welcome.

The Hazard of Experts

The demands for "high-quality" childcare have a hidden hazard associated with them: the syndrome of the experts. "Low quality" childcare is not likely to be dominated by education and child develment professionals. But the high quality day-care undoubtedly will use a variety of professionals. The natural experts, the parents, have been left at home (or sent off to their own jobs), while the children are grouped together under the care of strangers. But the experts can easily intimidate and overwhelm the parents. The day-care staff are professionals, in the sense of being paid for what they do.[25] They may have the authority of research studies standing behind their classroom practices and educational opinions.

Parents of modest education and income are at an inherent disadvantage in these confrontations. If the scientific studies say it is harmful to children to have too many siblings, then maybe it is. If the experts say there is no harm in leaving the baby at the day-care center, then maybe it is all right. The advice of the experts can come to dominate the day-to-day decisions about the care of an individual child. Mother and father might very well know what is best for their child, but they cannot necessarily prove it to the satisfaction of the day-care center or school.

As children get older, this problem becomes more profound because the needs of the children multiply and the extent of their individuation becomes greater. Parents may know very well that their child is having difficulty reading or that their child needs a particularly tight disciplinary rein. But they may be unable to convince the school that the child needs special reading help or that the group of classroom peers are truly unsuitable. The parents can be bullied into going along with an unsatisfactory situation because they are unable to state all their reasons as clearly and forcefully as the school authorities can. I have heard school authorities say, without any hint of irony, "Sometimes a child has a bad year with a particular teacher. Maybe the next year will be better." In other words, some school authorities are willing to write off an entire year of a child's educational and emotional development.

Likewise, parents may receive foolish advice or unsound diagnoses from child development or educational specialists, apart from the educational structure itself. I have a friend who had specialists tell her that her speech-delayed child was probably autistic. She and her husband were devastated. Those "experts" went home at the end of the day totally unaccountable for the impact their words had on the parents. Although my friend was distraught, she was unconvinced. A tenacious and articulate academic, she went to other experts and sought other advice. She found that her son was not autistic and that her own instincts had been sound. But think of the less self-confident parents who might have consulted those same experts. Parents of modest means and education might very well be bullied into accepting whatever was given to them.[26]

Raising of children in groups can easily seduce us into viewing them in a scientific and detached way rather than in the personal and individual way their parents view them. Children are in danger of becoming statistics, averages or norms, rather than individuals. As this scientific way of looking at the children proceeds, it necessarily emphasizes the information that can be articulated, quantified, and explained. There is nothing wrong with doing scientific research into child development or educational methods. But it is wrong to treat children as if they were merely research subjects rather than seeing them as individual human persons. Parents and teachers who love the child can make use of scientific knowledge without dehumanizing the child. But what parents need to know to raise any particular child goes far beyond what can be studied by science and articulated in a carefully specified research conclusion.

We tend to forget that sending children away from the home for most of their waking hours is a relatively recent innovation. Segregating children into separate, child-only institutions is not the most obvious way to help them learn and develop as full adult members of the human race. The only adult attention that children receive in these institutional settings is the attention of people who are paid to take care of them. Most children through most of human history have been educated at home in the continual company of the adult members of their own families.

In previous generations, most children were raised without the benefits of modern child-rearing methods and scientific studies. Most mothers were good enough mothers simply because they were there for their children. These mothers knew far more than they could explain and did far more than they could articulate. Likewise, today most mothers are good enough mothers simply because they are there. Unfortunately, many are very likely intimidated by the experts with scientific studies and modern child-rearing methods. The increasing institutionalization of child rearing has transferred authority from the relatively inarticulate but committed parent to the articulate but uncommitted expert.

Conclusion

The temptation of the market as child-care provider is that people tend to rely upon it too much because it is convenient. In Silicon Valley, private schools offer parents the option of leaving even very small children on campus for any period of ten hours per day between the hours of 6:00 a.m. and 6:00 p.m. Ten hours away from home is exhausting for adults, but preschoolers are routinely asked to "work" ten hour days in their schools and day-care centers.

These services exist because people want them. I would never say that these places should be regulated out of existence. But there is something distorted about the wishes of adults in this case. People allow their priorities to become garbled and do what is convenient for themselves rather than what is best for the child. This is why I discuss the market as a substitute for the family. Many Americans think of personal liberty as being the freedom to do what they want as long as they refrain from the initiation of force and fraudulent activity. This is an insufficient statement of the individual's responsibility in a free society because parents have a positive responsibility to take care of their children. Completely delegating the care of children to hired help is not exactly an act of force or fraud. It is, however, an extremely negligent act.

A free society cannot long survive if large numbers of people choose to discharge their parental duties in this most perfunctory way. The market is a wonderful institution because it gives us what we want. When our desires are skewed, the market will satisfy them just the same. The market sometimes appears unpleasant because it reveals a part of us that we might prefer not to see. But even this unpleasantness represents a virtue of the market. For, when we see the truth about ourselves, we can change. We can change how we behave and even what we want.

PART IV

LOVE AND LIBERTY

∞ 9 ∞

The Personal Ethics of a Free People

ALLING FOR PEOPLE to use paid day-care moderately and prudently may seem an unwarranted intrusion into their private lives. But in another sense admonitions about personal conduct are libertarian arguments par excellence.[1] It would be pointless to present a reasoned argument for or against particular private actions unless the listener were an active moral agent, capable of making decisions of social importance. We can all think of a hundred things the government should do or stop doing. But if we wait for the politicians to get themselves together to do all the right things, we will be waiting forever. It makes practical sense to do what we can as individuals.

The self-restraining individual is the basis of free institutions, both economic and political. The self-restraining individual is not born but made inside a loving family. There is no realistic alternative to the loving family as a foundational institution for a free society. When economics is the topic under discussion, advocates of minimal government and free markets have always understood that there are nonnegotiable realities in the human condition. We actively resisted socialist attempts to remake the economy, as if human nature were infinitely malleable. We accepted the fact that the economy

161

has a logic of its own and that this internal logic places constraints upon the ability of even the most powerful government to control the outcomes of the market process.

Free market advocates have shouldered the thankless task of pointing out that the socialist emperor has no clothes. When the Left tried to create the "new socialist paradise," in which scarcity had disappeared, peopled by "new socialist men," who had forgotten that they had ever experienced pride in ownership, we were among the first to protest that this experiment, no matter how superficially appealing, was doomed from the outset. Free market economists and libertarians are the ones who continually remind the public that we cannot all click our heels together three times, wish very hard, and be magically transported into a world in which economic incentives do not matter.

It is time to face up to the comparable facts about family life. We cannot afford to take a completely laissez-faire attitude toward the family and the issues that surround it. There are deep realities in the human condition that we ignore at our peril.

We are born as helpless infants with a specific set of needs and a developmental timetable that are both pretty much hardwired by nature. Children need to be weaned from their natural self-centeredness. They need parents who can provide them with stability and love. Children need parents who love each other. Children born to single mothers, children of divorced parents, children in perpetual day-care may not be impoverished in the material sense. But they are living in a kind of socioemotional poverty. These basic realities of the human condition cannot be wished away or evaded through some technological trick.

Advocates of free markets have always been aware that the system of individuals pursuing their own self-interest in a decentralized market cannot be opened up to just anyone with any preferences. Members of street gangs, people who expect something for nothing, and pathological liars behave as if their interests are incompatible with the interests of the wider society. Such people cannot be safely turned loose to pursue their own self-interest, and every advocate of the market knows it.

This is why advocates of minimal government need to take the issues surrounding marriage and children seriously. Children who do not receive the necessary adult help in maturing may very well become the types of people who cannot participate in a free and open society. Every society has a certain number of such people, to be sure. But if we embrace ideas about marriage and children that produce a large enough number of such people, a free society will not be able to absorb them all without damaging its basic institutions of minimally regulated markets and popular political participation.

America has had some ambivalence about the meaning of freedom and liberty. Is liberty essentially a political condition of minimal government? Or is liberty a social condition that allows people unlimited freedom of action, subject to the prohibition on the use of force or fraud? Many Americans have replied that our national ethos includes both of these strands of thought. Surely one's decisions about marriage, sexual conduct, childbearing, and child rearing are among the most private and personal decisions of a persons life.

But family structure is an area in which unlimited freedom of action may very well be in conflict with minimal government, for the minimal state cannot exist without a substantial component of self-restraint and self-government within the citizenry. This internalized ethic cannot come into existence in the absence of loving families taking personal care of their own children.

The reader might wonder whether I advocate that the state enforce these familial obligations. A reader trained in economics might expect me to make an economic argument that the government is the best institution to subsidize and promote these family obligations since their performance has such a great effect on other people's lives. But I am not going to make those kinds of arguments. I do not set up as an ideal a world in which the government has unlimited power

to create good people out of bad beginnings, or to control the outcomes of personal decisions, or to create a good society.

The government cannot force a husband to love his wife. The
state cannot issue a restraining order to prevent a woman from nagging her husband or children. All the state can do is to make it costly
to divorce or to engage in physical combat. That is something, of
course. But it is a long way from the full commitment of love and
generosity that is really required in a lifelong marriage. The lifetime
of caring for children requires much more that the shear absence of
violence or profound neglect that are the limits of what the state can
actually enforce.

My ideal world is a world in which the vast majority of the population understands the importance of family life, for its own good and
for the good of the greater society. My aspiration is a world in which
people continue to support the ethos of loving families, even when
they do not live up to the demands of love themselves. We would not
try to talk our way out of our obligations by claiming that the norms
do not really apply to us just to assuage our consciences. My ideal
world is one in which the government proposes a reasonable basic
"contract" for marriage because people want the kind of family life
that it represents. The government would establish reasonable legal
norms because the majority of people actively support them.

These are my ideals precisely because I am a libertarian in my
political philosophy. I mistrust government just as all political libertarians do. Arguing that there is such a thing as objectively moral
conduct does not mean it is prudent or just to assign the primary task
of enforcing that standard to the government.

I take seriously the insight from voting theory that a world of
diverse preferences is unstable. Imagine the unlikely event that the
day after tomorrow I formed a voting coalition powerful enough to
impose a desirable set of legal institutions surrounding marriage and
children. That coalition would still have to manage all the opposition such a move would surely generate. We could count on opposi-

tion from the large number of people who make a living from some portion of the social chaos. We could also count on opposition from some percentage of those who have limited contact with their children and do not want to feel guilty about it or who do not want to be forced to change. These groups would certainly try to pass additional legislation that would offset the effects of my legislation.

Voting would likely produce unstable outcomes because people have such a diversity of preferences and views. Since the underlying problem is the diversity of preferences, I believe it is more prudent to address people's preferences directly. This requires efforts in the cultural and social sphere rather than in the political sphere. Convincing people to vote differently is a different proposition from trying to convince them that they should think about their own experience differently and that they should live differently. This cultural effort requires different tools and, I think, an entirely different spirit.

Finally, and most importantly, this is my ideal world because my central claim is that the social order must be held together with love. Love's most important characteristic is that it cannot be compelled. Love's most important work takes place in the interior of the individual person, where it cannot be observed or monitored. Love's greatest power flows from the fact that it is freely chosen.

Because of the nature of the state, and because of the nature of love, the state cannot create the conditions of love. The opposite might be true: the state can create conditions that make it much more difficult for family love to flourish. And it is certain that a society of loving families would choose different political and legal institutions than a society of fragmented families and radically individualized persons. But the state cannot create loving families out of nothing.

Even with all the assurances that I do not aspire to state enforcement of family norms, I am sure many readers are still uneasy. Love, even freely chosen, implies self-imposed limitations on our behavior. Some readers might not be convinced that it is necessary, or in their own interest, to tighten the conditions for divorce, for instance. Others might not be prepared to sacrifice career goals to stay home with children.

In this section, I try to show that the decision to love is reasonable.

10

What Is Love?

EVERYONE AGREES that love has some mysterious features. We believe that loving is a good thing, yet we sometimes find it costly to do what love seems to require. We want to be loved, yet we have to admit we sometimes resist being loved. Let us begin with a vision of a loving person to see if we can find answers to some of these puzzles.

A Vision of a Loving Person

Suppose a person sees us accurately, sees us as we really are, in all our imperfection as well as our glory. He sees us in our embarrassment, as well as in our pride. He sees our shame as well as our accomplishments. He sees our vices as well as our virtues. He sees us in the peak of our adult strength. He sees in that adult the helpless child we once were. He remains with us in our incapacitated old age. He sees us in all our humanity, which is to say in all our dignity and imperfection.

Suppose that while the person sees us accurately, he also supports us. He does not abandon us because we disappoint him. He does not judge us harshly even when we fail. At the same time, it is not

167

exactly accurate to say that he accepts us as we are, for he loves us too much to want us to remain the way we are. He wants us to change for the better. He is willing to stay with us while we change for the better, while we struggle, while we suffer. He is willing to offer encouragement that is grounded in reality rather than a shallow boosterism. This is a love we would like to accept.

We can say that this person truly loves us. Yet this description does not specify particular actions the loving person performs. We cannot tell from the description exactly what the person does for us or whether he gives us any particular resources or gifts. I have described the person's disposition toward us. From that disposition, we might reasonably expect the person to spend time with us or give things to us. But these particulars depend on the needs and capabilities of the two people as well as on the kind of relationship between them. The actions inspired by love depend upon the context and will vary tremendously.

There are three components of the loving person's disposition toward us: the loving person sees us as we really are; he stands in solidarity with us; and he desires that we change for the better. This description can readily apply to the love of a parent for a child. Parents often see their children far more clearly than the children see themselves. Loving parents do not abandon their children, even in their deepest troubles. They are not content that their children should remain babies, even though babies are much cuter and easier than teenagers. Parents want their children to grow and mature.

This description applies as well to relationships between people who are more nearly equals in strength and capacity. Friends and spouses want many of the same kinds of things for each other. We sometimes think that we want our friends and spouses to overlook our faults. But we know in our heart of hearts that the friend who sees our faults, wants us to overcome them, and remains our friend all the same is more loving than the person who covers for us or helps us kid ourselves.

I will have more to say about these elements of love in the next chapter in which I talk about the costs of love. For now, let me summarize these elements by offering a very old definition of love that captures all three. "To love is to will and to do the good of another."[1]

The loving person must have a clear picture of who the other person really is in order to know what would be good for him. Overlooking serious faults does not allow us to will the good of the other person because we are not letting ourselves see who he really is in the first place. The loving person must continue to care about the person with or without his faults. Willing the good certainly involves a desire that the person change for the better.

What Is the Will?

We must say a few words about the idea of willing and how it relates to other ideas of choice and decision. To will means approximately to want, with this difference: to will implies a commitment of the intellect, whereas to want may include desires of a more impulsive or transitory sort.

The term "will" is used in two different senses. Sometimes the term is used as a verb, as in "to will." In this sense, to will means, approximately, to want. The word is also used as a noun, as in "it required the full force of his will to refrain from punching the IRS agent in the nose." When used in this sense, the will refers to a faculty of the mind. The will is the intellectual capacity that directs one's actions towards a particular end. The will (the noun) moves the person from thought to action. To will (the verb) involves a commitment to act, whereas simply wanting something need not imply any commitment to act.

The concept of the will might be unfamiliar to a person who is accustomed to thinking like an economist, as so many advocates of the free market are. Economists tend to be empiricists: they are interested in what they can observe. The will, being a faculty of the mind, is not directly observable. We might be able to observe some consequences of acts of the will, but we will often be left to infer from observing a person's actions what he actually willed.

The concept of the will is also alien to economists because the will shapes our capacity for future moral acts.[2] In other words, the acts of the will that take place in the interior of the person shape the person's future preferences. Economists and their fellow travelers are typically reluctant to examine processes that change (or claim to change) a person's preferences.

A person can will something that he does not finally do. The fact of willing it, even if the action itself was disrupted or interrupted or otherwise frustrated, still carries moral significance. It is also possible for a person to will things that are outside the range of his abilities, and for the fact of his willing it, to make an observable, tangible difference in his behavior and in his life.

Suppose a person decides to rob a bank. He makes all the plans to rob the bank. He obtains the things he needs, makes the preparations, and rehearses the robbery many times in his mind. Then, when the day comes to actually rob the bank, something unforeseen happens to prevent him from carrying out these plans. The planning for the bank robbery has moral significance, even though something outside of the would-be robber prevented him from carrying out his plan. He has made it more likely that in the future he will plan and carry out such acts.

We are, by our thoughts, shaping our own values. We can easily imagine the thought "I shall rob a bank" popping randomly into our heads. We are not morally accountable for things that pop randomly into our heads. But we deceive ourselves if we believe the entire planning process is random. Getting the materials, engaging accomplices, and planning the route for the purpose of robbing a bank are hardly random acts. We become more accountable with each step we take. With each of these actions and thoughts, we are turning our wills more and more toward the end of robbing a bank and away from some other end.

In addition, people invent reasons, justifications, and rationalizations for what they want to do. At some level, we all know that robbery is not good. Yet once we turn our will toward something, we must convince ourselves that it is a good. "The bank got its money from stealing from people." "I shall use it for a better purpose than the bank or its customers." And so on.

A person can will things that are not currently possible for him to do. The fact of his willing it can make an observable, tangible difference in his behavior and in his life. Our definition of love will provide us with an apt illustration: to love is to will the good of another.

Economists have a tendency to be irreverent at about this point in the discussion: "Sure, you say you will the good of another. But prove it. Talk is cheap. To say you will the good of another, without being willing to bear the slightest cost to bring it about, is meaningless chatter. Surely you can come up with some better definition of love than something that refers only to unobservables and cheap talk."

The economist has a point. To say you will some good for another person and then take no steps to bring it about is indeed cheap talk. It is fair to say that the person who takes concrete actions to bring about the good of another wills it more truly, and so loves more truly, than the person who simply professes his love. The economist is not wrong in insisting upon visible manifestations of love.

We are limited in our ability to act in the material world. We only have so much time allotted to us in this life. We cannot, in the nature of things, give every good thing to every person for whom we care. In this realm of scarcity, resource allocation is of course, necessary and important. We have to make decisions about how to allocate our time with our friends, family, community, and with strangers. The economist is correct to insist on this point.

But within the interior of the person we are not so limited. We can reasonably be said to "will" things that we have no capacity to bring about. We can increase our desire for good things for the people we love, even when we have no ability to make it so. We can will greater and greater goods for another person even when we cannot bring those goods into being. These interior acts are real and important. Indeed, these interior acts may be the most real and most important aspects of a person's moral life. For with these interior acts, we create dispositions in ourselves, and we become something different than we were before.

When It Is Difficult to Love

Imagine a man who has learned that his wife is terminally ill. Suppose he has already done all that he can do to bring about her cure. He has found the best doctor known to him and followed every instruction. He has stayed beside his beloved. There truly is nothing more he can do. Here is the question: Does love for the other person extend beyond all he could do? He wishes for her recovery with all his heart and mind, yet has no power to bring it about. Does his interior disposition matter, even in situations where he has no capacity to act?

Consider these possible responses . "Oh well, I've done all I can do. She's a goner. Never mind. I'll show up, I suppose. But I shall think about it and engage myself in it as little as I possibly can." Or, how about this one: "Oh well, I've done all I can do. I can't stand to see her suffer or linger. So, I won't come to see her. I will her good, I suppose you could say. But what good am I to her? She is sick and dying and there is nothing I can do about it. I am out of here." Or, how about this one: "Oh well, I've done all I can do. We're all dead in the long run. Let's kill her and be done with it."

We cannot observe his interior state directly. But these attitudes lead to actions in a very direct way. One man sits as a steely statue.

One man doesn't show up. The last man kills his wife. I think we may justifiably say that the love these men feel for their wives is quite limited. Not only an economist would say "talk is cheap" if these men professed to love their wives.

Let's take a more complicated, and perhaps more common, reaction. "I can't think of anything to do for my dying wife. So, I'll hover over her, pretending to do something, to ease my own discomfort with my helplessness. I'll fuss, because I can't think of anything else to do."

Suppose at this point, he turns to his wife and says "I don't know what to do for you. I feel helpless. Please forgive me for all my fussing and buzzing around. It makes me feel better. Is there something I can do that will make you feel better?" If his wife responds that she would prefer that he not fuss over her, he might reply "If you want me to just sit here and be quiet, I will. That is awfully hard. I don't know if I can. But, I love you, so I will try. Please forgive me if I irritate you by buzzing around again. I don't know how to love you right now. It is just too hard."

Now, at last, this reaction is recognizably loving. Probably, we can imagine ourselves feeling such a thing, even if we can't imagine actually having the courage to confess our helplessness quite so bluntly. This is recognizable as a loving attitude, in a situation in which the person has already done all he can humanly do to bring about the good of the person whom he loves.

The ever observant economist interjects: "You said he had already done everything he could do for her. Now she is telling him that there is something else he can do for her, namely, sit down and be still. Keep his anxiety to himself. That looks like a pretty big cost to me. As a matter of fact, that might be more than I could imagine myself doing. She is asking an awful lot of him. That might even be as impossible as curing her."

And that is the point. He had already done all that he could do, as he understood it at the time. He did not realize that controlling his anxiety level was something else he could do for the sake of love.

It may be much harder than finding a doctor or paying the hospital bills. It may never have crossed his mind that his anxiety level mattered to his wife. But now he knows. So now the question is, what will he do with this information? This is the crucial step in our economic analysis, and, of course, the crucial moment for this man's love. What he does with that information reveals whether he really was doing all he could or not.

In the economic analysis, we ran out of things to say at first because we thought this unfortunate man had reached the limits of his constraints. We tentatively accepted his claim to love his wife. But we wanted to see what he would do when it cost him something to "will her good." "Her good" is presumably unlimited in some sense. He cannot satisfy all her desires, nor can he actually bring about her unlimited good, for he is a finite human being. If economists know anything, they know that finite human beings have to make some choices. People must allocate their finite resources in the face of unlimited desires, wants, and goods.

An economist would say that his wife has given him some new information about her good and that this new information has expanded his choice set. He is no longer up against the limits of what he can do to bring about her good. If he does the best he can do to sit still and stop fussing, we can say without hesitation that he loves her. His capacity to bring about the good for her is still limited. He might do a bad job of controlling his anxiety. He might reach the limits of his capacity in this dimension as well as all the others.

This is where the moral significance of "the will" enters into the picture. His will is in some sense unobservable. But when his will is oriented toward the good of his wife, he will make his best effort. New information comes into his view. It will come to him that he can bring about her good in more ways than he knew. In this process, he changes as a person. He changes what he is willing to consider a cost to himself and what he is willing to consider a benefit. He changes his preferences by reorienting his will. A man who sits like a statue, or who abandons or kills his sick wife, has excused himself from the possibility of learning more about what he could do for her.

This is why and how the definition of love works: "To love is to will and to do the good of another." Willing another person's good does not necessarily mean that you give every material thing you have to that person, although it might. Nor does it mean you give every minute of your time to the other person, although it might. Willing another person's good does not necessarily mean that you give him what he says he wants, although it might.

Willing another person's good means that you are prepared to do these things for him, if they do indeed bring about the other person's good and if they are within your capacity to perform. The fact that you turn your will toward another person's good means that you are primed and ready to do good if the occasion presents itself. What you actually do may reflect your constraints more than your will. This is how a person with fewer resources can be more loving than a person of greater material wealth, intellect, or physical strength.

By the way, this is one way to understand why people pray for each other. When we pray, we turn our will toward the good of that other person. In fact, people often feel moved to pray for someone when they do not know what else to do for him. They are allowing themselves to continue to care, in spite of their feelings of helplessness. We direct our attention to another person's good by seeing him in reference to the greatest good imaginable, which is God himself. After a while of doing this, sometimes it just comes to our minds what we can do for the other person. We might attribute this insight to divine inspiration. Or we might attribute it to the more mundane fact that we have allowed our wills to be focused on this person's good. We come to see things that were not evident to us before.

This is hard for economists to understand, because it is fundamentally not about the transfer of resources, although the transfer of resources may ultimately be involved or reasonably be expected. Neither "will" nor "good" corresponds directly to resources and their ownership.

To Love a Stranger

Does it then make any sense to say that I love someone I have never met and have no likelihood of ever meeting? Is it possible to will good to someone in an abstract sense? The answer is surely yes. It is possible for me to "love" Mother Teresa or Madonna in exactly this sense: I will that something good happens to each of them even if I have no power to bring about this good.

This abstract love matters for two reasons: First, you never know when the opportunity to actually do some good to the other person will come your way. By willing the good in the abstract, you are preparing your will in the material realm. You are ready should the opportunity, which now eludes you, come your way. Had you not prepared your will, you might overlook the opportunity to bring about a good for another person when it presents itself.

Second, you are doing something more general when you will the good of a stranger. You are shaping your own person and character by willing the good of another. You are making your self into a different kind of person than you were before. I realize that this concept is difficult for the economist, who so often assumes fixed preferences, to grasp. Nevertheless, I believe it is of the first importance in understanding love. For we shape ourselves by our interior life.

Conclusion

Some people might say that love is nothing but body chemistry, a mere chemical reaction, hardwired into our bodies by natural selection. Other people might say that love is an illusion, nothing but a male conspiracy to keep women contented so they can be oppressed. My approach is different. I say love is a decision.

Now, perhaps, we can begin to see how it is that love can become social glue, the force that keeps society together. Love is the force that moderates self-interest and makes it possible for self-interested people to live together without causing each other too much trouble. The fact that anyone loves another person means that he wills good to that other. Thus he puts the other, as it were, in the place of himself and regards the good done to the other as done to himself. In this way, love is a binding force since it aggregates another to ourselves and refers his good to our own.[3]

Let us return to one of our original questions. Why do we sometimes resist loving and being loved? Let me rephrase this question in an economist's language. What does it cost us to give love or to accept it? Outlining these costs helps us see the answer. Love is not a cheap good, either to receive or to accept.

11

The Costs of Love

IN THE LAST CHAPTER, WE ASKED, WHAT IS LOVE? To will the good of another appears to be largely an intellectual task, a job of the mind. In that case, we might wonder why love seems so elusive. If having the right thoughts assures us of love and being loved, and if love is such a great good, why isn't everyone just swimming in love? In this chapter, I offer an economist's approach to an answer. Love is scarce because it is, in some way, costly.

Let us first imagine ourselves as the giver of love. We might, somewhat irreverently call the giver of love the supplier of love. Let us ask the following questions: Is it true that we are willing to supply more love when we receive a greater reward for doing so? Put it another way: Are we less willing to give love when it is costly to us to do so? To answer these questions, we must reflect on the costs of giving love.

The Costs of Loving

Looking at the three components of love that we outlined in the previous chapter, we can analyze what it means to say "more love." More love could mean a more clear perception of the person as he really is. Another dimension would be a deeper acceptance of the person as he really is, while yet another component would be the more earnest desire that the person change for the better.

It seems that all these elements must increase simultaneously, for if our desire for positive change increases without an accurate vision of the person, then we may become worse than a nuisance, a backseat driver without a road map. If our desire for positive change increases without an increase in our solidarity with the person, then we become a shallow busybody, a coach on the sidelines shouting instructions, without any real commitment to the person or willingness to engage in the game. If our acceptance of the person increases, but not our desire for positive change, then we could become accomplices in our friend's self-deception rather than being a constructive force in his life. If our acceptance of the person increases without a willingness to remain in solidarity with the person, then we are more indifferent than genuinely friendly or loving. If our perception becomes more accurate, but our desire for change for the better does not increase, then we may become callous to the good itself. Finally, if our perception becomes more accurate, but our willingness to remain in solidarity with him does not, then we might turn our backs on our friend, giving him up for lost or declaring him to be no longer worth the effort. So when we say that our love increases, we must mean that all of these aspects increase in some simultaneous way.

We sometimes hear the expression "Love the sinner, but hate the sin." This admonition calls upon us to love another person in all three of these dimensions. We have to see the other person clearly enough to realize he is about to do something wrong or destructive. The adage enjoins us to maintain a loving disposition while still hoping that he improves his behavior. In my observation, this is actually very difficult.

Often we invoke this adage when we are about to overlook the person's behavior because we do not want the cost of a messy confrontation with him. We redefine the person's actions so as to avoid seeing the sin. The alternative position is just as difficult. If we really let ourselves see how bad a person's behavior is, we feel revulsion rather than love. It is easier to walk away from the person, perhaps with a self-righteous air. Facing the truth about a person's behavior and still maintaining a loving disposition toward him can be intolerably painful.

There are few things more difficult than watching a loved one engage in behavior that is destructive to himself or others. These situations tax our love as much as anything can. Even this brief examination is enough to suggest that love is costly.

As we examine each of these three components of love in more detail, we will see that increasing love in any of these dimensions is costly. This means that not everyone will be observed in possession of love or, perhaps more accurately, of a loving disposition.

Costs of Perception

The most basic cost of clearly seeing the other person is time. We have to spend time with the person, in effect gathering data so that we know the person. We have to spend time in reflection so we know the meaning of what we observed.

The cost of accurately perceiving another person also includes the cost of letting go of a false image of the person. We have an image of another person perhaps because that image in some way reflects upon ourselves. We would like to live in the truth about the other person, but we are afraid. Sometimes, we cannot imagine living without the lie. But we can have a kind of moment of truth, in which we breathe a sigh of relief as we finally face an unpleasant reality that we had been avoiding. We are willing to face reality, but since it costs us something to do it, we do not always do it immediately. It is possible for us to spend quite a bit of time in some degree of self-deception. Facing reality is a good, but it is a costly good.

The cost of this type of knowledge necessarily means that love will indeed be scarce. The devotion needed to develop this type of knowledge is necessarily time intensive. For the finite-lived person, love is scarce.

The cost of accurately perceiving another person implies that there is a difference in kind between intimate love and love among strangers, as described in the previous chapter. It is intelligible to say "I love Mother Teresa" or "I love Madonna." It is possible to sincerely wish them well. It is even possible and intelligible to say, "I love the poor." I can sincerely will that the individual members of this large, impersonal class of people have good things happen to them. But I cannot invest in knowing them to the same extent that I can invest in knowing my own mother. I cannot possibly know them as well or as clearly.

These limitations on our knowledge are deep and radical and cannot be willed away. No matter how much we will good for a stranger, we cannot know what is good for him. We cannot see him clearly enough to be of genuine service to him, except in the most general way. We cannot even pray our way out of this radical ignorance. We can be aware as we pray for a stranger that we do not know what he really needs: we do not know exactly what to pray for on his behalf. All we can reasonably do is to entrust him to the care of God, who knows better than we do what he actually needs.

Costs of Solidarity

What of standing in solidarity with the person, in spite of his flaws and struggles? If you could do this at no cost, would you? People do, in effect, stand in solidarity with others at minimal cost through prayer. Praying for another person is a low cost way of aligning ourselves with him, especially in his suffering. We know that it is of some comfort to our friend, even a nonbelieving friend, to know that we are praying for him. And the person engaged in prayer receives the benefit of a sense of unity with another person.

Apart from this, however, we must admit that aligning ourselves with a suffering or struggling friend is in general costly. This is one way that we recognize a friend, that he is willing to bear costs on our behalf. Sometimes, we feel helpless as we watch a friend struggle or suffer. That sense of helplessness pains us so much that we run from it.

We actually find it easier to stand by our friends when some specific task is required of us. Physical illness or bodily tragedies are often easier to manage than psychological distress or the inner anguish of emptiness. For our sick friends, we bring chicken soup, we pick up their kids from school, we visit them in the hospital. But we can be overwhelmed just from listening to a person in despair. We cannot think of anything to do, and we cannot stand his suffering, so we run from him.

The economist can easily see that bringing chicken soup involves costs of time and money. We could rather easily add up the costs of the soup, the transportation, the implicit value of time, and so forth. The costs of standing in solidarity with a friend in mental anguish, on the other hand, must be inferred indirectly. One way of making that inference is to realize that people usually prefer to bear the chicken soup costs rather than the psychic costs of dealing with a person in emotional distress. From this observation, we can infer that those psychic costs must be at least as great as the costs of delivering chicken soup. It is easier to run errands for a friend than to sit quietly with him. In fact, we are willing to do quite a lot of running in order to avoid the quiet sitting. This tells us just how very costly we find the quiet sitting. So we conclude that standing in solidarity with a friend while he strives for positive change is a costly activity.

Of course, standing in solidarity with a person requires that we have some idea why we are with her. In other words, we must have some idea what the good for another person truly involves. This leads us to the third component of increasing our love for another person: increasing our desire for positive change.

Costs of Increasing Our Desire for Positive Change

This set of costs is the most interesting and complicated. Often our desire for positive change is not exactly loving toward the other person. All too often, we want the other person to change for our own comfort and convenience. We want him to change things which are legitimate objects of personal preference, all the while pretending that they are objects of dire moral consequence.

We manage to fight over how to put the toothpaste cap on the tube, or how much spice to put in the food, or how to organize the socks in the drawer. Our families are not deceived by our claims to superior insight into the "one true way" to manage these household affairs. They recognize our desire for our own comfort, our desire to control everything and everybody in our environment no matter how we masquerade it as being in their interests to do it all our way. We spend a lot of time fussing, and self-righteous fussing at that.

We imagine that our family members' love for us ought to include an unlimited willingness to accommodate us. We can easily transform an innocent act that happens to irritate us into an act of unmitigated, premeditated evil. We can get ourselves twisted into a position of expecting total adaptation by the other person to our whims, all the while demanding complete tolerance of any failings of our own. We tell ourselves this is love.

One of the costs of love is separating our concern for the genuine well being of the other person from our own comfort. This is a non-trivial cost. For our own comfort is usually our most immediate consideration and escaping discomfort usually our priority. It takes much effort to resist the urge to react to our impulses.

As difficult as this is, refraining from such fussing is only the first and most basic cost of increasing our desire for positive change.

Allowing the person some latitude, acting toward him with some magnanimity of spirit, simply allows two people to be in the same room. It does not by itself create love between them.

The next step is to become truly aware of what the good for the other person is. It is something more than correcting a myriad of irritating habits. We have to have sufficient awareness of the good ourselves to be able intelligently to wish for it for other people. We must act upon the good for ourselves, even when doing so is costly to us. We could, for instance, yell at someone to pick up his socks, but we are not very credible if we are surrounded by our own mess. We could try to convince him that he needs, for his own good, to spend more time with the children. But this plea is likely to be viewed with suspicion if we are working sixty-hour weeks ourselves.

In this way, we can finally be brought to a genuine act of love. For if we are willing to bear some costs in order to achieve the good ourselves, we might actually persuade another person that our desire for positive change is genuine. If we do not desire the good enough to bear some costs ourselves, the other person has reason to be suspicious of us and our motives.

The less we trumpet our sacrifices, the more credible we are. People run like mad from a the self-created martyr, and with good reason. We cannot teach or lead another person to goodness without setting the example ourselves. We cannot lead credibly if we are at all times reminding the other person how much we are suffering on his or her behalf. The target of our suffering might well conclude that we are trying to induce an ever greater debt of guilt.

But quietly going about our business demonstrates that we regard this particular cost as worth bearing. The suffering is not really suffering at all if we are engaged in doing something good that is worth doing. The discomfort we feel arises from the fact that we had to suppress our inclinations and inconvenience ourselves. As a side benefit, the other person is more likely to be persuaded to change his behavior as a result of demonstration rather than pontification.

In this way, we can see a kind of "gains from trade" in the logic of love, as well as in the ordinary world of market exchange. Our initial motivation may have been our own discomfort with our friend's actions, words, beliefs, or priorities. Our effort to relieve our own uneasiness focuses initially on the other person; we come to realize that something is amiss in his approach. But if we continue to be focused on him and his problems, we may miss the opportunity not only to reach him but to grow ourselves. Instead of yelling at him about his dirty laundry, we pick up after ourselves, cheerfully. Instead of pleading with him to spend more time with the children, we start refusing business trips and extra work hours and spend more time with the kids ourselves.

If we pay the price ourselves, both for the good it produces for ourselves and as an act of love for the other person, then we have created a constructive cycle in which no one loses. "Gains from trade" is at the heart of the logic of love. But the gains do not arise from a carefully orchestrated exchange of goods or promises ensuring that neither party is exploited. The gains arise because one person takes the risk of making a generous first move. The first mover necessarily benefits, regardless of the reaction of the other person because the first move was a move toward the good. Neither indifference nor hostility on the part of the other person can ultimately erase the good that the first mover attained for himself. If no genuine good truly flows to the first mover, then perhaps he was just fussing after all.

The Suspicion Tax

In our society, we have a tendency to be suspicious of sacrifices, either the demand that one make sacrifices or the claim that someone else is actually making a sacrifice. We often look with suspicion upon the claim that someone actually did something for someone else without a guarantee or even a reasonable expectation of something in return. We have great difficulty accepting an unrequited, unsolicited act of love from another person because we are afraid of being duped, of being used, of eventually being exploited. We want to know "What's in it for you?" before we allow ourselves to be taken care of, before we accept love from another person. We are suspicious, too, about anyone who defends the proposition that making a sacrifice as an act of love is a desirable thing. We wonder: "What is this person's agenda? How is my generosity going to be exploited?" We want a guarantee before we are willing to make a move.

I believe this suspicion arises because we have had too many experiences of having our trust and generosity abused. Too many politicians have asked us what we can do for our country only to exploit our patriotism for their own advantage. Too many clergymen have asked us to contribute to the church only to build their own mansions instead. Too many mothers have manipulated their children with guilt into doing things for their comfort rather than for the children's lasting benefit. There is plenty of evidence for the cynical position that everyone is out for his own good despite his claims of and demands for sacrifice. In fact, we might be so bold as to say that the intuitive appeal of the economic analysis of self-interest derives largely from this experience. Adopting the cynical posture of *homo economicus* starts to seem sensible after enough experiences of betrayed generosity.

But there is a problem with acting entirely on the basis of these suspicions, however reasonable they might be. If these suspicions take over our minds and color our view of the human race, then there will be no room for love. We will not be in a position to accept an act of genuine generosity. This attitude increases the cost of accepting love. When the cost of something goes up, we usually expect that people will demand less of it.

An economist might reply that an increased price of something will usually call forth an additional supply. But we will not observe an increase in the supply of love when suspicious minds raise the cost of accepting love. Consider the likely response of the supplier, that is, the giver of love. The person performs a generous act or makes a profession of affection in perfectly good faith. Perhaps he neither explicitly nor implicitly demands reciprocity in kind. He is not trying to manipulate the other person into changing, even for the better. He just wants to do something nice for another person for no particular reason.

Now suppose this supplier of love receives the response, "You say you are doing something nice for me: what's in it for you?" or "You say you love me: prove it." This is not a response that is likely to call forth an additional supply. In fact, the person is most likely to give up or go away.

We hypothesized that the person did not expect anything particular in return. But he did need one kind of benefit for his efforts: he needed the experience of being visible to the other person. He surely wanted the other person to see him and his offers as they really were rather than as a cover for an agenda. But his attempt to perform a loving act failed because of the suspicion of its intended recipient.

Suspicion can be viewed as a "tax" on love. Suspicion increases the costs of accepting love; that is, it increases the price paid by the receiver of love. But suspicion does not correspondingly increase the price received by the provider of love. Suspicion increases the cost of producing or giving love, so that less love is offered. A lower quantity offered, a lower quantity accepted, even when both parties could potentially have benefited: like all taxes, suspicion generates tremendous losses.

The problem flows both from people who are unreasonably suspicious and from people who have, by their actions, given just reason for suspicion. But I believe there is another, more cerebral aspect to the problem. We live in a society that venerates science. One of the things science does best is to reject and verify hypotheses while adopting a relatively skeptical stance throughout the phases of experimentation and data gathering. The scientist can justify a noncommittal attitude. The scientist can reasonably demand proof.

But if a person carries these scientific attitudes into the realm of personal relationships, he can do great harm to himself and those around him. We cannot directly observe the interior of another person's heart. If we remain skeptical until the proposition of love has been proven to us, we will necessarily remain skeptical forever. All the data will never be in. Even a person who loves us very much will certainly disappoint us or hurt us some of the time. The demand for proof where no proof is really possible destroys genuine love, for we more or less expect that eventually our hypothesis that no one really loves us will be verified. In effect, we place the entire human race on perpetual probation. Perhaps this begins to account for the indescribable loneliness that is so much a part of modern life.

So, we see how the supply side of this good called love bears some similarities to ordinary economic goods. Love is costly to give or produce or supply. Some of these costs are material costs that can be readily observed. Many of the other costs of giving love are purely interior, intellectual, or psychological. Because of all these costs of loving, the world is not necessarily filled with loving people, even though love is indeed a valuable good. It is reasonable to believe that the greater the perceived cost of love, the less of it will be given.

Our discussion of the suspicion tax suggests that there is something very counterintuitive about love once we begin to analyze it. Suspicious people resist being loved. The truth is that many people resist being loved, at least some of the time. Usually, economists think that when someone gives us a good thing, we accept it eagerly.

When people refuse a good, it is because it is, in some way, costly for them to accept it. We need to look at what we might somewhat irreverently call the demand for love. Our analysis of the costs of loving began by asking what we mean by "more love." These same components of love will help us understand how it might be costly to be the recipient of love.

The Costs of Being Loved

An Increase in the Accuracy of Perception

An increase in the accuracy of another person's perception of us is not an unmixed blessing. Sometimes, we are delighted when another person sees us as we really are. We are enchanted when someone finally recognizes our good qualities or sees our skills and achievements. When seeing us accurately means seeing our good qualities more clearly, it is certainly easy for us to accept. It is not costly to receive love that is based on an accurate knowledge of the parts of us that make us proud.

But every person has bad points as well as good, faults as well as strengths. In any relationship of any duration and intensity, these less gratifying parts of ourselves eventually emerge. When the other person sees more of our faults more accurately, it is a different story.

Sometimes we have the experience that another person who knows us well can "see through us." He can see us clearly in spite of our best efforts to conceal ourselves. Sometimes this experience is deeply comforting. Other times the experience is profoundly unnerving, especially when we are embarrassed about the other person's vision. We have the sense that there is no place to hide in the presence of such a person. We are having a kind of "moment of truth" that we were not prepared for.

How we react depends in part on our own courage. But it also depends on the reaction we expect from the other person. I argued earlier that a true "increase" in love needs to include an increase in all three of the components. The cost to us of accepting an increase in the accuracy of the other person's vision depends on what we expect him to do with that information. If the person in his clear vision continues to stand beside us, in solidarity with us, we might be willing to reveal ourselves more fully and entrust ourselves to him more completely. If the person sees our faults, recognizes them as faults, and is willing to help us see our way through to positive change, we might be more willing to accept his perception of us.

By contrast, if the person's increased accuracy of vision leads him to reject us, we would be hard-pressed to describe him as loving. At the same time, this reaction from him would make it more difficult for us to accept his vision of who we are. We will be more likely to argue the facts with him, claim that we do not in fact possess those particular faults, even if we do. If the person is not fully loving, we are more apt to find it costly to accept even the components of love that he can give.

If the person's increased knowledge of us leads him to redefine what is good, we might actually be more willing to accept his vision. It would not, however, be as great a good for us. For instance, suppose a son tells his father that the father has a drinking problem. It would not be unusual for the father to resist hearing this information. He might be more willing to accept it if his son would modify his statement by saying that being an alcoholic is not so bad and by redefining the drinking issue for him, so that it does not appear in so bad a light. This statement might indeed make it less costly for the father to hear the truth about his acts, but only because his son has been less than truthful about their meaning. The son sees his father clearly but has not increased his father's desire for positive change. Strictly speaking, a person telling us an unpleasant truth about ourselves is giving us a good. He may not necessarily be doing it as an act of love, but the truth is still a good to us. It is just that this particular good may be too costly for us to accept.

The example suggests that some attitudes significantly increase the costs of accepting an increase in the accuracy of a person's vision of us. Every human person is imperfect, yet everyone wants to think well of himself. No one enjoys having attention called to his or her faults. There are a variety of strategies that people use to help manage the tension caused by the gap between our actual condition and the condition in which we would like to imagine ourselves.

One strategy is to redefine goodness so that it includes the imperfect act the person has already decided to perform. In our example, the son tried to redefine a drinking problem to be less of a problem. But this strategy is not based on reality. The father may still have car accidents or get liver disease no matter how his son helps him redefine the question of drinking.

Some people have an implicit philosophy that any negative information about themselves signifies that they are somehow defective. They seem to believe that the natural condition of the human person is to be without problems, without faults, without anxiety. Some interpret evidence of imperfection to mean that they are mentally ill or that they had a defective upbringing. A few years ago, it was almost fashionable to claim to be "codependent" or that one's "family of origin was dysfunctional."

Others have a more spiritual approach. These people believe that a person is either saved or not saved. They know perfectly well that everyone is imperfect. Yet being among the saved is supposed to regenerate the person, so that one is able to live a better life. Evidence of one's own imperfection might mean that one is not among the saved. People with this view sometimes lose sleep wondering whether they are among the saved.

One problem with all of these approaches is that they make it more costly for us to hear the truth about our own imperfection. This type of personal philosophy raises the stakes, so to speak, in admitting to ourselves or to others that we are less than perfect. If a person points out to us one of our faults, we may have a hard time accepting this information, even if it is the truth (maybe especially, if it is the truth). It takes almost superhuman love and solidarity on the part of the other person, to remain in friendship while conveying this kind of unpleasant information.

There is an alternative attitude that lowers the cost to us of receiving negative information about ourselves. We can recognize imperfection as a natural part of the human condition. When someone points out a fault, we can use it as an opportunity for growth, as it was perhaps intended to be. We can see this as evidence of our membership in the human race. This look at our own frailty can be an opportunity to really connect with the other frail human beings around us. This is very difficult and demonstrates clearly that accepting this component of love can be costly to us.

An Increase in Solidarity

There are two different things we might mean by an increase in solidarity. We might mean that the person has an increased willingness to spend time with us for no particular reason or that the person is more willing to give us time, encouragement, and support when we are in distress or trouble. Suppose all the person is willing to do is to spend more time with us; he is no more willing than before to confront us with the truth about ourselves, no more eager than before for positive change on our behalf. Suppose instead that we mean a person has an increased willingness to help us through times of trouble. It is certainly true that this can form the basis of a lasting friendship. We never forget that special person who stood by us when we were desperate, when we were alone, when we were helpless. The more helpless we are, often the easier it is for us to accept a person's solidarity with us. Sometimes our helplessness is the key to letting down our defenses and allowing another person to really matter to us.

It is a curious fact that we so often require a nightmare of a problem before we allow someone to help us. It must be that it is costly to us to accept certain types of help because we so often do it only when we truly have no other choice. We only let people help us or be close to us when our backs are against the wall.

Several factors seem to be at work. First, we sometimes resist knowing that we need help. We cherish our independence, our autonomy, our sense of power. We sometimes believe that accepting help is a sign of weakness. Second, we sometimes fear that we are accumulating a debt to the other person, a debt that we would not be willing or able to repay. An economist might think that people would be eager to grab all the help and support they could get, especially if it is offered for free. Indeed, sometimes we are. But at the same time, there seems to be a special cost associated with admitting weakness by accepting help from someone. This special cost is evidently higher to us when we know we cannot reciprocate. Being the recipient of an unrequited gift makes us feel helpless and indebted.

Some of the attitudes and ideas we adopt can make these psychic costs more acute. I once knew a woman who had embraced a particular form of feminism. She thought it was necessary that she and her husband keep accurate accounts of all the money and time spent on joint projects around the house. This woman was convinced that their relationship depended upon absolute equality of contribution.

Then a serious accident occurred which required the couple to have extensive negotiations with insurance companies and repairmen. The husband was more competent at this type of work. He undertook it, as far as I know, without particular complaint. The wife was profoundly uncomfortable with the fact that she had accumulated a debt to her husband that she would never be able to repay in kind. Because of her attitude to marriage, and I suppose toward life in general, it was costly to her to accept her husband's gift of effort on behalf of their household.

So there are some costs associated with accepting this form of love. We sometimes do find it costly to accept an increase in solidarity when it is offered to us by another person. I do not claim that these attitudes are reasonable or desirable. I simply put it down as a fact that we sometimes feel this way. Even if you do not feel this way yourself, no doubt you have known someone who does.

An Increase in the Desire for Positive Change

Increasing the desire for positive change is the most challenging aspect of receiving love. The supply side is the most complicated and interesting component of receiving love. We say we want to change for the better, but the truth is we sometimes enjoy our faults very much. We do not necessarily want someone to earnestly desire that we shape up. We might, in the abstract, recognize their desire as being for our own good, and as being an act of love. Still, we might very well resist receiving this form of love.

The examples are so obvious we scarcely need to belabor the point. St. Augustine famously said: "Lord, grant me chastity, but not just yet." Another example would be: "I love you: I want you to stop drinking." This is not usually something that a person can easily stand to hear, even if it is true. In fact, people are advised not to say such a thing to an alcoholic or addict precisely because it will increase his resistance to change. Nonetheless, the person who deeply desires for the beloved to be released from his faults or bad habits or addictions may very sincerely love him. But still, the person may find it very costly to receive that particular loving act.

Notice too that all of our comments about personal philosophies that increase the cost of hearing negative information about ourselves apply to this component of love as well. An attitude that says that my imperfection is evidence of defectiveness will increase the cost of my accepting another person's desire that I change for the better.

Is Love a Commodity?

This analysis of the costs of love may lead the reader to wonder whether I view love as a commodity that can be bought and sold. Love is a good, and it has some of the usual properties of goods. We want more love when it costs us less to accept it. We supply more when it costs us less to give it or when we receive a greater reward for giving it. There is a different issue at stake in whether love is a commodity and not just another good.

The issue is whether it makes sense to think of love as something that can be exchanged. In my analysis of the costs of love, the discussion focused on one person at a time, either the giver or the receiver. The costs faced by the person receiving love are not somehow transferred as income or benefits to the person who gave him the love in the first place. In fact, the costs of receiving love are centered almost entirely in the person receiving it and have almost nothing to do with the person giving the love. A person can find it very difficult and costly to accept an increase in solidarity. That costliness does not translate into a benefit received by the person giving the love. As a matter of fact, those costs of receiving love act more as a cost upon the giver of love. Just as I argued that suspicion is a kind of tax, so many of the other costs associated with receiving love act as taxes on love. This is one thing that distinguishes this intangible good, love, from ordinary material commodities. A cost to the receiver is not a transfer to the giver. Likewise, the cost to the giver of giving love does not necessarily count as a benefit to the person who receives the love.

The problem does not end with this, however. With ordinary commodities, it makes sense to think about transferring objects in exchange for one another. It makes sense because the objects are just that—objects. They can be readily alienated from their original owner and transferred to another owner. But intangible goods cannot be alienated in the same way. It does not make sense to think of the person who loves as separating himself from the love he has produced (even though he may have produced it at great cost to himself). The love is a part of who he is. This is especially evident when we recall our original definition of love, to will the good of another. An act of the will is not something that can be alienated or sold. It is, rather, a condition of the person. The person now finds himself in a condition of greater love. This can be true, and can be of benefit to him, even if the love is rejected by the person for whom it was intended. We can still will the good of another even if that person does not want us to. We can love a person more than he realizes. We are in the condition of loving the person independent of his reaction to us.

So, can it ever make sense to say that love is for sale? I promise to offer you certain benefits if you will agree to love me. If you genuinely will my good, I will pay you. Let's make it concrete: I will pay you a million dollars if you will my good. Let it be said at the outset that a million dollars would certainly get your attention. Every gold-digger since time immemorial can be described as having her head turned by the thought of a lot of money. You might very well be inclined to pay attention to my good in a way you would not otherwise have been willing to do. You might even tell me my faults if I sincerely asked you to do so.

This illustrates what is so tricky about the proposition that love can be bought. The problem for the millionaire buying a friend or a wife is simply this: what is he likely to actually get? He might get a certain kind of attentiveness. He might get a person's time. But he is not likely to actually receive the person's candor, even if it would be greatly to his benefit. The person is much more likely to tell him what he wants to hear rather than to tell him the truth.

The most likely scenario is that the person wills the good of having a million dollars. Willing the good of the other person is simply a means toward that end. Telling a person an unpleasant truth that he seems to need to hear almost always risks arousing his anger. If a person is willing to risk a million dollars by telling the truth, we could plausibly argue that this is a genuine act of love. But the willingness to risk the money can only reveal a love that was already present for some reason other than the million dollars. The prospect of obtaining a million dollars cannot produce the love necessary to risk the million dollars.

This is perhaps why very wealthy people sometimes wonder whether they have any real friends. It is certainly why a candid advisor is so valuable to a rich or powerful person. These people who have the capacity to be really candid with the rich or the powerful must love something other than the money or the power.

Conclusion

This final observation sets the stage for the last chapter of this section on love. Love is costly to produce. Love is costly to receive. Therefore, love will be a scarce good. However, love cannot be bought and sold. The attempt to do so can muddy the waters so greatly as to destroy even the possibility of real love.

We cannot pay another person to genuinely will our good. We can pay him to do certain things that we can observe. We can perhaps have a contract with him to provide certain benefits to us and perform certain services for us. But we cannot have a contract with someone to will our good, since we could never fully specify what this might mean. Nor could we know for sure whether he had performed his obligations under the contract to will us good.

In earlier chapters we argued that both the economy and the polity are, in some way, held together with love. The love of a parent for a child allows the child to learn trust. This trust allows the child to learn a great many things that an economy needs for its smooth functioning: delayed gratification, impulse control, cooperative behavior, promise keeping. A self-governing political order requires self-restraint and forbearance as well. People cannot take advantage of every opportunity to use the political system that comes their way, or the system will collapse.

We can now see how it really was love that allowed the parents to do so much for the child. The parents truly, and naturally, will the good of the child. The parents see the child very clearly. The parents certainly stand in solidarity with the child. The parents willingly bear costs on behalf of the child. The parents truly and earnestly desire for the child to change for the better.

The child has no choice but to become the focal point of a tiny community. Adults, however, do have a choice. They can bind themselves together through love in the sense of willing the good of another. Love can hold these little groups together more durably than any other form of self-interest because people have redefined their concept of the good to include the other person.

We now need to address a set of questions that is, in my observation, among the most frightening for people with libertarian inclinations. Do we lose our autonomy by loving another person? If we redefine our good to include the good of another, do we surrender or lose some part of ourselves? Is the decision to love, even when love is costly, a reasonable decision?

12

Why the Decision to
Love Is Reasonable

"IS THIS RELATIONSHIP SATISFYING?" "Do I feel nourished by this relationship?" People do not usually think of themselves as utilitarians in their personal lives, but these questions reflect an underlying, if unspoken, attitude that relationships should be evaluated on the basis of their usefulness to me. The question "What's in it for me?" is a more brutally blunt version of the same questions.

Love and Economics

Economists have articulated the utilitarian philosophy more fully than the average person, so it is worthwhile to take a moment to explain the economists' approach to love. I am not saying that every person who asks himself "Is this relationship worth the cost?" is a closet utilitarian or has been directly or indirectly influenced by economics. But looking carefully at the economists' model of love might give a clue as to why this approach is so often disappointing when used in ordinary life. The current economists' vision of love badly constricts our vision of human relationships. The economists who have tried to give an account of love have inverted the logic of love.

Economists' define altruism as the willingness of one person to bear costs on behalf of another. Altruism can be modeled in two different ways. First, I receive a benefit from seeing another person consume or possess certain things. If my happiness depends on your consumption or possessions as well as my own, then I will rationally choose to transfer some of my resources to you. The alternative formulation of altruism is that my happiness depends on your happiness no matter how you might define your happiness. This form of altruism means I give you what you want, whatever that might be. I might just give you money so you can spend the money yourself on what you want the most.

The contrast between these two approaches helps us see one of the elements missing from the economists' account. In the first model, my happiness depends on seeing you do or consume certain things. This model can capture the possibility that I value some genuine good for you independently of your understanding of your good or your desire for that good. I give my child an education not because he especially likes it at the time but because I believe it is for his greater good. By contrast, if I value only the other person's happiness, I do not retain an independent judgment about what is good for him. I give him whatever he wants.

We might have some dispute about which of these two approaches is the more genuinely loving. Some say the second is more loving because it is more respectful of the person's autonomy and judgment. Others say that the first is more loving, or at least can be more loving, especially when dealing with dependent children. But those who take this position face a difficulty: if we transfer a certain good to someone, we cannot be assured he will actually consume that good and not exchange it for something else. How can we ensure that a child will not spend his lunch money on candy?

We cannot completely prevent such transfers. Our happiness depends on seeing the other person consume a certain thing, but we cannot force him to consume it. We can attempt to influence his choices, but we cannot control them. If we attempt to control another person and his actions, we might legitimately wonder whether we have left the realm of love.

In both cases, we have attempted to account for the phenomenon of love by seeing the other person as something that contributes to our happiness. We increase our happiness either from seeing his consumption of particular goods or from seeing his happiness. We are treating the other person as if he were an object similar to ice cream or a baseball game. We give something to the other person because we receive happiness from doing so. We value the other person because he does something for us.

But ordinary people think of love as valuing the other person for himself and not for what he can do for us. A person whom we love is not an object, and love consists of more than a simple transfer of resources. Economists who reflect on their experiences as spouses, parents, and children can recognize this fact as readily as anyone else. Most people identify a parent who values his child for what the child does for him as a bad parent. A parent who does nothing but give material things is a bad parent. A lover who only gives presents is not really loving. Genuine love involves some kind of giving of the self. This is why giving time to another person is usually considered more loving than giving objects: there is more of the person in his time than in the gift of an object.

When we say in ordinary conversation that we give ourselves or give of ourselves to the person we love, we mean more than taking our objects of consumption and giving them to the other person to consume. We mean allowing ourselves to be changed by the experience of being with and valuing another person. If we take a utilitarian approach as economists so often do, we have difficulty understanding the giving of the self. Economists think of a person as a utility function, that is, a being that transforms objects and experiences into happiness in a predictable and stable way. With this definition of the self, it is hard to imagine what it would mean for a person to give of himself to another person.

Seeing love or altruism as a transfer of resources, even if the resource is time, can never do justice to the reality of love. For the transfer model is operating in the realm of scarcity, just as all conventional economic analysis does. In the realm of scarcity, the thought of giving the self to another person is alarming. We might have the image of our entire self being consumed by another person or simply being lost. But the person who gives as an act of love is enriched by it. The person who gives of himself is not consumed but enlarged. Describing this enrichment as an increase in his utility or happiness does not fully capture the reality of love.

Even the maximization of utility or happiness is no longer an accurate description of the loving person's objective. The loving person no longer really knows what will make him happy because he does not and cannot know in advance exactly what the other person's good will be. By loving, the person commits himself to the unknown. The person is opening himself to a path he cannot by its nature predict. The person becomes willing to change and to allow himself to be changed by the experience of loving.

A critique of the utilitarian approach to love may not be enough to fully satisfy the doubtful. Even if a person agrees that it is unreasonable to make minute-to-minute calculations about whether being in a particular relationship is worth the cost, he still may not want to engage in a loving relationship in the first place. Love can be a costly business. Why should he bear these costs associated with loving another person?

It can be reasonable for a person to make sacrifices for the sake of love. It can be costly for a person to love, yet still be in the person's best interest to be the giver of love. Because both of these things can be simultaneously true, the decision to love does not require that a person surrender his autonomy. On the contrary, it is in the act of loving that a person most truly discovers who he really is, what he really wants, and what finally will make him happy.

Differences in the Need for Love

The benefits of love can be seen by reflecting upon people who, for various reasons, resist being loved or resist loving. For the most part, the costs these people thought they would have to bear from love were psychic costs. The suspicious person did not want to trust. The egalitarian wife did not want to be in debt to her husband. The alcoholic preferred to have a conspiracy of silence with his son. Most of us do not want our faults and weaknesses to be exposed. We want to keep those parts of ourselves safely hidden so that we do not have to be vulnerable, we do not have to be embarrassed. Many of these barriers to love can be broken by a change in attitude, a new way of thinking about our relationships.

The alternative to love is to live in a state of spiritual and emotional solitary confinement. It must be said that many people live in exactly this condition. These people do not let anyone else matter to them. They are obsessed with themselves, with their own projects and careers. They have nothing but superficial contact with other people. They live in a crowd of strangers.

People have a tremendous variety in their need for love and companionship. Some people are naturally gregarious and want to have other people in their vicinity. They can easily incorporate the good of others into their own view of the good. Other people are naturally easygoing. Even if they are not especially gregarious, they can accommodate the good of other people fairly easily.

Still others focus intensely on their own activities and interests. These people have a tendency to become upset if things do not happen on their own terms. These people can be very difficult to tolerate. They have a difficult time adjusting their view of the good to accommodate others, even those for whom they have high regard.

Their need to control outcomes can actively interfere with the love in their lives. Love can become very scarce for them. And yet, precisely because love is relatively scarce in their lives, they might appreciate it all the more. They have to let themselves surrender the reins of controlling everything in their environment. Only then can they genuinely will the good of another that does not happen to correspond immediately to their own good. When they finally allow someone else to matter to them, that person takes on tremendous value to them. These intense people may have only a very few friends.

Still others seem to have almost no capacity at all for willing the good of others. They are often very fragile. They cannot incorporate the good of another into their own good because they are so very needy. They cannot imagine how to accommodate others. If these people are part of a family at all, it is the other family members who must accommodate them.

Most people are connected to the rest of the human race by a thousand gossamer strands of love and affection. For some people, these connections are so automatic, so cost free, so easy that they would never question them. Their strands of affection, habit, temperament, and memory are so numerous and sturdy that they appear to be connected to humanity by steel cables. They are able to give to, and receive from, many people on many different levels.

But there are some people who are hanging on only by a few threads. Everything and everyone upsets these people. They can destroy a long-standing relationship in a momentary fit of temper. Others describe the experience of being around them as "walking on eggshells." One never knows what will set them off. No one can feel secure or comfortable in their presence. Even people who love them cannot be truly intimate with them. Perhaps they are attached only to their mother, or to one sibling, or to a spouse.

There is something unnatural about these people, which we can easily recognize when we see it in an extreme form in someone else. We are much less likely to recognize ourselves in this description. If someone points out to us that we are acting as if we are above the entire human race, we resist hearing it. If someone suggests that we need to consider a point of view other than our own, we do not necessarily welcome the observation. Yet most people, some of the time, behave as if they were the only person in the universe who matters. Most of us, some of the time, need to have someone confront us on this point.

The pitiful person off on his own suggests to us that love is valuable to us. The fact that we do not necessarily want to know that we are acting like a loveless person suggests that we know this is not a good way to live. The antisocial person seems unnatural even to those of us who find ourselves feeling antisocial some of the time.

Gains from Loving

When a person lives in spiritual solitary confinement, unconnected to the rest of the human race, he is literally at the center of his own little universe. There are two problems with this. First, it is not the truth: no human being is the center of the universe. Little children think this way, but we recognize this as immature thinking. The adult who lives as if he were the center of the universe is a person who is in for numerous disappointments, large and small. The rest of the universe has a way of not cooperating with his plans or with his image of himself.

For instance, we can sometimes wake up in the morning very satisfied with ourselves. We imagine that we are perfect people: nothing wrong with us, no faults, no weaknesses. Then some other people enter the room, maybe some little people. All of a sudden, we wonder whether we shall survive breakfast without screaming at someone. Our self-assurance no longer seems so assured. The truth is that these other people are just as worthy, just as important, just as valuable as we are. Yet, from a minor irritation we can manage to resist the idea that they amount to anything at all in comparison with our august selves. The idea that we are at the center of the universe is simply not very realistic.

We have a second problem with placing ourselves at the center of our own little universes: we can only be part of a very small universe. This is exactly the issue that loving can address so powerfully. When we come to encompass another person's good within our own good, our universe expands to include the other person and his good. This necessarily forces us to take a wider view of the world than we would have if we considered only our own good.

Love allows us to become more than we currently are. When we will the good of another person, we need to know more than just ourselves: we must learn about the other person. We need to learn what he values, what he enjoys, what makes him happy. There are tremendous "gains from trade" from the experience of really caring about another person. The experience of loving allows us to grow as no other experience can.

Loving a child truly exposes our faults. When a little child matters to us, and we have some responsibility for his or her development, all our faults take on a greater weight. I have to ask myself: what if my daughter whines like I do? (It is especially unnerving when she comes out with a complaint in exactly the same words, and with exactly the same gestures that I use. It is very embarrassing to see how much more fitting my faults appear in a five year old, than in an adult.) All of a sudden, I see myself with new clarity, and correcting a minor character flaw takes on a whole new urgency.

No one knows us like the people we grew up with—our parents, our siblings. The love from and for these people transforms us in more ways than we can even think about. Once I remarked to my older brother that my little daughter was becoming bossy. "She is just like our sister Joan," I said. Jerry burst into laughter. He could hardly get a full sentence out as he pointed at me. "Bossy like Joanie. What about you?" What could I say? He was right. He was not giving me a hard time about it: it was just the truth. I am bossy. There is no place to hide from your siblings. That observation, made in a spirit of fun and acceptance, helped me to track that particular unappealing quality in myself far more willingly than just about anything else could have.

A person who loves us can offer us realistic encouragement. A mother's loving suggestions can steer us into a direction that benefits us. When we are little, we want to please our mother. We trust her to have our best interest at heart and to know what she is talking about. Her encouragement can blend into insistence without our ever realizing it. We may not even consider the possibility that she is mistaken or that she is putting her own interests ahead of ours.

As we grow older, we may lose some of our trust in her. We may become suspicious of her motives. But every once in a while we have that same experience of relaxing into her care and her judgment. Sometimes we are more able to do this the less she insists, the more gently she suggests. At the end of the day, we can see that she was right all along. If she is wise, she may not even insist upon taking credit for or explaining what happened. But we both know.

In short, the experience of loving and being loved expands our world. By allowing another person to matter to us, we find out more about who we really are. Being with a person who matters to us holds up a mirror for us. Sometimes we like what we see, sometimes we do not. We discover our faults and have the opportunity to correct them. We find out what we are capable of, both in the physical realm and in the interior of our own minds. In this sense we can speak of gains from loving. But our gains are not of the sort that economists typically speak. Love does not increase our happiness by increasing our consumption of goods and services. The experience of loving changes what we consider a cost and what we consider a benefit.

Economists measure happiness by increases in utility, which presumes a stable utility function. Changes in what a person considers a cost or a benefit change the utility function itself, so there is no longer a stable measuring rod for evaluating changes in happiness.

The economist's description that comes the closest to describing the impact of love is that love makes us better off by expanding the set of goods with which we are familiar and which are available to us. But even this description does not fully do justice to the benefits of loving. The experience of love makes us more fully human by enlarging the soul.

Another Analogy with the Market

I have considered loving relationships among intimates. We can compare the benefits from these deep relationships with the more superficial benefits that economists ordinarily refer to as "gains from trade" in the market realm. Although the shopkeeper's relationship with his customers is not nearly as intense as his relationship with his wife, although the potential happiness of marriage far overshadows the potential happiness the revenue from his business might generate for him, there are some similarities between the two aspects of his life.

Recall that our definition of love is "to will the good of another." The love between spouses or the love of a parent for a child can encompass willing the complete good in every aspect of another person's life. But we can apply the definition to willing another's good in a more limited way and apply the same kind of reasoning. The purpose of this exercise is not to trivialize love or to reduce married life to a commercial transaction. Nor is my purpose to elevate the motivations of commerce to the sublimity of marriage.

Instead, my purpose is to appeal to those influenced by economic reasoning. Such people can easily understand the potential benefits of inconveniencing oneself for the sake of another person in a commercial transaction. Even the person who deals with others in impersonal transactions can sometimes be persuaded that it is in his interest to change his assessment of what behavior is in his interests and to surrender some small part of his autonomy to his customers.

It is this willingness to change that is the relevant analogy between commerce and romance. It is not that love can be reduced to a trade between strangers. Rather, it is that the willingness to change for the sake of another is the element common to both love and business.

Free market economists are fond of pointing out that commercial activity has a way of forcing people to become other-regarding. The market compels the shopkeeper to care about the needs of his customers. He thinks about what products would meet their needs at reasonable prices and provides those products. The successful shopkeeper considers how his customers would like to be treated and treats them accordingly. To this extent, we may say that he "loves" his customers. He wills only a very limited part of their good, perhaps. But he does will their good within the scope of his business activity. His interests, activities, and attention have been expanded to the exact extent that he wills the good of another.

I hasten to add that one can have gains from trade without love. A person in commerce can have benefit from trade without having any genuine regard for others. People can use their customers, employees, and suppliers simply as means to an end. Such people care about the people they do business with only to the extent that they are useful to them. They treat other people as if they were objects. This is the stereotypical bloodthirsty capitalist to which critics of commerce so often point.

Superficially, the cutthroat businessman and the other-regarding businessman may appear to be doing the same things. They both hire employees, buy goods, transform goods into something more useful to consumers, and sell the new goods to the public. But if we spend very much time in close contact with them, we will detect some subtle differences. Employees enjoy working with one firm and complain about the other. Customers are loyal to one kind of firm and not necessarily to another.

But the bloodthirsty capitalist misses something, just as the loveless individual does. Both are missing the opportunity to broaden their horizons to encompass a wider good. A person can make money by considering the needs of others more successfully than his competitors. Or a person can make money by ignoring everything and everyone except his own plans for success.

Participation in commerce has the potential to be genuinely ennobling. Commerce does not necessarily enlarge the soul and ennoble every individual who participates in it, any more than marriage or parenthood necessarily deepens every individual. Libertarians cannot be indifferent to people using each other, in business or in marriage. We know that people can legally get away with behaving in a cutthroat fashion and the market will only partially correct their behavior. Likewise, we know that people can live in loveless marriages that are little more than commercial transactions. Both marriage and commerce are potentially ennobling, but neither is automatically so. It requires effort, as well as some reflection and insight, to obtain the full moral enrichment possible in either a business relationship or a personal relationship. It would be unnecessary to observe that commerce induces people to be other-regarding if it were self-evident or automatic. The potential is there, but it is possible for people to miss out. Libertarians, of all people, need to point people in the direction of the higher goods that are latent in both commerce and married life.

I hope this analogy with the market will help some readers understand the seemingly paradoxical nature of love. It is costly to love. The act of loving can feel like a sacrifice of the self. Yet at the same time the act of loving produces numerous benefits that make it worthwhile to bear those costs. This what makes the decision to love reasonable.

We can also come to understand how we do not really lose ourselves, even though we might do things that seem like sacrifices of our autonomy. By loving, we discover more of who we are. When we live in isolation, we might imagine that we are autonomous, independent, and free. In point of fact, we sometimes scarcely know who we are.

We are not confronting reality in the same intense way that the experience of love demands of us. We miss the reality of other people and the reality of the impact that we have upon other people. If we live in isolation, we really only know a small corner of ourselves, our capabilities, our faults, our strengths, even our capacities for enjoyment.

This, finally, is the real benefit and power of love. Love is a transforming experience. Love helps us become more than we currently are and moves us toward the full realization of our potential as human beings. This is why love has always been so mysterious and unpredictable.

Love in the Modern Mind

Love is especially mysterious if we embrace the theory that only the material world is real or that only observable things are real. For most of love's work takes place in the interior of a person's heart and mind. Some aspects of love are observable, to be sure. But the unobservable, interior aspects must be at work before the exterior manifestations of love really appear. Materialism has trouble seeing love.

Love is also incomprehensible to a science like economics which assumes that people have fixed preferences, tastes, and desires. Love's most important work is to transform the person in exactly the dimensions that economists usually treat as fixed. The experience of loving and being loved changes what we consider a cost and a benefit. The key fact about love is that we change our preferences under its influence. Economics has trouble seeing love or understanding what it has seen when it does occasionally have a sighting.

If we take the view that only the material world is real, we will not only have trouble seeing love, we might also be afraid of it. The economic view of the world focuses upon the allocation of scarce resources among competing wants. Many resources, including time and attention, are material and therefore scarce.

However, some of love's most important aspects are not driven by scarcity. The person's will for the good of another is not and need not be scarce in any meaningful way. A person can turn his will toward things that are completely outside his set of possible actions. This turning of the will is not frivolous; nor is it mere sentimentality. The person is preparing himself to act in the event that his choice set expands. The person is priming his will so that when the opportunity to do good presents itself he is ready to do it.

There need not be any scarcity at all in this dimension of love. As a matter of fact, thinking in terms of scarcity disrupts the process. Focusing upon scarcity can cause the person to experience himself as impoverished or on the edge: "I am not capable of doing any good to this person. I shall stop thinking about his good at all. I am not going to waste my time willing the good that I have no capacity to bring about. I shall just demoralize myself if I do." This kind of thinking is impoverishing as well as being unreasonable. We do not know in advance whether we have actually exhausted all possibilities for doing good to the person we love.

In short, love proceeds from an abundance. Love is not a material good that is necessarily limited in quantity. Love proceeds from the interior of a person and acts upon the world around him.

Still, this might not be enough to satisfy the doubtful. For everyone knows that there are plenty of times when the demands of love are exhausting. In these times, it is hard to believe that love is abundant. We feel that love is in such short supply that we cannot see how to keep loving even if we believe that it would be in our interest in some abstract way. We cannot demand of ourselves that we do the impossible, no matter how appealing it might seem to be.

When Love Seems Scarce

When a family faces a crisis like death or serious illness, or a moral crisis like a family member being arrested, the family can go to pieces. Everyone is needy, but there is not enough love inside the established relationships of the family to fill everyone's needs. I need more from my spouse, but he needs more from me. At times like these, people can reach for something outside the relationship to support them. There are plenty of perfectly harmless and helpful things one can do. People in distress can turn to a trusted friend for support. Maybe the nuclear family reaches out to the members of the extended family for help.

But in their desperation, people sometimes take much more drastic and potentially dangerous steps. People abandon their families by placing emotional or physical distance between themselves and the rest of the family. People comfort themselves in these crisis situations by entering into addictive behaviors such as alcoholism, drug addiction, or compulsive eating, working, or shopping. The individual uses the addiction to take his mind off his troubles or to try to fill up his emptiness. Marriages can go to pieces as one spouse seeks support from someone outside the marriage, thinking that more love brought in from outside the relationship will finally be enough to satisfy.

Whatever kind of crisis brought the family to this condition, it has now become a moral crisis. People are choosing to do things that they know are wrong, but they feel they cannot help themselves. They feel that no one is really available to help them.

We can get ourselves into a moderately desperate condition under much less desperate circumstances. The children are whining and the in-laws are demanding. Or is it the other way around? It goes on, day after day, without any relief. We can feel like we are on the edge, simply from the stress of dealing with day-to-day problems without respite. Even without anybody sick or dying, we can feel like we are going to lose it.

What to do? I can only report what I do. I offer it as a suggestion that people can use or not, and endorse or not, as they see fit.

Going to the Source

There is one source of love that we can always count on, that is always in infinite supply and readily accessible to us: the love of God. When we feel completely drained by the demands of others, we can place ourselves in the presence of God and allow ourselves to be filled up with his love. We can face the demands of daily life more readily because we are less needy ourselves. We find it possible to make more realistic demands on other people because we no longer need them to do and be everything for us. We do not need to insist that other people be completely available, always understanding, and infinitely supportive. If we let God be God, we can let other people be human.

There is a peculiarly Catholic way of looking at this because Catholics tend to be quite literal and rather earthy about it. According to Catholic theology, Jesus is really present in the consecrated host. In Catholic practice, the consecrated host is kept in the tabernacle of every Catholic church. When we go into the church, and see the little red candle burning beside the tabernacle, we believe that Jesus is really there. We place ourselves physically in the presence of God, not just metaphorically, not just spiritually, but really.

During a personal crisis, I once had a priest tell me to kneel in front of the Blessed Sacrament (that's what we call the consecrated host) so that I could feel the love of God pour over me. I later noticed that other people at that parish were kneeling close to the tabernacle, too. I surmise he had told quite a few other people the same thing. I know of another priest who advises children to say their prayers as close to the tabernacle as possible so they can "snuggle up to Jesus."

I realize that non-Catholics think this is all rather mysterious and strange. But this is the essence of what we mysterious Catholics are doing: we are going into church for a refill of love. We are allowing ourselves to be filled up with the love of God.

A skeptic might think it is nothing but a trick of the imagination.

But he would have to admit it is a good trick. It would have to be a pretty convincing thing that would make it possible for people who believe it to live out their obligations in a deeper spirit of love than would otherwise be possible for them.

Nobody does Eucharistic theology quite like Catholics do. Nobody does theology of grace quite like Catholics do, either. But still, Christian and Jewish believers of all denominations know that the love of God is available to them. Believers of all sorts have plenty of ways of placing themselves in the presence of God and his love. By connecting ourselves with the source of love, we can restore the disposition to love after it has been taxed seemingly down to nothing. Whatever their forms of expression or their forms of popular piety, believers know that the love of God is the one resource that is truly infinite in supply. If we allow ourselves to be connected to it, we need not end up in a position of scarcity or desperation.

What about the non-believer? It is sometimes said that "there are no atheists in foxholes." The import of that remark is that a desperate situation can bring a person to abandon an intellectual commitment to atheism. It is my observation that people going through personal crises sometimes feel as wretched as a nineteen-year-old in a foxhole. Yet, we seldom hear people say "there are no atheists in divorce courts" or "there are no atheists in juvenile detention homes." For some reason, many of us do not allow ourselves even the urgent prayer of the soldier.

Without attempting to answer every possible objection, or pretending to know every possible reason for reluctance, let me offer this observation to the non-believers among my readers. Perhaps you think it is a kind of intellectual weakness to pray to a god whose existence has not been proved to your satisfaction. Consider this: you cannot prove God does not exist. And even if there is no God, prayer is a harmless thing to do (unlike many of the things people do in desperation.) Why not give the universe the benefit of the doubt? The worst that can happen is that you feel foolish afterward.

You do not know whether there is any loving being who is listening to you. You do not feel any presence; you don't receive any message or any comfort. On the other hand, you can take consolation from the knowledge that you have allied yourself on the side of love. There may come a time in your life when it is wise to regard being on the side of love a higher priority than the fear of being duped. From that perspective, there is no shame in crying out with the psalmist: "Out of the depths I cry to thee, O Lord! Lord, hear my voice!. . . O Israel, hope in the Lord! For with the Lord there is steadfast love, and with him is plenteous redemption."[1]

From the time of the American Founding to the present hour, Americans have debated and pondered the contribution that religion might make to the success of our unique experiment in self-government. One common theme is that religion instructs free people in the requirements of moral behavior. Many of the Founders were convinced that without the foundation of religious instruction, the great masses of ordinary people would be unable to discover and maintain the knowledge of what a good and free society really needed them to do.

Another common theme is that without the fear of judgment after death, and the prospect of everlasting punishment, even people who knew what they were supposed to do might choose not to do it. The fear of justice after death keeps people from continually figuring out what they can get away with by looking forward to the end of life when it no longer matters whether other people can extract punishment. The fear of eternal punishment raises the stakes for bad behavior. Even if I might get away with it in some earthly sense, I will surely pay for my crimes after death—with compound interest.

Without taking anything away from these two considerations, I would suggest a third that may be even more basic for the Judeo-Christian religious tradition in a free society: our connection with the loving God makes it possible for us to keep the commandments. The love of God rejuvenates us so that we can continue loving, even when it seems impossible. A society of free people requires more human connections, more generosity, and more love than almost any other kind of society we can imagine. Surely the existence of an inexhaustible supply of love, available to anyone for the asking, is of more than passing importance for a society like ours.

With all due respect to others who have participated in this debate, I must say that in my opinion this aspect of what religion contributes to our lives has been shortchanged in public discussion. We ought not to confine our discussion of the role of God and religion to defining morality and imposing penalties. If we do, we are in danger of reducing God to a cosmic Napoleon marching through the universe, handing down legal codes and terrorizing everyone into obedience. A skeptic can be forgiven for asking "Who needs God for that? We can do that ourselves." It is possible that we could figure out a reasonable moral code for ourselves without special divine revelation. It is possible that the government could attempt to replicate the terror of hell by increasing the punishments for crimes. But how could the government replicate the infinite love of God?

I realize that this claim that God actually does something for us is likely to be greeted with skepticism, for this is a more supernatural aspect of religion than the ones we are accustomed to talking about in public. Our non-believing neighbors might be willing to indulge us in a religion that is merely an intellectual belief system or a backdrop for an ethical code. But I open myself to ridicule by divulging that God actually does something for me.

A light-hearted skeptic might voice his concern this way. "Oh, so God talks to you, does he? What did he say to you this morning?" Without claiming any special, private revelation, a believer can tap the resevoir of public revelation to discover that God is, in a general way, talking to him through the ancient traditions and texts. A skeptic might worry that a person who thinks God is talking to him can confuse his own desires with some vast divine plan. But I have never received instructions from God to march into Luxemburg or Poland

and proclaim myself queen. I usually receive messages like "call your mother once in a while," "quit whining at your husband," or "you need to apologize to your son." Belief in God does not teach me that I am the center of the universe.

God tells me that I am his precious child and that what I do matters. I freely admit that this part of the conversation empowers me. At the same time, meditating upon God has a way of reminding me that other people are also his precious children and that I am no more important than they are. The person with whom I am about to quarrel, the person who is not giving me all that I think he should, the person who is making unreasonable demands upon me, all of these people are just as important to God as I am. That thought can be humbling, even arresting. It is certainly not a thought that gives me unlimited sanction to do anything I want to other people.

Parents try to teach their little children to have regard for others, even while conveying to them that they are uniquely important. This combination of concepts helps the child have a balanced perspective on his relationship to other people. This lesson taught in all the sand boxes and playgrounds of the world captures in microcosm a deep and pervasive reality that we must face throughout our lives. Our status as God's precious children does not give us the license of a spoiled brat. After all, he has lots of other children. In this way, there is a close parallel between an adult's dialogue with God and the child's conversation with his parents.

The voice of God is the voice of the loving parent telling us both that we are important to him and that we must have regard for other people. When our parents tell us that other people are just as important as we are, we sometimes do not quite believe them. For we know that our own parents favor us. They mean what they say in an abstract way, but when push comes to shove between us and another child, they would surely show partiality to us. But the divine parent is the ultimate "impartial spectator."[2] When he reminds us that the other person is just as valuable as we are, he really means it. Our quarrel is a dispute between siblings from God's point of view. Both parties to the quarrel are his children.

In a free society, people need to have a realistic perspective on their relationship to the rest of the human race. The American experiment in self-government will surely falter unless the vast majority of the people possess a reasonable view of their own value and dignity as persons coupled with a similar view of the value and dignity of others. Those of us who have some experience in being in a relationship with God owe it to our countrymen to offer an honest account of that experience.

At the core of our relationship with God is love. He loves me and I love him. Through that experience, I can be filled up with love so I can come through for other people when the demands of love might otherwise seem impossible. I feel confident that I am not the only person who has ever had this kind of experience. Surely this is a significant contribution of religion to the functioning of a well-ordered democracy.

Conclusion

Like the observation that we are born as helpless babies, the observation that the love of God is central to the civilization built upon the Judeo-Christian tradition is so obvious that we can easily overlook it. The time has come to focus anew on these ancient truths.

We observed in the first section of this book that a community or society forms naturally around a helpless baby. The baby has no choice but to be part of a community: he cannot survive any other way. Here I am making a stronger argument. Love creates a society out of autonomous adults. But even people who do have a choice can find it reasonable to exercise their choice in favor of welcoming another person into their world. People become linked to one another by the act of caring about each other. In their caring, they form a little society.

The decision to love entails costs for the person who loves. The person voluntarily assumes these costs. No one forces a person to love and to bear the costs associated with a loving relationship. In short, love is a decision, and the decision to love is reasonable. With the grace of God, we can live out the commitments we make for the sake of love.

A Civilization of Love

W E STARTED WITH BABIES and have ended with transcendent love, with a policy detour along the way. All the while, Adam Smith has been in the background. Let us bring him forward for a moment.

I placed a quotation from Adam Smith's first book, *Theory of Moral Sentiments*, at the front of this book. Smith observed that a society based upon merely utilitarian considerations could function, while a society based upon love would flourish. But a group of people who were always ready to injure one another could not survive as a society at all. He concluded that justice was more fundamental to the foundation of society than love since love could be dispensed with while justice could not.

Smith did not realize that without love present in the background, a much larger fraction of people would be always ready to injure one another. He seems to have assumed that people develop a sense of justice naturally. The conditions of his particular time and place induced him to inquire into the nature and causes of the wealth of nations even while those same circumstances allowed him to take sympathy or empathy for granted. Nothing in the social environment of his time led him to inquire into the nature and causes of the disposition to cooperate.

During Smith's time, no doubt, some men abandoned their wives, fathered children out of wedlock, or were dominating tyrants in their homes. No doubt some women delegated the care of their children to strangers, bore children out of wedlock, or drove their families to distraction with nagging. But in Smith's very Calvinist eighteenth-century Scotland, such people were regarded with disdain and bore the censure of the community. It would have been rare to find people defending or excusing behavior that disrupted family life in such profound ways.

Perhaps his time was too harsh. But our time has swung to the opposite extreme. Today, it is the Calvinist divines who bear the brunt of social disapproval. Meanwhile, even the most destructive behavior is excused not only by the law but even by social mores.

Adam Smith could take for granted a set of guiding cultural and social norms. He took for granted that "the man within the breast," as he sometimes called the conscience, was formed in enough detail to guide an individual in the numerous fine points of daily living. Smith thought that the process of looking at the behavior of other people and reflecting upon one's own behavior could guide the most detailed niceties of human interaction: in one striking passage, Smith talks about the appropriate amount of enthusiasm to display over an unexpected turn of good fortune.[1] The people of Smith's acquaintance evidently had consciences robust enough that he could safely assume that gloating was universally regarded as bad manners.

Smith could construct a moral theory based upon sentiments or feelings because most of the people of his time and place had very well-developed moral sensibilities. In such a society, people's natural desire to think well of themselves would lead them to avoid doing things that would be revolting if they saw someone else doing them. This self-restraining person was in the background of Smith's later and more famous work, *An Inquiry into the Nature and Causes of the Wealth of Nations.*

But we are not born with a fully grown "man within the breast" to guide our actions. We do not become Smith's "impartial spectators," judges of the moral worth of our own behavior, immediately after birth. We are all born as helpless babies.

Smith was correct to assume that all of us, with an insignificant number of exceptions, have the capacity to one day form these kinds of moral judgments and to restrain ourselves by conscience. He was correct in his assessment that the person with these two abilities is the most lofty example of humanity, the fullest expression of the potential that lies within each of us. In these two senses, the self-restraining person is "natural." But Smith was mistaken if he supposed that we automatically progress from infancy to this majestic condition. Becoming the kind of reflective individual who both has regard for others and the ability to think for himself requires vast amounts of human effort from the individual himself and from the adults who contribute to his upbringing.

Smith's ideas about self-regulating social systems have influenced generations of Americans, even those who have never heard of him. Smith's ideas are like wallpaper in our minds, in the background of our world coloring our environment, though we do not always notice them. We only notice the wallpaper when it has begun to yellow or fray, which even the best wallpaper hung with the best workmanship will eventually do.

Perhaps it is time for a little sprucing up. For Adam Smith's mind had its own wallpaper which he did not need to look at very closely. We can no longer take for granted the conditions of family life and connectedness that he took as settled. Every generation has a new set of problems with which to grapple. Our new problem is that the family bonds that earlier generations of political theorists could take for granted have become so weakened that the very fabric of social life is threatened. In our current environment, we cannot assume that children will receive the moral or even the material support they need to develop a regard for others, the ability to restrain themselves, and a sense of right and wrong.

Little babies are bundles of impulses and desires. They do not automatically respect the rights of other people, make long-range plans, make and keep promises, or offer equivalent value for value in transactions. In short, babies are not guaranteed to become full participants in the free market or in participatory self-government. Children must be taught to do these things.

Babies and children do not learn all these things from didactic, classroom-type instruction. Explicit instruction is sometimes helpful and even necessary. It would be a mistake to dispense with all such verbally transmitted, adult-directed moral education. But that kind of formal instruction does not completely substitute for experience and example. Babies absorb profound, if inarticulate, moral lessons through their connections with other members of the human race. Babies come to know that they matter, and they come to allow other people to matter to them. They come to know that human contact is the great good upon which their very survival depends. As they mature, children learn from example, and this requires that they spend significant amounts of time with adults who provide worthy examples.

People do not provide this sort of connection, example, or instruction to babies out of some sort of cleverly redefined self-interest. People take care of babies because they love them. If the parents for some reason fail to take care of their own children, the possible alternatives really are second-best imitations. These facts are so obvious that we do not notice them and almost trip over them.

Templeton Prize winner Michael Novak has observed that a free society consists of three kinds of liberty: economic liberty, political liberty, and moral-cultural liberty.[2] The free society requires three sets of institutions that correspond with these liberties: the market economy with secure property rights, free political institutions with constitutionally limited government, and reasonable cultural and social institutions. Each of these three institutions supports the other two, while at the same time checking their excesses.

We might compare the free society to a three-legged stool. The surface of the stool represents all the choices and activities of all the people in the society. No one in the society is inherently more worthy or better than anyone else. People go about their business, protected from unreasonable encroachments from other people. Each of the three kinds of liberty, with its corresponding institutions, represents the legs of the stool upon which stand all the activities and interactions within the society.

Libertarians have tended to focus upon maintaining the free market and limited government legs of the stool and have allowed the moral-cultural leg to decay. Culture seems to be the result of the choices of the millions of individuals in the society. Perhaps for this reason those with libertarian inclinations have been hesitant to say very much about culture. We think that the kinds of choices that go into building and sustaining families are quintessentially private choices and as such should be respected, left to each person's preferences and not second-guessed.

Libertarians sometimes argue that any peaceful act is acceptable. While this may be perfectly correct as a statement of political philosophy, it is not true as a statement of moral or cultural philosophy. For some peaceful acts are objectively better than others, in the sense that some acts have a greater probability of making us happy. Other peaceful acts are morally wrong, even if they are and ought to be legally permissible. People need to have some tools of moral discernment, and this moral compass is more important in a libertarian, free society than in almost any other because individuals are left with such broad liberty.

But moral and cultural license will not necessarily correct itself in the way that the competitive mechanism of the market tends to correct certain kinds of economic miscalculations. Business establishments that systematically misperceive the demands of consumers or that overprice products will eventually be driven from the market by other firms that perform these tasks more effectively. Firms that underpay their workers will eventually find that other firms bid away the most talented members of the workforce. This creates an incentive for the firm to make itself more attractive to potential workers or risk bankruptcy.

There is no particular reason to think that people making poor decisions in their family lives will be unable to continue in the "family business." As we all know, people are perfectly capable of going through an entire life with skewed preferences and ideas, doing things that bring misery to themselves and those around them. We need sensible ideas that will help people to live out their family commitments with some happiness and pleasure precisely because the habits of mind we bring to our family lives are so deeply ingrained. If we need to change our actions, words, and thoughts (and who does not, at least some of the time?), a well-considered defense of family as a great social and personal good can help.

Just as the economic and political legs require well-articulated defenses from those who love liberty and defend the dignity of the human person, so does the moral-cultural leg. A three-legged stool with one short leg is not a firm foundation for anything. While libertarians have been criticizing the Federal Reserve, attacking the tax code, and denouncing regulatory agencies, many moral presumptions inconsistent with liberty have quietly taken root in the social life of the country. Many good and decent people have unwittingly accepted some disastrous cultural assumptions.

Marxism may be dead, but many of its underlying social assumptions linger in the background of the attacks on the family, from both welfare statism on the left and radical individualism on the right. Marxism has produced its own wallpaper of the mind. Even those who detest marxism may find traces of it in their own thinking. This wallpaper was never very pretty to begin with and has only survived when it has had something more attractive pasted over the top of it. So it is worthwhile to peel back some of the layers and get a good look at a few of these lingering pernicious presuppositions, so we can clear them away once and for all.

For instance, marxist social class theory views differences between people as inevitable engines of conflict, while free market economics sees those very same differences as possibilities for gains from trade. Marxist materialism asserts that the essence of the social problem is providing for the physical well-being of the workers. Libertarianism, by contrast, recognizes that the set of things people naturally and normally want include far more than the mere survival of the body and the possession of material objects. At the core of marxism is a utopianism that suggests that creating a perfect world is not only a possibility but a moral imperative. Advocates of limited government, on the other hand, realize that perfection is not an option and try to make the best of imperfect situations. Libertarians recognize that any institutions they establish or laws they pass will be imperfect.

Take, for instance, the widespread assumption that relations between men and women will necessarily be characterized by mistrust, exploitation, and suspicion. This assumption colors public policies in areas as diverse as sexual harassment, workplace discrimination, and divorce law. But this mistrust is even more insidious outside the arena of public policy. Mutual suspicion poisons our relationships, handicaps our marriages, and distorts our images of one another. We have almost lost the vision of marriage as providing the opportunity for the natural complementarity of men and women to flower.

Few people would defend marxist materialism either in its old extreme form or in its more harmless-looking welfare state form. No one really believes that the government can solve all the problems of the poor by providing for their material needs. Free market advocates have done reasonably well at making the public policy case that taking care of the bodily needs of the poor will never be enough, either for the good of the poor or for society as a whole. But a kind of bankrupt materialism lives on in some of the most private decisions of ordinary people, and here I am not thinking primarily of the poor. There are far too many people who believe that their moral worthiness is somehow dependent on how much money they make or on the prestige of their job titles. There are people who delude themselves into thinking that their childcare arrangements are adequate if the children are fed, warm, dry, and properly medicated.

After the failure of the socialist experiment and the manifest problems of the welfare state, most people have been innoculated against utopian public policy. But honestly, isn't it sometimes a variety of utopianism that leads people to throw away perfectly good marriages to perfectly decent human beings in the hope that some other person or life will finally bring perfect happiness? There is sometimes an element of utopian thinking when we hear the recently divorced say things like "He just wasn't the right man for me" or "The marriage just didn't work out." People sometimes walk away from their parents, siblings, and even children thinking that they will finally be happy if only they could choose different intimates. How much happier we might be if we worked with the imperfect people on hand rather than continually switching around, looking for perfection. I am not attacking marxism to flog a dead horse. I am just trying to show that this particular dead horse is still flogging us more than we might realize.

Our attention needs to be turned toward the moral and cultural sphere not so much to legislate the particular outcomes of private decisions but to encourage personal choices that will promote a stable, free society. Our objective ought to be to persuade people that such responsible behavior is good, reasonable, and ultimately in their own interest.

I am committed to the proposition that persuasion, not legislation, is the appropriate tool because my central claim is that the social order must be held together with love. Love's most important characteristic is that it cannot be compelled. It can never be a fit subject for government activity. Love's most important work takes place inside the interior of the individual person, where it cannot be observed or monitored. Love's greatest power flows from the fact that it is freely given.

The loving family is surely the foundation of the moral and cultural leg of a free society, just as property rights and contract law are the foundations of the economic leg, and constitutionally limited government and freely elected rulers are of the political leg. Loving families are just as essential to a free society as property rights and a constitution. The moral and cultural tools of a free people include persuasion based upon reason and evidence, as well as the cultivation of appropriate "habits of the heart" from birth to adulthood.

The virtues and habits that support family life are often difficult to live by. There are periods over the lifetime of a marriage when it is hard to live in fidelity to one person. It can be difficult to overlook the faults of the people we live with. It is hard to keep silent when we are longing to tell somebody off. It sometimes seems to be easier to go to the office, where we might occasionally have our egos stroked, than to stay home to take care of a bunch of snot-nosed, whiny, demanding kids.

A recent book by Arlie Russell Hochschild speaks to this conflict between what we want and what we think we ought to want. The book's title captures the problem: *The Time Bind: When Work Becomes Home and Home Becomes Work.*[3] The premise of the book is that men and women alike spend excessive time at work because they are more comfortable there than at home. The people interviewed for the book found the workplace to be emotionally safer and more fulfilling than their own homes.

To the extent that this provocative thesis is true, it is very sad and presents a bold challenge to anyone who would theorize exclusively about the economic and political spheres of life. What kind of "good life" is it that promises economic prosperity and political liberty if we cannot enjoy those blessings in the company of those we love? If

we are running away from home, where are we going? If we run away
from the people whom we love and who love us, to whom shall we
run?

All too often, people end up running to the government or to
other impersonal institutions. Can we really believe that the numerous calls for government support for divorce and single parenthood
would have gotten off the ground if everyone were happy in his family? These proposals have some credibility because everyone can
think of someone he knows who is unhappily married. Similarly, the
proposals to assign ever greater responsibility to state-run schools for
ever more detailed aspects of child development derive much of their
appeal from the fact that everyone can think of someone who is not
doing such a great job of caring for her kids.

I believe that my proposals for living inside a loving family are
not only good for society in some grand sense but also for the individuals themselves. I do not think that I will get very far in persuading people of that unless I acknowledge that some of what I advocate
is in fact costly to act upon. It is more persuasive and more truthful
to admit that these things are costly and to explain why the costs are
worth bearing.

I take as my role model in this regard one of the great twentieth-
century heroes of economic liberty, Milton Friedman. Friedman
spent many years arguing for a stable and predictable monetary policy
as both the cure for inflation and one of the necessary foundations
of a prosperous economy. His critics pointed out that slowing the
growth of the money supply would create hardship in the form of
unemployment and economic dislocation. If Friedman had responded by claiming that there would be no unemployment, his critics would have dismissed him as a lunatic (which they probably
wanted to do). Instead, he agreed that there would be costs to his
proposals, but he showed why he expected the costs to be short term
and the benefits to accrue over a longer term. He patiently, over the
course of many years, continued to explain why the short term costs

would be worth bearing. Inflation is no longer a serious economic problem in this country, in part due to Friedman's candor and persistence.

A limited government and free market cannot exist without a substantial component of self-restraint among the citizenry. This internalized ethic cannot come into existence in the absence of loving families taking personal care of their own children. Scholars sometimes conceptualize the promise-keeping ethic as though its primary impulse were rational and its primary foundation were utilitarian. I believe this is a mistake. We academics have always lived in a society in which most people already lived by these basic norms.

But it seems that promise keeping for purely rational and utilitarian reasons cannot supply the foundation for contracts and ethical behavior that a free society really requires. For there are many occasions on which it is privately rational to break promises and contracts. When these temptations arise, something more powerful and more primal than rational calculation must overrule the urge to follow one's own self-interest, narrowly defined. The internal voice must say "We don't do that kind of thing" before the calculation process ever gets started. That internal voice is the voice of the loving parent: the parent who proved trustworthy, long before we ever even could begin to demand proof or reasons for anything.

It is not sufficient to reduce family obligations to a species of contractual obligations which may be renegotiated at will by consenting adults. The children who result from the union are not consenting adults, by definition. The needs of the children are not simply social constructs that can be redefined for the convenience of the adults. Some childhood needs are universal and non-negotiable.

We are not free to choose any type of social arrangements, for some social arrangements are self-contradictory and unsustainable. Every advocate of the free market and limited government knows that we are not "free to choose" a prosperous society that has no private property rights. I would add that neither are we free to choose a

society in which every generation completely renegotiates its definitions of family relationships, obligations, and virtues. Some familial
obligations are inherent in the relationship of parent and child. Some
virtues are indispensable.

Love is the key to fulfilling these obligations and inculcating these
virtues. Love of the parents for the child keeps them engaged in the
never-ending job of meeting the child's needs. Love of the parents
for each other keeps them working as a team so they are not overwhelmed by the task.

The child learns to trust his parents not because he reasons from
first principles that they are generally reliable sources of information.
He trusts them because their loving actions have allowed him to feel
safe. The loving act takes the place that a rational argument might
take for an adult: it is utterly persuasive. From the parents' actions
toward him, he learns that making a generous first move is not the
behavior of a sucker but of the kind of fully human person that he
would like to be. From their love of each other, he learns that cooperation between people is not only possible but quite wonderful.

Economics has been a successful social science because it focuses
on things that are true: human beings are self-interested and have the
capacity for reason. But it is equally true that we have the capacity
to love. This capacity is no less human and no less defining of who
we are. Too much of our public discourse has proceeded as if these
two great realities of the human condition, reason and love, were in
conflict with each other. The Right favors the cold, calculating, tough-
minded approach of the intellect: man is essentially a Knower. The
Left favors the warm, fuzzy, emotional approach of the heart: man is
essentially a Lover. Yet the Left at its most extreme has given us the
impersonal state and its bureaucracy as the answer to social problems.
At the same time, the Right at its most extreme has given us the irra-
tionality of trying to reduce man to the sum of his bodily needs.

We sometimes even see this dichotomy expressed in terms of

gender. Men are rational; women are emotional. Yet the point of marriage is to help people cross that divide. We marry someone different from ourselves in part because he or she will help us moderate ourselves.

Inside the home, the family as a whole has the benefit of being able to call upon both these deep realities of the human condition. Mother may very well react to her son's staying out past curfew by worrying about his safety and smothering him with hugs when he finally gets home. Father may very well calculate that it is in his son's long-term interest to get the verbal equivalent of a swift kick in the pants. The son probably needs both. Marriage at its best allows people to cross this divide, at least inside the home.

It is time to cross this divide in the sphere of public discourse as well. The consequences of going off the deep end into either the direction of love or reason and ignoring the other can be grim indeed. The French Revolution raised an altar to the "Goddess Reason." But that revolution, putatively based on reason, produced one of the most irrational, chaotic, and bloody periods in French history. The Russian Revolution tried to establish the dictatorship of the proletariat in which everything would be owned in common. That revolution produced oceans of blood and ushered in a new period of material privation unequaled even in Russian history.

We might argue that the American Revolution was the most successful of the modern revolutions because it preserved the underlying social and cultural order even while it created reasonable economic and political institutions. The family was surely among the key components of that underlying cultural order. Families were then and are now held together by a thousand ties of affection, obligation, and habit. The love in these families was and is the kind of love I have talked about: willing the good of another. This is love that is more than mere sentiment and more than the erotic urges of the body. Love is a decision.

Like all decisions, the decision to love can be guided by reason. This would seem to be the key to avoiding the extremes of trying to build a society exclusively on either the intellect or the heart. Love guided by reason and reason informed by love are more realistic and therefore more humane approaches. The tragic history of the last two centuries coupled with the relative success of the American experiment suggests that it would be prudent to avoid either extreme of trying to build a society on reason alone or on sentiment alone.

What will we have then? We will have a society in which people can work, be productive, and enjoy material prosperity—and at the same time a society in which people can relax into the comfort of those who love them and the comforts of home. It will not be a perfect society. But it might be a society in which families stay together and work out their problems. We will have a society that is worth living in—and worth dying for. In short, we will have a civilization of love.

Notes

Introduction: Homo Economicus *and the Noble Savage*

1   This syndrome is known as the Kaspar Hauser syndrome, or psychosocial dwarfism. See Harold I. Kaplan, M.D. and Benjamin J. Sadock, M.D.,
eds., *Comprehensive Textbook of Psychiatry/VI*, vol.2, 6th ed. (Baltimore:
Williams and Wilkins), chapter 40 and sections 43.3, 47.3.

2   Dava Johnson and Margaret Hostetter, "Planning for the Health Needs of
Your Institutionalized Child," in *International Adoption: Challenges and
Opportunities*, eds., Thais Tepper, Lois Hannon, and Dorothy Sandstrom,
eds. (Meadow Lands, PA: Parent Network for the Post-Institutionalized
Child, 1999), 15.

3   See Kaplan and Sadock, *Comprehensive Textbook of Psychiatry*, section
43.3, "Reactive Attachment Disorder of Infancy or Early Childhood." The
locus classicus is the work of John Bowlby, *Attachment and Loss. Vol. 1:At-
tachment* (New York: Basic Books, 1969). Also, Mary Ainsworth, Mary
Blehar, Everett Waters, and Sally Wall, *Patterns of Attachment: A Psychological Study of the Strange Situation* (New Jersey: Lawrence Erlbaum Associates, 1978).

4   Foster Cline, *Understanding and Treating the Severely Disturbed Child* (Evergreen Colorado: Evergreen Consultants, 1979). Richard J. Delaney and
Frank Kunstal, *Troubled Transplants: Unconventional Strategies for Helping Disturbed Foster and Adopted Children* (National Child Welfare Resource Center: University of Southern Maine, 1993). Carole A. McKelvey,
ed., *Give Them Roots and Let Them Fly: Understanding Attachment
Therapy* (The Attachment Center at Evergreen: 1995) .

5   The terminology of "trust bandit" is used by Ken Magid and Carole McKelvey, *High Risk: Children without a Conscience* (New York: Bantam Books, 1987). Foster W. Cline, *Conscienceless Acts, Societal Mayhem: Uncontrollable, Unreachable Youth and Today's Desensitized World* (Golden CO: Love and Logic Press, 1995); Nancy Thomas, *When Love is Not Enough: A Guide to Parenting Children with Reactive Attachment Disorder* (Glenwood Springs, CO: Families by Design, 1997).

6   For an overview of some of the most common difficulties found in post-institutionalized children, see Ronald S. Federici, *Help for the Hopeless Child: A Guide for Families* (Alexandria, VA: Ronald Federici and Associates, 1998), and Tepper, Hannon, and Sandstrom, eds., *International Adoption: Challenges and Opportunities.*

7   For an overview of the Socialist Calculation Debate, see Trygve J.B. Hoff, *Economic Calculation in a Socialist Society* (Indianapolis: Liberty Press, 1981) and Don Lavoie, *Rivalry and Central Planning: The Socialist Calculation Debate Reconsidered* (New York: Cambridge University Press, 1985.) In the final stages of editing this work, I discovered a newly released nine-volume survey of the Socialist Calculation Debate: Peter Boettke, ed., *Socialism and the Market: The Socialist Calculation Debate* (London: Routledge, 2000).

8   Frederick A. Hayek, "The Use of Knowledge in Society," *American Economic Review* 35:4 (1945): 519-30; and *Law, Legislation and Liberty, Vol. 1, Rules and Order* (Chicago: University of Chicago Press, 1973).

9   Frederick A. Hayek, *The Fatal Conceit* (London: Routledge, 1989), vol. 1 of *Collected Works*, ed. W. W. Bartley III (London: Routledge, 1989).

1   The Baby and Society

1   John Galt, Danny Taggert, and Fransisco D'Anconia are characters in Ayn Rand's *Atlas Shrugged* (New York: Bobbs Merrill, 1957). Howard Roark is the hero of *The Fountainhead* (Indianapolis: Bobbs Merrill, 1968, 25th anniversary edition).

2   Perhaps Jean-Jacques Rousseau is guilty of the most dramatic gap between "real babies" and "hypothetical babies" in intellectual history. Rousseau is the single person most responsible for the view of the infant as a "noble savage" whose proper development requires only freedom from unnecessary restraint. Rousseau fathered five children, all of whom he placed in a foundling hospital shortly after birth. One wonders how the intellectual history of the West would have unfolded if Rousseau had actually raised even a single one of those children himself.

3   The Five Nations of the Iroquois were organized in this matrilinear fash-

ion. See Anthony F. C. Wallace, *The Death and Rebirth of the Seneca* (New York: Random House, 1972).

4   For a discussion of the resources allocated among past and current wives, and the economic hierarchy so created, see Leonore Weitzman, *The Divorce Revolution* (New York, NY: Free Press, 1985).

5   The prohibition on divorce is explicit in the synoptic Gospels, (Matthew 19:3-9; Mark 10:1-12) and in the Pauline letters, especially I Corinthians 7. For a modern treatment of these texts, and their impact on the whole course of the conjugal relationship, see Karol Wojtyla, *Love and Responsibility* (San Francisco: Ignatius Press, 1993).

6   The forerunner of the Invisible Hand can be seen in passages of Adam Smith's earlier work (1759), *The Theory of Moral Sentiments*, ed. D. D. Raphael and A. L. Macfie (Indianapolis: Liberty Fund, 1984) but the classic, fully developed treatment appears in Smith's *An Inquiry into the Nature and Causes of the Wealth of Nations*, ed. Edwin Canaan, (Chicago: University of Chicago Press, 1976). Hayek's most developed treatment of the spontaneous order concept can be found in *Law, Legislation and Liberty: Vol. 1, Rules and Order.*

7   The analysis of the Cycle of Trust and Cycle of Rage is based upon the pioneering work of Foster Cline, *Understanding and Treating the Severely Disturbed Child* and *Hope for High Risk and Rage Filled Children: Reactive Attachment Disorder*, (Evergreen, CO: EC Publications, 1992). See also his collection of essays, *Give Them Roots: Then Let Them Fly: Understanding Attachment Therapy* (Evergreen, CO: The Attachment Center at Evergreen, 1995).

8   David Schmidtz, *Rational Choice and Moral Agency* (Princeton: Princeton University Press, 1995), 218.

2   *The Prisoners' Dilemma*

1   The classic reference showing the stability of the tit-for-tat strategy is by Robert Axelrod, *The Evolution of Cooperation* (New York: Basic Books, 1985).

2   Margaret Brinig has done the most systematic work on the differences in time preferences between men, women and children, as well as on the development of the length of time preferences. See her articles "Why Can't a Woman be More Like a Man? Or, Do Gender Differences Affect Choice?" in Rita Simon, ed., *Neither Victim or Enemy* (Lanham, MD. University Press of America, 1995), and "Does Mediation Systematically Disadvantage Women?" *William &Mary Law Review* 2:1 (1995).

3   For an extensive development of the idea that trust has vast economic and

social significance, see Francis Fukuyama, *Trust: The Social Virtues and the Creation of Prosperity* (New York: Free Press, 1995).

4   John H. Kagel, Raymond Battalio, Howard Rachlin, and Leonard Green, "Demand Curves for Animal Consumers," *Quarterly Journal of Economics*, 96 (1981) 1-16, and Raymond C. Battalio, John H. Kagel ,and Don N. McDonald, "Animals' Choices over Uncertain Outcomes: Some Initial Experimental Results," *American Economic Review*, 75 (1985) 597-613.

5   For a discussion of why it might be that animals do not trade, see David Levy, *The Economic Ideas of Ordinary People* (London: Routledge, 1992), 17-33.

6   Oliver E. Williamson and Sidney G. Winter, *The Nature of the Firm: Origins, Evolution and Development* (New York: Oxford University Press, 1991).

7   An accessible discussion of the economics of contracts can be found in Robert Cooter and Thomas Ulen, *Law and Economics* (Glenview, Ill.: Scott Foresman, 1988). See also Oliver Williamson, "Transaction-Cost Economics: The Governance of Contractual Relations," *Journal of Law and Economics* 22 (1979): 233.

An advanced textbook treatment of the problem can be found in David M. Kreps, *A Course in Microeconomic Theory* (Princeton: Princeton University Press, 1990), especially chapter 16. In his examples of moral hazard in contracts, the "first best" contract is the one the two parties could use if they trust each other. If they cannot trust each other to perform their part of the contract faithfully, they have to devise an "incentive compatible" contract that has performance incentives and penalties built into it. The incentive compatible contract is less profitable for the employer and less remunerative to the employee than the contract they could have used if they could trust each other. The examples in the text illustrate the financial losses to both parties to the contract.

8   Randall Collins, *Weberian Sociological Theory* (Cambridge: Cambridge University Press, 1986), 52-4.

9   See for instance Michael S. Bernstam and Alvin Rabushka, *Fixing Russia's Banks: A Proposal for Growth* (Stanford: Hoover Institution Press, 1998).

10 James M. Buchnan and Gordon Tullock, *The Calculus of Consent: Logical Foundations of Constitutional Democracy* (Ann Arbor: University of Michigan Press, 1962), and James M. Buchanan, *The Limits of Liberty: Between Anarchy and Leviathan* (Chicago: University of Chicago Press, 1975).

11 See Gordon Tullock, "The Welfare Costs of Tariffs, Monopolies and Theft," *Western Economic Journal*, 1967; Anne Kreuger, "The Political Economy of the Rent-Seeking Society," *American Economic Review* 64 (1974): 291-

303. For a survey of recent work on rent seeking, see Robert Tollison, "Rent-Seeking: A Survey," *Kyklos* 35 (1982): 575-602.

12 See for instance, my "The Modern State as an Occasion of Sin: A Public Choice Interpretation of the Welfare State," *The Notre Dame Journal of Law, Ethics and Public Policy* 11 (1997): 531-48.

3 Contracts in Libertarian Thought

1 For one of the earliest and still best treatments of these points, see Frederic Bastiat, "The Law," originally published in 1850, anthologized in *Selected Essays on Political Economy* (Irvington-on-Hudson, New York: The Foundation for Economic Education, 1964).

2 Frederick A. Hayek, "Liberalism," in *New Studies in Philosophy, Politics, Economics and the History of Ideas* (Chicago, Unviersity of Chicago Press, 1978), 119-51. For an interpretation that emphasizes the classical liberal reaction against religion as well as against absolutism, see Pierre Manent, *An Intellectual History of Liberalism*, trans. Rebecca Balinski (Princeton: Princeton University Press, 1995).

3 Francois Furet, *The Passing of an Illusion: The Idea of Communism in the Twentieth Century*, trans. Deborah Furet (Chicago: University of Chicago Press, 1999). See especially chapter 6, "Communism and Facism."

4 John Locke, *Two Treatises of Government*, originally published in 1698, ed. Peter Laslett (New York: Cambridge University Press, 1960); Etienne de la Boëtie, *The Politics of Obedience: The Discourse of Voluntary Servitude* (New York: Free Life Editions, 1975).

5 Furet, *The Passing of an Illusion*. See also my review of Furet, "The Appeal of the Empire of Lies," *The Independent Review* 5:2 (Fall 2000): 283-93.

6 Robert Filmer, *Patriarcha and other Writings*, ed. Johanne P. Sommerville, (Cambridge: Cambridge University Press, 1991).

7 Locke, *Two Treatises of Government*. The First Treatise is devoted to showing why Filmer's analogy between the family and the monarch does not work.

4 Why Marriage Is Not a Contract

1 Joan R. Kahn and Kathryn A. London, "Premarital Sex and the Risk of Divorce," *Journal of Marriage and the Family* 53 (November 1991): 845-55; Elizabeth Thomson and Ugo Colella, "Cohabitation and Marital Stability: Quality or Commitment?", *Journal of Marriage and the Family* 54 (May 1992): 259-67; Jan E. Stets, "The Link Between Past and Present In-

timate Relationships," *Journal of Family Issues* 14:2, (June 1993): 236-60; Steven L. Nock, "A Comparison of Marriages and Cohabiting Relationships," *Journal of Family Issues* 16:1 (Jan. 1995): 53-76; Vijaya Krishnan, "Premarital Cohabitation and Marital Disruption," *Journal of Divorce and Remarriage* 28:3/4, (1998): 157-70.

2   Jennifer Roback Morse, "Counter-Cultural Womanhood: Why I am Not a Feminist," *Vital Speeches of the Day*, December 15, 1997.

3   Jennifer Roback Morse, "Moral Agnosticism as a Human Rights Problem: The Problem of Self-Deception," in Rita J. Simon, ed., *Neither Victim Nor Enemy: Women's Freedom Network Looks at Gender in America*, (Lanham, MD: University Press of America, 1995), 191-201.

4   *Black's Law Dictionary* defines a partnership as "A voluntary contract between two or more competent persons to place their money, effects, labor and skill, or some or all of them, in lawful commerce or business, with the understanding that there shall be a proportional sharing of the profits and losses between them."

5   This analysis was inspired by that found in Ian Macneil, "The Many Futures of Contract," *Southern California Law Review* 47:691 (May 1974).

6   On the economics of sharecropping, see Jennifer Roback, "Southern Labor Law in the Jim Crow Era: Exploitive or Competitive?", *University of Chicago Law Review*, 61:4 (Fall 1984): 1161-92; Joseph Reid, "Sharecropping as an Understandable Market Response: The Post-Bellum South," *Journal of Economic History* 33 (1973).

7   This distinction is due to Frank Knight, *Risk, Uncertainty and Profit* (Boston: Houghton, Mifflin, 1933).

8   Economists use the term "specific capital" to refer to knowledge and skills that are useful only to one specific enterprise. For an overview of the difference this makes for the organization of the business firm, see the papers and references collected in Williamson and Winter, *The Nature of the Firm: Origins, Evolution and Development.*

9   There is now some empirical evidence to suggest that workers behave less cooperatively, less generously, when they believe their employer does not trust them. Bruno S. Frey, " Does Monitoring Increase Work Effort?: The Rivalry with Trust and Loyalty," *Economic Inquiry* 31 (October 1993): 663-70.

5   The Irreplaceable Family

1   Richard McKenzie, *The Home: A Memoir of Growing up in an Orphanage* (New York: Basic Books, 1996), esp. 97-112.

2   Thomas S. Monaghan, "Why I am Still Catholic," *Crisis* 15:8 (September 1997): 22-26.

3 Patrick F. Fagan, "The Child Abuse Crisis: The Disintegration of Marriage, Family, and the American Community," *Backgrounder no. 1115* (Washington, D.C.: Heritage Foundation, June 3, 1997) observes that social workers are called upon to be simultaneously "good cops" and "bad cops," therapists and policemen. Social workers have the responsibility for terminating parental rights, but this responsibility is commingled with a mandate to preserve the family if possible. This mandate for family preservation comes from the Adoption Promotion and Child Welfare Act of 1980. See Fagan's "It Takes a Family: The Adoption Promotion Act of 1997," *Executive Memorandum no. 477* (Washington, D.C.: Heritage Foundation, April 23, 1997).

   See also the report by Conna Craig, "'What I Need is a Mom'," *Policy Review* (Summer 1995): 41-49, of a case in which a biological mother was coached by the local department of social services as to how to keep her parental rights, even though she did not want to care for her child, and even rejected a judge's offer of custody.

4 According to Craig, Conna in "What I Need is a Mom," "Under federal law, states cannot obtain federal funds for foster care unless 'reasonable efforts' are made to keep members of the family of origin together ('family preservation') or to reunite the family ('family reunification'). But the federal government nowhere defines 'reasonable efforts,' and only a few states have specific statutes. It is a classic catch-22: Children are not free to be adopted until every reasonable effort is made to return them to their biological parents. But almost no one seems to know what constitutes a reasonable effort, that is, what services must be offered to parents who need outside help."

5 See, for instance, Respondent #3 in Richard McKenzie, "Orphanages: Did They Throttle the Children in Their Care?", Center of the American Experiment Symposium, May 1995, 12. His survey of the orphanage alumni found that 93 percent preferred the orphanage to the prospect of foster care (10).

6   The Mother of All Myths

1 In 1996, 31.6 percent of children lived in single-parent families. In 1995, of the children who lived only with their mothers, 36.5 percent were children of divorced parents, 35.5 percent were children of never-married mothers, and 23.6 percent were children of mothers who were married, but whose spouses were absent. Only 4.2 percent of children in mother-only families were children whose fathers had died. See Wade F. Horn, *Father Facts*, 3rd ed. (Gaithersburg, MD: The National Fatherhood Initiative, 1997), 14-15.

2 For an overview of the data and the issues, two good general sources are, David Blankenhorn, *Fatherless America: Confronting our Most Urgent Social Problem* (New York: HarperCollins, 1995) and Patrick F. Fagan and Robert Rector, "The Effects of Divorce on America," *Backgrounder no. 1373* (Washington, D.C.: The Heritage Foundation, June 5, 2000).

3 Sara McLanahan and Karen Booth, "Mother-Only Families: Problems, Prospects and Politics," *Journal of Marriage and the Family*, 51:3 (August 1989): 557-80, review the relevant literature. Irwin Garfinkel and Sara S. McLanahan, *Single Mothers and Their Children* (Washington, D.C.: Urban Institute Press, 1986), 30-31, cite research showing that daughters of single parents are 53 percent more likely to marry as teenagers, 111 percent more likely to have children as teenagers, 164 percent more likely to have a premarital birth, and 92 percent more likely to dissolve their own marriages. Their chapter 2, "Problems of Mother-Only Families," offers a succint summary of the problems. See also Blankenhorn, *Fatherless America*, chapter 2, "Fatherless Society."

4 Deborah A. Dawson, "Family Structure and Children's Health and Well-Being: Data from the 1988 National Heath Interview Survey on Child Health," *Journal of Marriage and the Family* 53 (August 1991): 573-84. Similar results were found by Judith S. Wallerstein, Shauna B. Corbin, and Julia M. Lewis, "Children of Divorce: A 10 Year Study," in Hetherington, E. Mavis, and Josephine D. Arasteh, *Impact of Divorce, Single Parenting and Stepparenting on Children* (Hillsdale: N.J.: Lawrence Erlbaum Associates, 1988), 197-214. This is a follow-up study of fifty-two couples who had been divorced ten years previously and their children. Among those between the ages of nine and nineteen at the time of divorce (now nineteen to twenty-nine), only two-thirds were in college or had graduated from college or were seeking advance degrees. (The national norm is that 85 percent of high school grads go directly to college.) The authors note that this may be due to abrupt end to child support payments at age 18.

5 Dawson, "Family Structure and Children's Health and Well-Being."

6 Suet-Ling Pong, "Family Structure, School Context, and Eighth Grade Math and Reading Achievment," *Journal of Marriage and the Family* 59 (August 1997): 734-46.

7 Dawson, "Family Structure and Children's Health and Well-Being."

8 Ronald L Simons, Kuei-Hsiu Lin, Leslie C. Gordon, Rand D Conger, and Federick O. Lorenz, "Explaining the Higher Incidence of Adjustment Problems Among Children of Divorce Compared with Those in Two-Parent Families," *Journal of Marriage and the Family* 61 (November 1999): 1020-33.

9 McLanahan and Booth, "Mother-Only Families: Problems, Prospects and Politics," 565.

10 The classic statement of this position can be found in Richard Dawkins, *The Selfish Gene* (New York: Oxford University Press, 1976).

11 Fagan, "The Child Abuse Crisis." Fagan's argument relies upon an important British study: Robert Whelan, *Broken Homes and Battered Children: A study of the relationship between child abuse and family type* (London: Family Education Trust, 1993). See also Martin Daly and Margo Wilson, "Discriminative Parental Solicitude: A Biological Perspective," *Journal of Marriage and the Family* (May 1980): 282; Michael Gordon and Susan Creighton, "Natal and Non-natal Fathers as Sexual Abusers in the United Kingdom: A Comparative Analysis," *Journal of Marriage and the Family* 50 (February 1988): 99-105. See also, the information contained in Blankenhorn *Fatherless America*, 40, n.58. Leslie Margolin, "Child Abuse by Mothers' Boyfriends: Why the Overrepresentation?" *Child Abuse and Neglect* 16 (1992): 541-51 finds similar results for the U.S.

12 Patrick Fagan, "The Child Abuse Crisis."

13 See for instance, Murray S. Straus, "Sexual Inequality, Cultural Norms and Wife-beating," *Victimology* 1 (1976): 54-76, and R. Stark and J. McEvoy, "Middle Class Violence," *Psychology Today* 4 (1970): 52-65.

14 Kersti Yllo and Murray S. Straus, "Interpersonal Violence Among Married and Cohabiting Couples," *Family Relations* 30 (1981): 339-47. Jan E. Stets and Murray S. Straus, "The Marriage License as a Hitting License: A Comparison of Assaults in Dating, Cohabiting and Married Couples," *Journal of Family Violence* 4:2 (1989), show that cohabiting couples have higher assault rates than either married or dating couples. Likewise, Nicky Ali Jackson, "Observational Experiences of Intrapersonal Conflict and Teenage Victimization: A Comparative Study Among Spouses and Cohabitors," *Journal of Family Violence*, 11:3 (1996), shows that cohabiting couples are more likely to engage in violence, even accounting for prior violence in the individual's family of origin.

Even relatively recent and detailed studies frequently fail to distinguish between married couples and cohabiting couples. For instance, one study of the clients of a counseling program for abusive couples, gives a demographic breakdown of the population in the study, including age, ethnicity, income, and education. But the researchers do not report whether the couples were married or living together. From the discussion of the case studies, the reader can infer that the researchers knew whether the couple was married. By grouping the married couples with the cohabiting couples, researchers treat what could be a testable hypothesis, namely that married men and cohabiting men are equally likely to batter their partners, as an assumption. See William A. Stacey, Lonnie R. Hazlewood, and Anson Shupe, *The Violent Couple* (Westport, Conn.: Praeger, 1994), table 4.1, 87.

15 The safest living arrangement for children is to live with both biological parents who are married to each other. Children living with their mother married to a stepfather are six times more likely to be seriously abused by the stepfather than are children who live with their biological parents who are married to each other. But either kind of married parents (biological or step) are safer for children than either kind of cohabiting, unmarried parents (biological or boyfriend). See Fagan, "The Child Abuse Crisis."

16 Nicholas Zill, "Behavior, Achievement and Health Problems Among Children in Stepfamilies: Findings from a National Survey of Child Health," in Hetherington and Arasteh, 325-68.

17 Dawson, "Family Structure and Children's Health and Well-Being."

18 Frank L. Mott, Lori Kowalski-Jones, and Elizabeth Menaghen, "Paternal Absence and Child behavior: Does a Child's Gender Make a Difference?" *Journal of Marriage and the Family* 59 (February 1997): 103-18.

19 Paul R. Amato and Fernando Rivera, "Paternal Involvement and Children's Behavior Problems," *Journal of Marriage and the Family* 61 (May 1999): 375-84.

20 Elizabeth C. Cooksey and Michelle M. Fondell, "Spending Time With His Kids: Effects of Family Structure on Fathers' and Children's Lives," *Journal of Marriage and the Family* 58 (August 1996): 693-707. For pre-teens, there was a statistically significant negative impact on grades of living in a single-father household, or living with a stepfather who has biological children living in the same household. For teens, the statistically significant negative impact came from living either in a single-father household, or in a household with a stepfather who does not have biological children in the household.

21 Dawson, in "Family Structure and Children's Health and Well-Being," shows the children in stepfamilies generally having greater emotional difficulties than children of single-parent households. Sara McLanahan and Karen Booth, in "Mother-Only Families: Problems, Prospects and Politics," find that remarriage does not fully repair the loss to the children of divorced mothers. Frank Furstenberg also summarizes the evidence in "History and Current Status of Divorce in the United States," *The Future of Children* 4:1 (Spring 1994): 37.

22 This paragraph is based on the analysis in Blankenhorn, *Fatherless America*, 138-41.

23 James S. Coleman, et. al., *Redesigning American Education* (Boulder, CO: Westview Press, 1997), 18-24.

24 James Q. Wilson, quoted in Blankenhorn, "Fatherless America," Center of the American Experiment, January 13, 1993.

25 Douglas A. Smith and G. Roger Jarjoura, "Social Structure and Criminal

Victimization," *Journal of Research in Crime and Delinquency* 25:1 (February 1988): 27-52. See especially table 2, 41.

26 Blankenhorn, *Fatherless America*, 41, references in notes 65-68.

27 See Blankenhorn, *Fatherless America*, especially 117-23 for examples of experts who propose androgynous parenting to one degree or another.

28 Robert S. Weiss, *Staying the Course: The Emotional and Social Lives of Men Who Do Well at Work* (New York: Free Press, 1990), 170-76. See also, Blankenhorn, *Fatherless America*, 219-21.

29 Paul R. Amato and Alan Booth, *A Generation at Risk: Growing up in an Era of Family Upheaval* (Cambridge, MA: Harvard University Press, 1997), 197-203 (quotation in the text, 201).

30 Margaret F. Brinig and Douglas W. Allen, "These Boots are Made for Walking: Why Wives File for Divorce," *American Law and Economics Review* 2 (2000), 126, examine the reasons offered for divorce in Virginia, one of the few states that allows people to offer cruelty as a grounds for fault divorce. Only 6 percent of those filing for divorce cited cruelty as a reason. Another survey of 256 people who had been divorced at one time or another asked "What was the principle reason you got a divorce?" Sixteen percent reported drug or alcohol problems as the principle reason, while only 5 percent reported abuse as the principle reason. Fully 47 percent listed "basic personality differences or incompatibility" as the principle reason for their divorce, while 17 percent listed marital infidelity and 10 percent reported disputes about money or children. *Statistical Handbook on the American Family*, Bruce A. Chadwick and Tim B. Heaton, eds. (Phoenix, AZ: Oryx Press, 1992), table c3-6, 98.

31 Yllo and Strauss, "Interpersonal Violence," 339-47.

32 Lisa Schiffren, "Is That All There Is?" and F. Carolyn Graglia, "We're All Tramps Now: Why We Lost the Sexual Revolution," both in *The Women's Quarterly*, Autumn 1997, No. 13.

33 Furstenberg, in "History and Current Status of Divorce in the United States," 30-43, shows that second marriages are more likely to end in divorce than first marriages. Frank Furstenberg and Andrew Cherlin, *Divided Families* (Cambridge, MA: Harvard University Press, 1991), 86-88, show that second marriages have a higher probability of failure than first marriages, especially during the first five years.

34 Lloyd Cohen, "Marriage, Divorce and Quasi-Rents, or, 'I Gave Him the Best Years of My Life'," *Journal of Legal Studies* (June 1987).

35 Brinig and Allen, "These Boots are Made for Walking," 126, argue that the favorable treatment of mothers in custody disputes accounts for the greater willingness of women to initiate divorce.

36 Wendy Shalit, *The Return to Modesty: Discovering the Lost Virtue*, (Touchstone Books: 2000).

7   *Big Brother and Big Daddy*

1   I made a variant of this argument in "Chopping the Family Tree," *Forbes* (October 5, 1998): 86.

2   Isaac Ehrlich and Jian-Guo Zhong, "Social Security and the Real Economy: An Inquiry into Some Neglected Issues," *American Economic Review, Papers and Proceedings* 88:2 (May 1998): 151-57, show that a higher level of governmentally provided pensions is correlated with lower propensities to get married and higher divorce rates, as well as lower birth rates.

3   Of mothers who receive AFDC payments, 48 percent have never been married, and 39 percent of mothers receiving Food Stamps have never been married. *Statistical Abstract of the United States, 1997* (Washington, D.C.: U. S. Dept of Commerce, 1997), 387.

4   To convince you that the instability is real, I offer the following standard example. Suppose there are three voters, X, Y and Z, and three possible policies A, B, and C, among which they must choose. Suppose further that voter X ranks the policies from most preferred to least preferred as follows: A, B, C. Voter Y ranks the policies B, C, A. Finally, voter Z ranks the policies C, A, B. The outcome of the election depends upon which two policies are pitted against each other. If the voters must decide between A and B, voters X and Z will prefer A, and voter Y's preference for B will be defeated. If on the other hand, the election is between B and C, voter Y will join together with X to support policy B. So A beats B and B beats C. One might naturally assume that A would beat C. But take another look at the preference ordering. In an election between A and C, voter X is defeated by a coalition of voters Y and Z, and C beats A.

The references on this point are legion. The vote cycle was evidently first discovered in the eighteenth century by the Marquis de Condorcet. The first modern expositions of the problem were Duncan Black, *The Theory of Committees and Elections* (New York: Cambridge University Press, 1958) and Kenneth Arrow, *Social Choice and Individual Values,* 2nd ed. (New York: Wiley, 1963). When the problem emerged in the modern literature, the reaction of both the economics and political science professions was to attempt to prove the proposition false. However, the voluminous literature seems to show that the problem is real and pervasive. Richard McKelvey, "Intransitivies in Multi-dimensional Voting Models and Implications for Agenda Control," *Journal of Economic Theory* 12 (1976) is the standard reference.

For experimental demonstration of sensitivity of voting outcomes to various details of institutional design, see Morris P. Fiorina and Charles

Plott, "Committee Decisions under Majority Rule: An Experimental Study," *American Political Science Review* 72 (1978): 575-98. In this study, students were induced to have preferences over the positions of dots on the blackboard. Charles Plott and Michael Levine, "A Model of Agenda Influence on Committee Decisions," *American Economic* Review 68:146-60, is an experimental study of an airplane club's decisions about which planes to purchase. The chairman of the meeting used agenda control to induce the club to vote for his most preferred alternative.

5   For an argument showing the appeal of moral relativism for good people with guilty consciences, see Morse, "Moral Agnosticism as a Human Rights Problem: the Problem of Self-Deception."

6   The economic theory of bureaucracy is an underdeveloped field. The field has scarcely advanced since the classic works by William Niskanen, *Bureaucracy and Representative Government* (Chicago: Aldine, 1971) and Gordon Tullock, *The Politics of Bureaucracy* (Washington: Public Affairs Press, 1965). Most empirical work in the study of bureaucracy utilizes these works, either implicitly or explicitly.

7   Joseph D. Reid Jr. and Michael M. Kurth, "The Rise and Fall of Urban Political Patronage Machines," in *Strategic Factors in Nineteenth Century American Economic History: A Volume to Honor Robert W. Fogel,* ed. Claudia Goldin and Hugh Rockoff (Chicago: University of Chicago Press, 1992), 427-45, argue that civil service bureaucracies were less directly accountable to particular voters than patronage machines. (See especially 432-34 and 445.) See also Gary Libecap and Ronald Johnson, "Patronage to Merit and Control of the Federal Government Labor Force," *Explorations in Economic History* 31:1 (Jan. 1994): 91-119, especially 93-8.

8   Even in that relatively straightforward situation, a bureaucracy still faces daunting problems. See my "The Modern State as an Occasion of Sin."

9   Social isolation is a major correlate of child abuse. Social isolation can be measured by the number of continuing relationships outside the home, the length of time the family lives in the same neighborhood, and memberships in organizations outside the family. For a summary of this research, see Richard J. Gelles and Murray Straus, "Violence in the American Family," in *Crime and the Family,* Alan Jay Lincoln and Murray A. Straus, eds. (Springfield, IL.: Charles C. Thomas Publishers, 1985), 103-4.

10 One way of understanding the problems of single-parent families is that these families have lower levels of social capital. This is conceptual framework used in N. M. Astone and S. S. McLanahan, "Family Structure, Parental Practices, and High School Completion," *American Sociological Review* 56 (1991): 309-20.

11 James S. Coleman, "Social Capital in the Creation of Human Capital," *American Journal of Sociololgy* 94 (1988): 95-120.

12 Suet-Ling Pong,"Family Structure, School Context, and Eighth Grade Math and Reading Achievment." Parents were asked about their involvement in their child's school, as well as their interaction with other parents in the school. The question asked of the parents was: How many parents of your child's friends do you know? This measure was called "parental social relations" or "parental acquaintances."

13 Coleman used this notion of social capital to account for the superior academic performance of students in Catholic high schools over public schools. Coleman argued that Catholic schools provided a richer, more dense network of social connections than public schools. James S. Coleman and T.B. Hoffer, *Public and Private High Schools: The Impact of Communities* (New York: Basic Books, 1987).

14 See the very sensitive review of Christopher Lasch's views of the marginalization of women's unpaid community work by Mary Ann Glendon, "The Man Who Loved Women and Democracy," in *First Things*, 70 (February 1997): 40-3, reviewing *Women and the Common Life: Love, Marriage and Feminism* by Christopher Lasch, edited by Elisabeth Lasch-Quinn.

8   Institutionalizing Childhood

1 The argument in this chapter appeared in abbreviated form in my "Why the Market Cannot Raise Our Children For Us," *The American Enterprise* (May/June 1998).

2 For an example of exactly such a free market analysis, see Darcy Olsen, "The Advancing Nanny State: Why the Government Should Stay Out of Child Care," *Cato Institute Policy Analysis No. 285*, October 23, 1997.

3 I once gave a lecture based on the material in this book at a college campus. One young woman raised her hand and gave a long description of her work as a nanny to the children of two-earner professional couples. Her assessment was that her employers were preoccupied with themselves to the detriment of the children and that some of the children she had cared for were in danger of becoming juvenile delinquents. She wanted copies of my talk to leave on the kitchen table of her employers. I never heard from her again after she received copies of the talk. I wonder what happened.

4 For studies reporting adverse effects of infant day-care, Patricia Morgan, *Who Needs Parents? The Effects of Childcare and Early Education on Children in Britain and the USA* (London: Institute of Economic Affairs, 1996), 25-6.

5 Hayek, "The Use of Knowledge in Society," and *Law, Legislation and Liberty, Vol. 1, Rules and Order.*

6   For British examples of claims that the tax revenues generated by work-
    ing women would more than offset the cost of child care, see Janet Bush,
    "The Child is the Father of the Man," *The Times*, December 24, 1993, and
    Bronwen Cohen and Neil Fraser, *Childcare in a Modern Welfare System*
    (London: Institute for Public Policy Research, 1991), cited by Patricia Mor-
    gan, *Who Needs Parents?*, 6-7.

7   David Gilmore, *Manhood in the Making: Cultural Concepts of Masculin-
    ity* (New Haven: Yale University Press, 1990), 43, makes the same point for
    Spanish men and Italian men doing menial work for the sake of their
    families.

8   Frank L. Mott, "Developmental Effects of Infant Care: The Mediating Role
    of Gender and Health," *Journal of Social Issues*, 47:2 (1991): 139-58.

9   Peter Barglow, Brian E. Vaughn, and Nancy Molitor, "Effects of Maternal
    Absence Due to Employment on the Quality of Infant-Mother Attachment
    in a Low-risk Sample," *Child Development* 58 (1987) 945-54. Jay Belsky
    and Michael J. Rovine, "Non-maternal Care in the First Year of Life and
    the Security of Infant-Parent Attachment," *Child Development* 59 (1988):
    157-67. Jay Belsky and David Eggebeen, "Early and Extensive Maternal
    Employment and Young Children's Socioemotional Development: Chil-
    dren of the National Longitudinal Survey of Youth," *Journal of Marriage
    and the Family* 53 (November 1991) 1083-110.

10 See Morgan, *Who Needs Parents?*, 40-2.

11 Judith L. Rubenstein and Carollee Howes, "Social-Emotional Develop-
    ment of Toddlers in Day Care: The Role of Peers and of Individual
    Differences," in *Advances in Early education and Day Care*, Sally Kilmer,
    ed. (Greenwich, CT: JAI Press, 1983), 13-46; Jay Belsky and David
    Eggebeen, "Early and Extensive Maternal Employment and Young
    Children's Socioemotional Development."

12 Jay Belsky, Sharon Woodworth, and Keith Crnic, "Trouble in the Second
    Year: Three Questions about Family Interaction," *Child Development* 67
    (1996): 556-78. The NICHD Early Child Care Research Network, "Early
    Child Care and Self-control, Compliance, and Problem Behavior at
    Twenty-Four and Thirty-Six Months," *Child Development* 69:4 (August
    1998): 1145-70.

13 Morgan, *Who Needs Parents?*, 82.

14 Ibid., 87-8. Infants who entered out-of-home care before their first birth-
    day are significantly more likely to have insecure-avoidant relationships
    with their mothers at twelve months, and also at eighteen months, com-
    pared with either home-reared children, or those whose mothers started
    work later. This pattern continues through three and a half years. While
    only the insecurely attached home-care children had difficulties when they
    started school, the day-care children, regardless of attachment classifica-

tion had difficulties (82). Another study, Peter Barglow, "Effects of Maternal Absence Due to Employment on the Quality of Infant-Mother Attachment in a Low-risk Sample," showed that of the 54 infants of mothers at work more than 20 hrs, 31.5 percent were insecure-avoidant, while 54 percent were secure. Of the 56 infants cared for by their mothers, only 9 percent were insecure-avoidant, and 71 percent were securely attached.

15 Jay Belsky and Michael J. Rovine, "Non-maternal Care in the First Year of Life and the Security of Infant-Parent Attachment," 157-67. Of those children in full-time care, 47 percent were insecurely attached, 35 percent of children in high part time care (20-34 hours) were insecurely attached, 21 percent of those in day care 10-20 hrs were insecurely attached, and 25 percent of those with exclusive maternal care were insecurely attached.

16 Ibid.

17 Ibid., 164.

18 C. Violata and C. Russell, "Effects of Non-Maternal Care on Child Development," paper presented at the Canadian Psychological Association, British Columbia, 1994; cited in Morgan, *Who Needs Parents?*, 84.

19 The NICHD Early Child Care Research Network, "The Effects of Infant Child Care on Infant-Mother Attachment Security: Results of the NICHD Study of Early Child Care," *Child Development* 68:5 (October 1997): 860-79, quote from 876.

20 Actually, the debate seems to center around just how great the increased risks of insecure attachments are. The "pro-child-care camp" (for want of a better term) cites studies showing that the increased risk of anxious attachment for children in child care is only 8 percent greater than for children reared at home. (Alison Clarke-Stewart," Infant Day-Care: Maligned or Malignant?" *American Psychologist* 44 (Feb. 1989): 266-73.) The "anti-child-care camp" (again, for want of a better term) cites studies showing increased risks of insecure attachment of up to 22 percent for children in non-maternal care over children raised at home. For a summary of the controversy, see Robert Karen, *Becoming Attached: First Relationships and How They Shape our Capacity to Love* (New York: Oxford University Press, 1998), 313-44.

21 Morgan, in *Who Needs Parents?*, 83, reports the differential effects for boys. Belsky and Eggebeen, "Early and Extensive Maternal Employment," show differences between shy and non-shy children.

22 For a particularly egregious example of intemperate criticism, see the discussants of Jay Belsky and David Eggebeen, "Early and Extensive Maternal Employment." Their study shows children who have been cared for by their mothers to be less likely to be "maladjusted" than children whose mothers either began full-time work during their first year of life or those whose mothers began full-time work during their second year. Their

critics argue that the home-care mothers are significantly different from the employed mothers, and that this might account for the observed differences in outcomes for the children. (This problem, called selection bias, is common in social science statistical work.)

These differences between the two groups ought to have made the home-care children *at greater risk*, not lower risk, for being maladjusted. The mothers who were not employed at all during the first three years were more likely to be below the poverty line, to be teenagers at the time of their first birth, to be single mothers, and to have low self-esteem. The full-time mothers also had less education, lower IQ, and lower income. All of these factors should work to make this group more likely to have poorly adjusted children. However, Belsky and Eggebeen found that the children of full-time mothers are less likely to be maladjusted than the children whose mothers worked full-time.

23 See my commentary on these particular headlines in "The Truth About Day Care," *Forbes* (December 14, 1998): 220.

24 Morse, "Government Nannies," *Forbes* (March 6, 2000): 102.

25 The parents are literally amateurs, in that root of the word "amateur" is *amare*, to love. They care for the children out of love, not for the money.

26 Thomas Sowell reports other such incidents in his *Late-Talking Children* (New York: Basic Books, 1997).

9   The Personal Ethics of a Free People

1   Douglas B. Rasmussen has given an account of the distinction between personal ethics and libertarian political philosophy in "Community vs. Liberty?" in *Liberty for the Twenty-First Century: Contemporary Libertarian Thought*, Tibor R. Machan and Douglas B. Rasmussen, eds. (Lanham, MD: Rowman and Littlefield, 1995). His discussion is an abstract philosophical account and does not take up any of the specific issues related to family life that I discuss in this chapter.

10   What Is Love?

1   Thomas Aquinas, *Summa Theologica*, 1.20.3.

2   Some moral theologians consider this the defining quality of a moral choice. An act of moral significance is one that shapes our capacity for future acts. See Germain Grisez and Russell Shaw, *Fulfillment in Christ: A Summary of Christian Moral Principles* (Notre Dame, IN: University of Notre Dame Press, 1991), 19-21: "As a result of one's choice, one has a greater affinity for the good one has chosen than for the other good (or goods) not chosen (20).

3   Thomas Aquinas, *Summa Theologica*, 1.20.1 ad 3.

12   *Why the Decision to Love Is Reasonable*

1   Psalm 130, Revised Standard Version, Catholic edition.
2   The "impartial spectator" is Adam Smith's term for the conscience within the heart of every person, in his first great work, *The Theory of Moral Sentiments*. He also sometimes calls the conscience "the man within the breast."

Conclusion: A Civilization of Love

1   Adam Smith, *Theory of Moral Sentiments*, Raphael and Macfie, eds. (Indianapolis, Ind.: Liberty Press, 1984), 1.11.5.2.
2   Michael Novak, *The Catholic Ethic and the Spirit of Capitalism* (New York: Free Press, 1993).
3   Arlie Russell Hochschild, *The Time Bind: When Work Becomes Home and Home Becomes Work* (New York: Metropolitan Books, 1997).

Bibliography

Aquinas, Thomas, *Summa Theologica*, trans. Fathers of the English Dominican Province (Westminster, Md.: Christian Classics, 1948).

Ainsworth, Mary, Mary Blehar, Everett Waters and Sally Wall, *Patterns of Attachment: A Psychological Study of the Strange Situation* (New Jersey: Lawrence Erlbaum Associates, 1978).

Amato, Paul R. and Alan Booth, *A Generation at Risk: Growing up in an Era of Family Upheaval*, (Cambridge, Mass.: Harvard University Press, 1997).

——— and Fernando Rivera, "Paternal Involvement and Children's Behavior Problems," *Journal of Marriage and the Family* 61 (May 1999): 375-384.

Arrow, Kenneth *Social Choice and Individual Values* (New York: Wiley, 1963), 2nd. ed.

Astone, N.M. and McLanahan, S.S. "Family structure, parental practices, and high school completion," *American Sociological Review* 56 (1991): 309-20.

Axelrod, Robert, *The Evolution of Cooperation* (New York: Basic Books, 1985).

Barglow, Peter, Brian E. Vaughn, Nancy Molitor, "Effects of Maternal Absence Due to Employment on the Quality of Infant-Mother Attachment in a Low-risk Sample," *Child Development* 58 (1987): 945-54.

Bastiat, Frederic, *Selected Essays on Political Economy*, (Irvington-on-Hudson, New York: The Foundation for Economic Education, 1964).

Battalio, Raymond C., John H. Kagel and Don N. McDonald, "Animals' Choices over Uncertain Outcomes: Some Initial Experimental Results," *American Economic Review* 75 (1985): 597-613.

Belsky, Jay and Michael J. Rovine, "Non-maternal Care in the first Year of Life and the Security of Infant-Parent Attachment," *Child Development* 59 (1988): 157-67.

Belsky, Jay and David Eggebeen, "Early and Extensive Maternal employment and Young Children's Socioemotional Development: Children of the National Longitudinal Survey of Youth," *Journal of Marriage and the Family* 53 (November 1991): 1083-1110.

Belsky, Jay, Sharon Woodworth, and Keith Crnic, "Trouble in the Second Year: Three Questions about Family Interaction," *Child Development* 67 (1996): 556-78.

Bernstam, Michael S., and Alvin Rabushka, *Fixing Russia's Banks: A Proposal for Growth*, (Stanford: Hoover Institution Press, 1998).

Black, Duncan, *The Theory of Committees and Elections* (New York: Cambridge University Press, 1958).

Blankenhorn, David, *Fatherless America: Confronting our Most Urgent Social Problem*, (New York: HarperCollins, 1995).

Boettke, Peter, ed., *Socialism and the Market: The Socialist Calculation Debate*,(New York, Routledge: 2000).

Bowlby, John, *Attachment and Loss. Vol. 1: Attachment*, (New York: Basic Books, 1969).

Brinig, Margaret, "Why Can't a Woman be More Like a Man? Or, Do Gender Differences Affect Choice?" in *Neither Victim or Enemy*, Rita Simon, ed. (Lanham, Md.: University Press of America, 1995).

———, "Does Mediation Systematically Disadvantage Women?" 2 *Wm.&Mary L. Rev. 1.* (1995).

——— and Douglas W. Allen, "These Boots are Made for Walking: Why Wives File for Divorce,"*American Law and Economics Review* 2 (2000).

Buchanan, James M., *The Limits of Liberty: Between Anarchy and Leviathan* (Chicago: University of Chicago Press, 1975).

———— and Gordon Tullock, *The Calculus of Consent: Logical Foundations of Constitutional Democracy,* (Ann Arbor: University of Michigan Press, 1962).

Chadwick, Bruce A. and Tim B. Heaton, ed. *Statistical Handbook on the American Family,*(Phoenix, Ariz.: Oryx Press, 1992).

Clarke-Stewart, Alison "Infant Day-Care: Maligned or Malignant?" *American Psychologist* 44 (Feb. 1989): 266-73.

Cline, Foster, *Understanding and Treating the Severely Disturbed Child* (Evergreen, Colo.: Evergreen Consultants, 1979).

————, *Hope for High Risk and Rage filled Children: Reactive Attachment Disorder,* (Evergreen CO: EC Publications, 1992).

————, *Conscienceless Acts, Societal Mayhem: Uncontrollable, Unreachable Youth and Today's Desensitized World,* (Golden CO: Love and Logic Press, 1995);

Cohen, Lloyd, "Marriage, Divorce and Quasi-Rents, or, 'I Gave Him the Best Years of My Life'," *Journal of Legal Studies,* June 1987.

Coleman, James S. "Social Capital in the creation of human capital," *American Journal of Sociology* 94 (1988): s95-s120.

———— and T.B. Hoffer, *Public and Private High Schools: The Impact of Communities* (New York: Basic Books, 1987).

Coleman, James S., Barbara Schneider, Stephen Plank, and Katherine Schiller, *Redesigning American Education* (Boulder, Colo.: Westview Press, 1997).

Collins, Randall, *Weberian Sociological Theory* (Cambridge: Cambridge University Press, 1986).

Cooksey, Elizabeth C. and Michelle M. Fondell, "Spending Time With His Kids: Effects of Family Structure on Fathers' and Children's Lives," *Journal of Marriage and the Family* 58 (August 1996): 693-707.

Cooter, Robert and Thomas Ulen, *Law and Economics* (Glenview, Ill.: Scott Foresman, 1988).

Craig, Conna, "'What I Need is a Mom'," *Policy Review,* Summer 1995, pp. 41-9, Daly, Martin and Margo Wilson, "Discriminative Parental Solicitude: A Biological Perspective," *Journal of Marriage and the Family,* May 1980: 282.

Dawkins, Richard, *The Selfish Gene* (New York: Oxford University Press, 1976).

Dawson, Deborah A., "Family Structure and Children's Health and Well-Being: Data from the 1988 National Heath Interview Survey on Child Health," *Journal of Marriage and the Family* 53 (Aug. 1991): 573-84.

de la Boetie, Etienne, *The Politics of Obedience: The Discourse of Voluntary Servitude*, (New York: Free Life Editions, 1975).

Delaney, Richard J. and Frandk Kunstal, *Troubled Transplants: Unconventional Strategies for Helping Disturbed Foster and Adopted Children*, (National Child Welfare Resource Center: University of Southern Maine, 1993).

Ehrlich, Isaac and Jian-Guo Zhong, "Social Security and the Real Economy: An Inquiry into Some Neglected Issues," *American Economic Review, Papers and Proceedings*, 88:2, (May 1998): 151-57.

Fagan, Patrick F. "The Child Abuse Crisis: The Disintegration of Marriage, Family, and the American Community," *Backgrounder, No. 1115* (Washington, D.C.: Heritage Foundation, June 3, 1997).

———, "It Takes a Family: The Adoption Promotion Act of 1997," *Executive Memorandum no. 477* (Washington, D.C.: Heritage Foundation, April 23, 1997).

——— and Robert Rector, "The Effects of Divorce on America," The Heritage Foundation Backgrounder, No. 1373, Washington, D.C. June 5, 2000.

Federici, Ronald S. *Help for the Hopeless Child: A Guide for Families*, (Alexandria, Va.: Ronald Federici and Associates, 1998).

Filmer, Sir Robert *Patriarcha and other Writings*, ed. Johann P. Sommerville, (Cambridge: Cambridge University Press, 1991).

Fiorina, Morris P. and Charles Plott, "Committee Decisions under Majority Rule: An Experimental Study," *American Political Science Review*, 72 (1978): 575-98.

Frey, Bruno S., "Does Monitoring Increase Work Effort?: The Rivalry with Trust and Loyalty," *Economic Inquiry* 31 (October 1993): 663-70.

Furet, Francois, *The Passing of an Illusion: The Idea of Communism in the Twentieth Century*, trans. Deborah Furet (Chicago: University of Chicago Press, 1999).

Furstenberg, Frank, "History and Current Status of Divorce in the United States," *The Future of Children* 4:1 (Spring 1994): 37.

———— and Andrew Cherlin, *Divided Families* (Cambridge, Mass.: Harvard University Press, 1991).

Garfinkel, Irwin and Sara S. McLanahan, *Single Mothers and Their Children*, (Washington, D.C.: Urban Institute Press, 1986).

Gelles, Richard J. and Murray A. Straus, "Violence in the American Family," in *Crime and the Family*, Alan Jay Lincoln and Murray A. Straus, eds. (Springfield, Ill.: Charles C. Thomas Publishers, 1985), pp. 103-4.

Gilmore, David, *Manhood in the Making: Cultural Concepts of Masculinity* (New Haven, Conn.: Yale University Press, 1990).

Glendon, Mary Ann, "The Man Who Loved Women and Democracy," in *First Things* 70 (February 1997): 40-3.

Gordon, Michael, and Susan Creighton, "Natal and Non-natal Fathers as Sexual Abusers in the United Kingdom: A Comparative Analysis," *Journal of Marriage and the Family*, 50 (February 1988): 99-105.

Graglia, F. Carolyn, "We're All Tramps Now: Why We Lost the Sexual Revolution," *The Women's Quarterly* 13 (Autumn 1997).

Grisez, Germain and Russell Shaw, *Fulfillment in Christ: A Summary of Christian Moral Principles*, (Notre Dame, Ind.: University of Notre Dame Press, 1991).

Hayek, Frederick A., "The Use of Knowledge in Society," *American Economic Review* XXXV:4 (1945): 519-30.

————, *Law, Legislation and Liberty, Vol. 1, Rules and Order* (Chicago: University of Chicago Press, 1973).

————, *New Studies in Philosophy, Politics, Economics and the History of Ideas*, (Chicago: University of Chicago Press, 1978).

————, *The Fatal Conceit* (London: Routledge, 1989), Vol. 1 of Collected Works, edited by W.W. Bartley III.

Hochschild, Arlie Russell, *The Time Bind: When Work Becomes Home and Home Becomes Work* (New York: Metropolitan Books, 1997).

Hoff, Trygve J.B., *Economic Calculation in a Socialist Society*, Indianapolis: LibertyPress, 1981.

Horn, Wade F., *Father Facts*, 3rd ed. (Gaithersburg, Md., The National Fatherhood Initiative, 1997).

Jackson, Nicky Ali, "Observational Experiences of Intrapersonal Conflict and Teenage Victimization: A Comparative Study Among Spouses and Cohabitors," *Journal of Family Violence*, Vol. 11, No. 3, (1996).

Johnson, Dana, and Margaret Hostetter, "Planning for the Health Needs of Your Institutionalized Child," in *International Adoption: Challenges and Opportunities*, Thais Tepper, Lois Hannon, and Dorothy Sandstrom, eds. (Meadow Lands, Penn.: Parent Network for the Post-Institutionalized Child, 1999).

Kagel, John H., Raymond Battalio, Howard Rachlin, and Leonard Green, "Demand Curves for Animal Consumers," *Quarterly Journal of Economics* 96 (1981): 1-16.

Kahn, Joan R. and Kathryn A. London, "Premarital Sex and the Risk of Divorce," *Journal of Marriage and the Family* 53 (November 1991): 845-55.

Kaplan, Harold I. M.D. and Benjamin J. Sadock, M.D.,ed., *Comprehensive Textbook of Psychiatry/VI*, Vol.2, 6th ed.(Baltimore: Williams and Wilkins.)

Karen, Robert, *Becoming Attached: First Relationships and How They Shape our Capacity to Love* (New York: Oxford University Press, 1998).

Knight, Frank, *Risk, Uncertainty and Profit* (Boston: Houghton, Mifflin, 1933).

Kreps, David M., *A Course in Microeconomic Theory* (Princeton, N.J.: Princeton University Press, 1990).

Kreuger, Anne, "The Political Economy of the Rent-Seeking Society," *American Economic Review* 64 (1974) 291-303.

Krishnan, Vijaya "Premarital Cohabitation and Marital Disruption," *Journal of Divorce and Remarriage* 28:3/4 (1998): 157-70.

Lavoie, Don, *Rivalry and Central Planning: The Socialist Calculation Debate Reconsidered* (New York: Cambridge University Press, 1985).

Levy, David, *The Economic Ideas of Ordinary People* (London: Routledge, 1992).

Libecap, Gary, and Ronald Johnson, "Patronage to Merit and Control of the Federal Government Labor Force," *Explorations in Economic History*, 31:1 (Jan. 1994): 91-119 .

Locke, John, *Two Treatises of Government*, Peter Laslett ed. (New York: Cambridge University Press, 1960).

Macneil, Ian, "The Many Futures of Contract," *Southern California Law Review* (47:691) May 1974.

Magid, Ken, and Carole McKelvey, *High Risk: Children without a Conscience* (New York: Bantam Books, 1987).

Manent, Pierre *An Intellectual History of Liberalism*, translated by Rebecca Balinski (Princeton, N.J.: Princeton University Press, 1995).

Margolin, Leslie "Child Abuse by Mothers' Boyfriends: Why the Overrepresentation?" *Child Abuse and Neglect* 16 (1992): 541-551.

McKelvey, Carole A., ed., *Give Them Roots and Let Them Fly: Understanding Attachment Therapy* (The Attachment Center at Evergreen: 1995)

McKelvey, Richard, "Intransitivities in Multi-dimensional Voting Models and Implications for Agenda Control," *Journal of Economic Theory* 12 (1976).

McKenzie, Richard, *The Home: A Memoir of Growing up in an Orphanage* (New York: Basic Books, 1996).

————, "Orphanages: Did They Throttle the Children in Their Care?" Center of the American Experiment Symposium, May 1995, 12.

McLanahan, Sara and Karen Booth, "Mother-Only Families: Problems, Prospects and Politics," *Journal of Marriage and the Family* 51:3 (August 1989): 557-80.

Monaghan, Thomas S. "Why I am Still Catholic," *Crisis*, 15:8 (September 1997): 22-6.

Mott, Frank L., Lori Kowalski-Jones, and Elizabeth Menaghen, "Paternal Absence and Child behavior: Does a Child's Gender Make a Difference?" *Journal of Marriage and the Family* 59 (February 1997): 103-118.

Morgan, Patricia, *Who Needs Parents? The Effects of Childcare and Early Education on Children in Britain and the USA* (London: Institute of Economic Affairs, 1996).

Morse, Jennifer Roback, (See also, Roback, Jennifer),"The Modern State as an Occasion of Sin: A Public Choice Interpretation of the Welfare State," *The Notre Dame Journal of Law, Ethics and Public Policy* 11 (1997): 531-48.

―――――, "Counter-Cultural Womanhood: Why I am Not a Feminist," *Vital Speeches of the Day*, December 15, 1997.

―――――, "Moral Agnosticism as a Human Rights Problem: The Problem of Self-Deception," in *Neither Victim Nor Enemy: Women's Freedom Network Looks at Gender in America*, ed. Rita J. Simon (Lanham, Md.: University Press of America, 1995), 191-201.

―――――, "The Appeal of the Empire of Lies," *The Independent Review*, 5:2 (Fall 2000): 283-293.

Mott, Frank. L., "Developmental Effects of Infant Care: The Mediating Role of Gender and Health," *Journal of Social Issues* 47:2 (1991) 139-58.

NICHD Early Child Care Research Network, "Early Child Care and Self-control, Compliance, and Problem Behavior at Twenty-Four and Thirty-Six Months," *Child Development* 69:4. (August 1998): 1145-1170.

―――――, "The Effects of Infant Child Care on Infant-Mother Attachment Security: Results of the NICHD Study of Early Child Care," *Child Development* 68:5 (October 1997): 860-879.

Niskanen, William, *Bureaucracy and Representative Government* (Chicago: Aldine, 1971).

Nock, Steven L., "A Comparison of Marriages and Cohabiting Relationships," *Journal of Family Issues* 16:1 (Jan. 1995): 53-76.

Novak, Michael, *The Catholic Ethic and the Spirit of Capitalism* (New York: Free Press, 1993).

Olsen, Darcy, "The Advancing Nanny State: Why the Government Should Stay Out of Child Care," *Cato Institute Policy Analysis No. 285*, October 23, 1997.

Plott, Charles, and Michael Levine, "A Model of Agenda Influence on Committee Decisions," *American Economic Review* 68: 146-60.

Pong, Suet-Ling, "Family Structure, School Context, and Eighth Grade Math and Reading Achievment," *Journal of Marriage and the Family*, 59 (August 1997): 734-746.

Rand, Ayn, *Atlas Shrugged* (New York: Bobbs Merrill, 1957).

—————, *The Fountainhead* (Indianapolis: Bobbs Merrill, 1968).

Rasmussen, Douglas B., "Community vs. Liberty?", in *Liberty for the Twenty-first Century: Contemporary Libertarian Thought*, Tibor R. Machan and Douglas B. Rasmussen, eds. (London: Rowman and Littlefield, 1995).

Reid, Joseph "Sharecropping as an Understandable Market Response: The Post-Bellum South," *Journal of Economic History* 33 (1973).

————— and Michael M. Kurth, "The Rise and Fall of Urban Political Patronage Machines," in *Strategic Factors in Nineteenth Century American Economic History: A Volume to Honor Robert W. Fogel*, ed. Claudia Goldin and Hugh Rockoff (Chicago: University of Chicago Press, 1992), 427-445.

Roback, Jennifer (see also Morse, Jennifer Roback) "Southern Labor Law in the Jim Crow Era: Exploitive or Competitive?", *University of Chicago Law Review* 61:4 (Fall 1984): 1161-92.

Rousseau, Jean-Jacques, *A Dissertation on the Origin and Foundation of the Inequality of Mankind*, trans. and ed. Maurice Cranston (London: Penguin Books, 1984).

Rubenstein, Judith L., and Carollee Howes, "Social-Emotional Development of Toddlers in Day Care: The Role of Peers and of Individual Differences," in *Advances in Early education and Day Care*, Sally Kilmer, ed. (Greenwich, Conn.: JAI Press, 1983), 13-46.

Schiffren, Lisa, "Is That All There Is?" *The Women's Quarterly* 13 (Autumn 1997).

Schmidtz, David, *Rational Choice and Moral Agency* (Princeton, N.J.: Princeton University Press, 1995).

Shalit, Wendy, *The Return to Modesty: Discovering the Lost Virtue* (New York: Touchstone Books, 2000).

Simons, Ronald L., Kuei-Hsiu Lin, Leslie C. Gordon, Rand D Conger, and Federick O. Lorenz, "Explaining the Higher Incidence of Adjustment Problems Among Children of Divorce Compared with Those in Two-Parent Families," *Journal of Marriage and the Family* 61 (November 1999): 1020-1033.

Smith, Adam, *The Theory of Moral Sentiments*, ed. Raphael, D.D. and A.L Macfie, (Indianapolis: Liberty Fund, 1984).

————, *An Inquiry into the Nature and Causes of the Wealth of Nations* ed. Edwin Canaan (Chicago: University of Chicago Press, 1976).

Smith, Douglas A., and G. Roger Jarjoura "Social Structure and Criminal Victimization," *Journal of Research in Crime and Delinquency* 25:1 (February 1988) 27-52.

Sowell, Thomas, *Late-Talking Children* (New York: Basic Books, 1997).

Stacey, William A., Lonnie R. Hazlewood, and Anson Shupe, *The Violent Couple* (Westport, Conn.: Praeger, 1994).

Statistical Abstract of the United States, 1997 (Washington, D.C.: U.S. Dept of Commerce, 1997).

Stets, Jan E., "The Link Between Past and Present Intimate Relationships," *Journal of Family Issues* 14:2 (June 1993): 236-260.

————, and Murray S. Straus, "The Marriage License as a Hitting License: A Comparison of Assaults in Dating, Cohabiting and Married Couples," *Journal of Family Violence* 4:2 (1989).

Stark, R., and J. McEvoy, "Middle Class Violence," *Psychology Today* 4 (1970): 52-65.

Straus, Murray S., "Sexual Inequality, Cultural Norms and Wife-beating," *Victimology* 1 (1976): 54-76.

Tepper, Thais, Lois Hannon, and Dorothy Sandstrom, eds., *International Adoption: Challenges and Opportunities*,(Meadow Lands, Penn.: Parent Network for the Post-Institutionalized Child, 1999).

Thomas, Nancy, *When Love is Not Enough: A Guide to Parenting Children with Reactive Attachment Disorder* (Glenwood Springs, CO: Families by Design, 1997).

Thomson, Elizabeth, and Ugo Colella, "Cohabitation and Marital Stability: Quality or Commitment?" *Journal of Marriage and the Family* 54 (May 1992): 259-67.

Tollison, Robert, "Rent-Seeking: A Survey," *Kyklos* 35 (1982): 575-602.

Tullock, Gordon, *The Politics of Bureaucracy* (Washington: Public Affairs Press, 1965).

————, "The Welfare Costs of Tariffs, Monopolies and Theft," *Western Economic Journal* (1967).

Wallace, Anthony F.C., *The Death and Rebirth of the Seneca* (New York: Random House, 1972).

Wallerstein, Judith S., Shauna B. Corbin and Julia M. Lewis, "Children of Divorce: A 10 Year Study," in Hetherington, E. Mavis, and Josephine D. Arasteh, *Impact of Divorce, Single Parenting and Stepparenting on Children* (Hillsdale: N.J.: Lawrence Erlbaum Associates, 1988), 197-214.

Weiss, Robert S., *Staying the Course: The Emotional and Social Lives of Men Who Do Well at Work* (New York: Free Press, 1990).

Weitzman, Leonore, *The Divorce Revolution* (New York: Free Press, 1985).

Williamson, Oliver, "Transaction-Cost Economics: The Governance of Contractual Relations," *Journal of Law and Economics*, 22 (1979).

————, and Sidney G. Winter, *The Nature of the Firm: Origins, Evolution and Development* (New York: Oxford University Press, 1991).

Wojtyla, Karol (Pope John Paul II), *Love and Responsibility* (San Francisco: Ignatius Press, 1993).

Yllo, Kersti and Murray S. Straus, "Interpersonal Violence Among Married and Cohabiting Couples," *Family Relations* 30 (1981): 339-47.

Zill, Nicholas, "Behavior, Achievement and Health Problems Among Children in Stepfamilies: findings from a National Survey of Child Health," in Hetherington and Arasteh, op.cit., 325-68.

SELECTED BIBLIOGRAPHY ON ATTACHMENT DISORDER

Every time I have given a talk on the subject of this book, I have had at least one member of the audience express an intense personal interest in attachment disorder. Based on that experience, I expect that a subset of my readers have an urgent need for information about attachment disorder. I have prepared this resource list with those readers in mind.

Inclusion on this list should not be considered an endorsement; rather, this list is intended only as a set of suggestions for finding the information relevant to your particular case.

BOOKS

Federici, Ronald S., *Help for the Hopeless Child: A Guide for Families*, (Alexandria, Va.: Ronald Federici and Associates, 1998) gives a good overview of the range of issues parents encounter with difficult adoptions.

Karen, Robert, *Becoming Attached: First Relationships and How They Shape our Capacity to Love* (New York: Oxford University Press, 1998) is the best single overview of the normal attachment attachment process.

Foster Cline is one of the pioneers in understanding and treating attachment disorder. His works include:

Cline, Foster W., *Conscienceless Acts, Societal Mayhem: Uncontrollable, Unreachable Youth and Today's Desensitized World*, (Golden, Colo.: Love and Logic Press, 1995);

————, *Hope for High Risk and Rage Filled Children: Reactive Attachment Disorder* (Evergreen, Colo.: EC Publications, 1992).

————, *Understanding and Treating the Severely Disturbed Child* (Evergreen, Colo.: Evergreen Consultants, 1979).

Cline's book with Cathy Helding, *Can This Child Be Saved? Solutions for Adoptive and Foster Families* (Franksville, Wis.: World Enterprises, 1999) includes a detailed resource list, as well as information about obtaining a detailed assessment that families can use to identify their child's problems.

Delaney, Richard J. and Frandk Kunstal, *Troubled Transplants: Unconventional Strategies for Helping Disturbed Foster and Adopted Children* (National Child Welfare Resource Center: University of Southern Maine, 1993) offers innovative strategies for dealing with troubled children.

I do not recommend that parents begin with Magid, Ken and Carole McKelvey, *High Risk: Children without a Conscience* (New York: Bantam

Books, 1987). This book is very scary. Read it after you have read something else.

ORGANIZATIONS AND WEBSITES

Parent Network for the Post-Institutionalized Child (PNPIC)
P O Box 613
Meadow Land, PA 15347
www.pnpic.org

A parent volunteer network devoted to disseminating accurate information about the consequences of institutionalization, and the strategies for
dealing with those consequences. They publish a newsletter and spon-
sor conferences.

The Attachment Center at Evergreen (ACE)
www.attachmentcenter.org
Box 2764
Evergreen, CO 80437-2764
303-674-1910

Association for Treatment and Training in the Attachment of Children
(ATTACh)
Box 9348
Newport Beach CA 95658
949-760-9109
www.attach.org

Association for Research in International Adoption
www.adoption-research.org

The two therapists whose conferences and writings have given me
the most help in dealing with the disorder on a daily basis are Nancy
Thomas and Deborah Hage. Here are their websites.

Deborah Hage:
www.debrahage.com/pwp/

Nancy Thomas:
www.sni.net/~phage/cwa/cwa_nancy.htm

Good luck and God bless.

RECENT WORKS

These books were published too recently to be cited in the text. Interested readers may consult them for the most recent statistical information and for arguments that complement those made in the text.

Hymowitz, Kay S., *Ready or Not: Why Treating Children as Small Adults Endangers Their Future— and Ours* (New York: Free Press, 1999).

Waite, Linda J. and Maggie Gallagher, *The Case for Marriage: Why Married People are Happier, Healthier and Better Off Financially* (New York: Doubleday, 2000).

Wallerstein, Judith S., Julia M. Lewis, and Sandra Blakeslee, *The Unexpected Legacy of Divorce: A 25-Year Landmark Study* (New York: Hyperion, 2000).

Index

absolutism 56, 60

accountability: and the will 170-1

adoption 86

aggression: father's response to 99-100, daycare 148-9

American: experiment 219, Founding 216, Revolution 233

androgynous parenting 100

arranged marriage 71

articulated knowledge: about child 156

atheism 215-6

atomistic individualism 28, 58-9

attachment 41, 112; clinical definition 149; daycare related to 149-52; developmental timetable for 12; parent/child 7, 12, 47; parental commitment 93; trust 33

attachment disorder 34, 64, 94; can't trust 43; cost-benefit calculations 44, described & defined 12-13

attacks on family 59, 61

authority: father's and monarch's compared 58; independent 97-8; mother's 98

autonomy 193, 198, 202; of commercial transactors 208-9

babies: helplessness of 223; fed like hamsters 22; need instruction 224 (*See* infants)

biological: family 83, 86; fathers 103

blood relationships: are not contracts 73

bureaucracy 113, 127-8; accountable to procedures 127

calculation 64, 202; about children 76; in marriage 70

capitalist: income-maximizing 138; stereotypical 209

Catholic 47, 214-5; nuns 85; schools 125-6,134-5

centrally planned economies: compared with parenting 143-8; Hayek's critique of 16

character flaws 106-7

child abuse 114, 127; defined by bureaucracy 128-9; fatherless girls 99; mediating institutions prevent 130-6; rates by family type 92-93

child protective services: 86, 87; types of errors 128-9

childcare: as menial work 29, 138, 147-8; claims of advocate 146; economies of scale in 139

A Note on the Author

Jennifer Roback Morse, a regular contributor to *Forbes* magazine and the *National Catholic Register*, is a research fellow of the Hoover Institution at Stanford University and a senior research scholar of the Social Philosophy and Policy Center at Bowling Green State University. The author of numerous articles in scholarly and popular journals, she taught economics for fifteen years at Yale and George Mason University before moving to California, where she combines motherhood with writing and lecturing.

This book was designed and set into type
by Mitchell S. Muncy
and printed and bound
by Thomson-Shore, Inc.,
Dexter, Michigan.

The text face is Minion Multiple Master,
designed by Robert Slimbach
and issued in digital form by Adobe Systems,
Mountain View, California, in 1991.

The cover illustration is *Breakfast in Bed* (1897) by Mary Cassatt,
The Huntington Library, Art Collections, and Botanical Gardens,
San Marino, California,
reproduced by agreement with SuperStock,
on a cover by FigDesign, Irving, Texas.

The paper is acid-free and is of archival quality.

30